HOW
PEOPLE
CHANGE

Resources published in cooperation with the
CHRISTIAN COUNSELING & EDUCATIONAL FOUNDATION
Susan Lutz, Series Editor

Edward T. Welch, When People Are Big and God Is Small: *Overcoming Peer Pressure, Codependency and the Fear of Man (P&R Publishing)*

Paul David Tripp, *Age of Opportunity: A Biblical Guide to Parenting Teens (P&R Publishing)*

Edward T. Welch, *Blame It on the Brain? Distinguishing Chemical Imbalances, Brain Disorders, and Disobedience (P&R Publishing)*

James C. Petty, Step by Step: *Divine Guidance for Ordinary Christians (P&R Publishing)*

Paul David Tripp, *War of Words: Getting to the Heart of Your Communication Struggles (P&R Publishing)*

Edward T. Welch, *Addictions – A Banquet in the Grave: Finding Hope in the Power of the Gospel (P&R Publishing)*

Paul David Tripp, *Instruments in the Redeemer's Hands: People in Need of Change Helping People in Need of Change (P&R Publishing)*

David Powlison, *Seeing with New Eyes: Counseling and the Human Condition through the Lens of Scripture (P&R Publishing)*

Edward T. Welch, *Depression – A Stubborn Darkness: Light for the Path (New Growth Press)*

David Powlison, *Speaking Truth in Love: Counsel in Community (New Growth Press)*

William P. Smith, *Caught Off Guard: Encounters with the Unexpected God (New Growth Press)*

Timothy S. Lane and Paul David Tripp, *Relationships: A Mess Worth Making (New Growth Press)*

Christian Counseling &
Educational Foundation

RESTORING CHRIST *to* COUNSELING &
COUNSELING *to the* CHURCH

HOW PEOPLE CHANGE

Timothy S. Lane

and

Paul David Tripp

New Growth Press

www.newgrowthpress.com

ISBN: 0977 0807-2-2

Printed in Canada

Acknowledgments

While several people have been instrumental in the writing of this book, in large part this book would not even exist without the leadership, vision, and insights of our friend and colleague, David Powlison. The content of this book grew out of a class that David has developed and taught for over twenty years. Each of us had the privilege of taking this class: one of us in 1984, when it was in its early form, and one of us as recently as 2000! (We won't name names or you will determine which of us is older!) Whatever strengths exist in this book belong to David; whatever weaknesses exist we humbly own.

One of the benefits we experience daily is to work in a place where the gospel and its application to life are talked about regularly. We also have countless opportunities to apply what we talk about to our own lives and relationships together. As in any community of believers, we do this imperfectly, yet God remains faithful and our friendships remain intact. Many thanks to David, Ed, Bill, Winston, Jayne, John, and Mike for your friendship, encouragement, and patience as we work and grow in grace together. You have had a profound effect on our lives and ministries.

We are grateful yet again for the work of Sue Lutz, who is not only a very gifted wordsmith but also has a deep understanding and appreciation for the content of the gospel. Because of that, she is a capable guide and helpful sounding board concerning the message of this and all of our books. She has even made this Acknowledgments page sound better!

On a practical note, we wish to thank Punch Marketing (Joan Johnson) for believing in this material and for her financial investment and encouragement throughout this process. Special thanks to Ray Burnette for the passion, creativity, and care he has demonstrated on our behalf. We're also grateful for our publishing partner, New Growth Press, for their commitment and dedication to this project.

Seldom in ministry do you have the opportunity to write; rarer still is the opportunity to write with a colleague who is also a friend! We have had this opportunity and privilege. We are amazed that we actually get paid to do this! Three years ago, we started co-writing a discipleship curriculum for local churches that laid the foundation for this book. At the time, we had no idea whether our writing partnership would work. We are thankful that it has, and that our appreciation for each other has grown through the process.

God has used our families in tremendous ways to remind us how much we need the grace we celebrate in this book. To our wives, Barbara and Luella, and our children, Hannah, Timothy, Kathryn, and Benjamin, and Justin, Ethan, Nicole, and Darnay: thank you for your patience as we continue to grow as husbands and fathers.

It is our hope that the same gospel we need every day will become clearer and more captivating as you read this book. As we come to the end of this project, we are very aware of how much we need what we have written. Simply because you can explain something with some degree of clarity does not mean that you have mastered it – or that it has mastered you. We remain, until the day we die or Christ returns, two sinners in need of grace. We thank God that this is what he gives us on a daily basis!

Timothy S. Lane
Paul David Tripp
September 2, 2005

CONTENTS

FOREWORD

The Word of God contains hundreds of thousands of words – but no photographs, drawings, maps, or charts. God's words are all words.

And yet, your Bible is a colorful picture book, a vivid storybook, and more. It's as multi-sensory as life itself. You are meant to see – in your mind's eye – the wildflowers tended by no one but God. You are meant to feel the apprehension as Esther steps into the Persian throne room uninvited. You are meant to feel the gladness of hosannas and the sting of mocking. You taste roasted grain, apples, raisin cakes, and honey – and become able to imagine how wisdom might be "sweeter than honey." You smell incense and cedar, fresh bread and lamp oil, blood and fire and smoke – and learn something about the mercies and glories of the LORD. As Jesus' life story unfolds, you sense the mounting hostility from religious leaders, the stunned disappointment in his disciples when he is killed, and then the dawning of indestructible joy as they realize he is alive and well.

God tells dramatic stories. He puts earthy metaphors to work. Reading and listening, you see moving pictures in your head. So the impact is visceral as well as conceptual. God speaks earthy, holy words in order to change you, not just to give you more information.

Compare the impact of the following sentences. First, "The Bible says that God loves people." Second, "I am the good shepherd. The good shepherd lays down his life for the sheep." Both statements are true. They even mean the same thing. But they don't do the same thing. The second statement gets to you, stays with you, works on you. That's because it comes with pictures and stories attached.

In the pages that follow, Tim Lane and Paul Tripp intend to teach you things about how the Christian life works. This isn't for theory, it's for real. So the truths they teach come with pictures and stories attached. Tim and Paul will tell you stories about real people, illustrating the ways that God's grace operates in our lives. In fact, frequently you will be asked to add your own story, to make what is taught personally relevant.

This book will also use one particular visual image throughout chapters 3-14 (chapters that mirror the lessons in the How People Change curriculum). It pictures two kinds of plants growing in the burning desert. The barren Thorn bush grows where there is no moisture. The Fruit tree flourishes where its roots tap a steady source of sweet water. The Lord, who laid down his life for us, is that spring of living water.

The authors asked me to write this Foreword because they borrowed their particular visual image from a course called "The Dynamics of Biblical Change" that I first developed in the 1980s. I'm honored to be credited by two respected colleagues who were formerly my students. But, of course, I can't take much credit. I also borrowed that visual image – from the Bible, in Jeremiah 17 – and simply adapted it into a more comprehensive metaphor for the Christian life. I hope that this picture will assist readers, helping you to take to heart and put into practice all that you will be reading in the chapters that follow.

In the wider world, as in the church, many voices cry out in our ears, "Listen to me! I'm important. I will give you happiness, health, money, knowledge, success, love." A few of those voices are in fact important and helpful. But most of those voices are simply hot air. At best, the things they offer are not nearly as important as they're made out to be. At worst, they get it all backwards.

What about How People Change? If the authors speak truly, then you need to listen. It's really important – a matter of life or death – whether or not you grow up into a wiser human being: "Nothing you desire can compare with her [wisdom]" (Prov. 3:15). In fact, there's only one thing more important. Here's how God himself weighs in on the question:

"Let not the wise man boast of his wisdom or the strong man boast of his strength or the rich man boast of his riches, but let him who boasts boast about this: that he understands and knows me, that I am the LORD who exercises kindness, justice and righteousness on earth, for in these I delight." (Jer. 9:23-24)

How People Change starts with God, and so avoids the fatal flaw in all the self-help books. You become profoundly different as you come to the growing realization, "It's not all about me." It's all about the One who is remaking us – each one and all together – into his image, and thus into a community that practices loving-kindness, justice, and righteousness in the earth. "In these things I delight."

David Powlison
July 2005

THE GOSPEL GAP

At first I was impressed. Phil was not only familiar with Scripture and systematic theology, he also owned an extensive library of biblical commentaries by the "who's who" of theological writers. There were few places I could go in Scripture and few theological references I could make that were new to Phil. Yet there was something dramatically wrong. If you were to turn from Phil's library and watch the video of his life, you would see a very different man.

Phil always seemed to be pointing out something wrong around him, yet he was successful at very little himself. He had the theological dexterity of a gymnast, but he lived like a relational paraplegic. His marriage to Ellie had been tumultuous from day one. He seemed completely unable to diagnose or correct the unending stream of problems that had sucked the oxygen out of this relationship. His relationships with his grown children were distant at best, and he always seemed to be embroiled in some drama with his extended family. He was never satisfied in his career, and he had been involved in four churches in three decades. The time he spent dealing with his own problems left little time for ministry to others.

The problem was that few seemed to know the "video" Phil. He and Ellie never fought publicly, never separated, and never considered divorce. They were faithful in church attendance and in giving. In Sunday school classes and Bible studies, Phil came across as knowledgeable and committed. Yet at home he was easily irritated and often explosive. Most of his free time was spent on the computer. He and Ellie rarely talked beyond the level of plans for the day, and even then his responses toward her were harsh and impatient. Terms like love, grace, and joy did not characterize Phil's life.

Ellie carried around a frustration with the church because she felt like no one really "got" Phil. He wasn't physically abusive, he wasn't addicted to substances or pornography, and he wasn't about to forsake his family, so he flew under the radar of pastoral care. Knowing how many people looked up to Phil, Ellie struggled every time he was asked to lead a Bible study or teach a theology class. She did everything she knew to resist becoming bitter and cynical, but she was beginning to lose the battle. Some days

Ellie would find herself at the kitchen table, lost in daydreams of a life without Phil.

Finally, Ellie told Phil she could not go on like this any longer. She knew she needed help, and she asked him to come along for counseling. At first, Phil angrily refused, but he eventually agreed to give it a try. During our first time together, I let them spend most of the time talking. There was something strange about their story, but I couldn't put my finger on it. It wasn't until I was driving home that it hit me: They had given me an extensive history, yet there was little or no reference to God. Here was a theological man and his believing wife, yet their life story was utterly godless!

Phil and Ellie had a huge gap in their understanding of the gospel. It was as if they were attempting to live with a gaping hole in the middle of their house. They walked around it every day. Things would fall into it, and the hole would get bigger, but they didn't seem aware that it was there. They didn't realize that other houses didn't have a hole, and that those that did needed to be renovated or demolished. Phil even had a "hole repair manual" that he had read thoroughly, but it hadn't led him to fix his. Ellie suffered from the dust, smell, and heat that drifted up from the hole, but she had no idea what to do about them. This was their Christianity.

I wish I could say that Phil and Ellie are alone, but I am convinced that there are many Phils and Ellies among us. Often there is a vast gap in our grasp of the gospel. It subverts our identity as Christians and our understanding of the present work of God. This gap undermines every relationship in our lives, every decision we make, and every attempt to minister to others. Yet we live blindly, as if the hole were not there.

Understanding the Gap

Second Peter 1:3-9 describes this gap better than any other passage.

> [3]His divine power has given us everything we need for life and godliness through our knowledge of him who called us by his own glory and goodness. [4]Through these he has given us his very great and precious promises, so that through them you may participate in the divine nature and escape the corruption in the world caused by evil desires. [5]For this very reason, make every effort to add to your faith goodness;

and to goodness, knowledge; [6]and to knowledge, self-control; and to self-control, perseverance; and to perseverance, godliness; [7]and to godliness, brotherly kindness; and to brotherly kindness, love. [8]For if you possess these qualities in increasing measure, they will keep you from being ineffective and unproductive in your knowledge of our Lord Jesus Christ. [9]But if anyone does not have them, he is nearsighted and blind, and has forgotten that he has been cleansed from his past sins.

Let's look at the symptoms of the gap. In verse 9, Peter points out that there are people who know the Lord, but whose lives fail to produce the expected fruit of faith. Their lives are not characterized by peaceful, loving relationships, a sweet, natural, day-by-day worship of the Lord, a wholesome and balanced relationship to material things, and ongoing spiritual growth. Instead, these believers leave a trail of broken relationships, a knowledgeable but impersonal walk with God, a struggle with material things, and a definite lack of personal growth. Something is wrong with this harvest; it contradicts the faith that is supposed to be its source.

Peter's words describe Phil and Ellie. They were "ineffective and unproductive" in many ways. The scars of conflict had so crippled their respect for each other that there was little trust or spontaneous affection left between them. They did not get along with their neighbors and left three churches badly. There was little tenderness or affection in their worship of God. Their Christianity seemed more an ideology than a worship-driven relationship, and God's practical call on their lives was more a duty to be performed than a joy to be pursued. It wasn't surprising that Phil and Ellie struggled with debt. Physical things had replaced spiritual things long ago. More than anything else, they seemed stuck. If you had recorded their complaints against each other ten years ago, the tape could have been seamlessly inserted into any of the arguments they had today.

Why are many Christians "ineffective and unproductive?" Peter provides the diagnosis in verse 9: they are nearsighted and blind, having forgotten that they have been cleansed from their past sins. They are blind to the power and hope of the gospel for today. What does this mean?

The good news of the gospel of Jesus Christ is a "then-now-then" gospel (see Figure 1.1) First, there is the "then" of the past. When I embrace

FIGURE 1.1 The Gospel Gap

Christ by faith, my sins are completely forgiven, and I stand before God as righteous. There is also the "then" of the future, the promise of eternity with the Lord, free of sin and struggle. The church has done fairly well explaining these two "thens" of the gospel, but it has tended to understate or misunderstand the "now" benefits of the work of Christ. What difference does the gospel make in the here and now? How does it help me as a father, a husband, a worker, and a member of the body of Christ? How does it help me respond to difficulty and make decisions? How does it give me meaning, purpose, and identity? How does it motivate my ministry to others?

It is in the here and now that many of us experience a gospel blindness. Our sight is dimmed by the tyranny of the urgent, by the siren call of success, by the seductive beauty of physical things, by our inability to admit our own problems, and by the casual relationships within the body of Christ that we mistakenly call fellowship. This blindness is often encouraged by preaching that fails to take the gospel to the specific challenges people face. People need to see that the gospel belongs in their workplace, their kitchen, their school, their bedroom, their backyard, and their van. They need to see the way the gospel makes a connection between what they are doing and what God is doing. They need to understand that their life stories are being lived out within God's larger story so that they can learn to live each day with a gospel mentality.

Three Kinds of Blindness

The "here and now" hole in the middle of our lives produces three fundamental forms of spiritual blindness. First, there is the blindness of identity. Many Christians do not have a gospel perspective on who they are. For example, Phil was a good theologian, but his personal identity was more rooted in knowledge and achievement than in the gospel. This lack of gospel identity shows up in two ways. First, many Christians underestimate the presence and power of indwelling sin. They don't see how easily entrapped they are in this world full of snares (Gal. 6:1). They don't grasp the comprehensive nature of the war that is always raging within the heart of every believer (Rom. 7). They're not aware of how prone they are to run after God replacements. They fail to see that their greatest problems exist within them, not outside them.

My work with teenagers has convinced me that one of the main reasons teenagers are not excited by the gospel is that they do not think they need it. Many parents have successfully raised self-righteous little Pharisees. When they look at themselves, they do not see a sinner in desperate need, so they are not grateful for a Savior. Sadly, the same is true of many of their parents.

Many believers also fail to see the other side of their gospel identity: their identity in Christ. Christ not only gives me forgiveness and a new future, but a whole new identity as well! I am now a child of God, with all of the rights and privileges that this title bestows. This is important because each of us lives out of some sense of identity, and our gospel identity amnesia will always lead to some form of identity replacement. That is, if who I am in Christ does not shape the way I think about myself and the things I face, then I will live out of some other identity.

Often in our blindness, we take on our problems as identities. While divorce, depression, and single parenthood are significant human experiences, they are not identities. Our work is not our identity, though it is an important part of how God intends us to live. For too many of us, our sense of identity is more rooted in our performance than it is in God's grace. It is wonderful to be successful at what God has called you to do, but when you use your success to define who you are, you will always have a distorted perspective.

Second, a "here and now" gap in the gospel also causes us to be blind to God's provision. As Peter states, in Christ we have been given "everything we need for life and godliness." Why does he use two words here, both "life" and "godliness"? The second word is meant to qualify the first. If Peter had simply said that God has given us everything we need for life, it would be easy to add the word "eternal" before it. This is how this passage is often interpreted. We find it much easier to embrace the gospel's promise of life after death than we do its promise of life before death! But when Peter says that God has given us everything we need for "godliness," we know that he is talking about life now. Godliness is a God-honoring life from the time I come to Christ until the time I go home to be with him.

Peter is saying that we cannot live properly in the present unless we understand the provision God has made for us. Many believers are blind to the fact that this provision runs deeper than the commands, principles, and promises of Scripture we normally associate with the pursuit of a godly life. It is even more fundamental than the conviction of the Holy Spirit or our legal forgiveness. God's provision for a godly life now is literally Christ himself! He has given us himself so that we can be like him.

Paul says in Galatians 2:20, "I no longer live, but Christ lives in me." Jesus is Emmanuel not only because he came to earth and lived with us, but because he actually lives within us now by his Spirit. His presence gives us everything we need to be who we are supposed to be and do what we are supposed to do.

Without an awareness of Christ's presence, we tend to live anxiously. We avoid hard things and are easily overwhelmed. But a clear sense of identity and provision gives us hope and courage to face the struggles and temptations that come our way.

A third form of blindness that a gospel gap produces is blindness to God's process. The New Testament is clear that our acceptance into the family of God is not the end of God's work in us, but the beginning. God has not called us to a life of "I have spiritually arrived" or "I am just waiting for heaven." Rather, he calls us to a life of constant work, constant growth, and constant confession and repentance. Making us holy is God's unwavering agenda until we are taken home to be with him. He will do whatever he needs to do to produce holiness in us. He wants us to be a community of joy, but he is willing to compromise our temporal happiness in order to increase our Christ-likeness.

Any time we find ourselves in difficulty or trial, it is easy to think we have been forgotten or rejected by God. This is because we do not understand the present process. God is not working for our comfort and ease; he is working on our growth. At the very moment we are tempted to question his faithfulness, he is fulfilling his redemptive promises to us. After all, it's not like there are only some people who really need to change. Change is the norm for everyone, and God is always at work to complete this process in us.

What Fills the Gap?

There is one thing that physical and spiritual holes have in common: They don't stay empty for long. A hole in the sand will quickly fill with water. A hole in a field will accumulate sticks and leaves. Holes always seem to get filled.

Under the main staircase in our house is a large walk-in closet. It is the bane of my wife's existence. Every six months or so, Luella summons the courage to attack this closet. She empties it completely, sorting its contents and uncovering the floor for the first time in months. She always says that she wants us to try to keep the closet in this pristine condition. I don't oppose the idea since I like being able to walk into it, but the closet always seems to fill up again. Our children visit and leave artifacts of their new existence in the closet. Packages come in the mail, and the boxes seem to mysteriously wind up in the closet. All the "stuff" that has no home somehow finds its way there. And before long, the closet door can barely shut, and Luella has to attack it again.

The gospel gap in many of our lives doesn't stay empty either. If we do not live with a gospel-shaped, Christ-confident, and change-committed Christianity, that hole will get filled with other things. These things may seem plausible and even biblical, but they will be missing the identity-provision-process core that is meant to fill every believer.

I like the term Paul uses for these counterfeits in 2 Corinthians 10:5. He calls them "pretensions." Not every lie is a pretense. A pretense is a plausible lie. I could tell you that I was a female Olympic gymnast. That would be a lie, but it would not be a pretense because it would lack plausibility. But if I dressed in a suit and stood in front of an office with a briefcase and a set of architectural drawings, I could probably fool you into thinking I was a building contractor.

The most dangerous pretensions are those that masquerade as true Christianity but are missing the identity-provision-process core of the gospel. They have their roots in the truth, but they are incomplete. The result is a Christianity that is mere externalism. Whenever we are missing the message of Christ's indwelling work to progressively transform us, the hole will be filled by a Christian lifestyle that focuses more on externals than on the heart. I believe that a war for the heart of Christianity is raging all around us, seeking to draw us away from its true core toward the externals.

What sorts of Christian externals tend to fill the gospel gap? They are all things that are part of the normal Christian life; each tends to attract us at different times and in different ways. Look for yourself in these descriptions. Is it possible that you have a gap in your gospel and that it has been filled in ways you didn't realize?

Christian Externalism: Things that Fill the Gap

Formalism

If you want to know the church calendar, just look at Jim's schedule. Whatever the meeting or ministry, Jim is there, Bible in hand. He's done his stint as a Sunday school teacher and regularly volunteers for short-term missions trips. He is faithful in giving and a willing volunteer when work needs to be done around the church. But Jim's world and God's world never meet. All of his church activities have little impact on his heart and how he lives his life.

God railed against the formalism of the Israelites (Isa. 1), and Christ condemned the formalism of the Pharisees (Matt. 23:23-28). Why? Because formalism allows me to retain control of my life, my time, and my agenda. Formalism is blind to the seriousness of my spiritual condition and my constant need for God's grace to rescue me. Jim sees his church participation simply as one healthy aspect of a good life. He has no noticeable hunger for God's help in any other area. For him, the gospel is reduced to participation in the meetings and ministries of the church.

8

Legalism

Sally is a walking list of dos and don'ts. She has a set of rules for everything. They are her way of evaluating herself and everyone around her. Her children live under the crushing weight of her legalism. To them, God is a harsh judge who places unreasonable standards on them and then condemns them when they can't keep them. There is no joy in Sally's home because there is no grace to be celebrated. Sally thinks that performing her list gives her standing with God. She has no appreciation for the grace given her in Christ Jesus.

Legalism completely misses the fact that no one can satisfy God's requirements. While Sally rigidly keeps her rules, her pride, impatience, and judgmental spirit go untouched. Legalism ignores the depth of our inability to earn God's favor. It forgets the need for our hearts to be transformed by God's grace. Legalism is not just a reduction of the gospel; it is another gospel altogether (see Galatians), where salvation is earned by keeping the rules we have established.

Mysticism

Christine careens from emotional experience to emotional experience. She is constantly hunting for a spiritual high, a dynamic encounter with God. Because of this, she never stays with one church very long. She is more a consumer of experience than a committed member of the body of Christ. Yet in between the dynamic experiences, Christine's faith often falls flat. She struggles with discouragement and often finds herself wondering if she is even a believer. Despite the excitement of powerful moments, Christine isn't growing in faith and character.

Biblical faith is not stoic; true Christianity is dyed with all the colors of human emotion. But you cannot reduce the gospel to dynamic emotional experiences with God. As the Holy Spirit indwells us and the Word of God impacts us, most of the changes in our hearts and lives take place in the little moments of life. The danger of mysticism is that it can become more a pursuit of experience than a pursuit of Christ. It reduces the gospel to dynamic emotional and spiritual experiences.

Activism

Shirley stands on the right-to-life picket line wondering why more Christians aren't there. Of course, Shirley feels the same about the protests at the adult bookstore and her work on the coming local election. These causes define what it means to be a Christian. Her constant refrain is, "Stand up for what is right, wherever and whenever it is needed." There is something admirable about Shirley's willingness to devote time, energy, and money to stand up for what is right.

But on closer examination, Shirley's Christianity is more a defense of what's right than a joyful pursuit of Christ. The focus of this kind of Christian activism is always on external evil. As a result, it can take on the form of a modern monasticism. The monastics essentially said, "There is an evil world out there, and the way to fight evil is to separate from it." But monasteries failed because they forgot to focus on the evil inside every monk who entered their walls!

Whenever you believe that the evil outside you is greater than the evil inside you, a heartfelt pursuit of Christ will be replaced by a zealous fighting of the "evil" around you. A celebration of the grace that rescues you from your own sin will be replaced by a crusade to rescue the church from the ills of the surrounding culture. Christian maturity becomes defined as a willingness to defend right from wrong. The gospel is reduced to participation in Christian causes.

Biblicism

John is a biblical and theological expert. His theological library includes rare, antique Christian volumes, and he is always seeking to buy first editions. John frequently uses phrases like "biblical worldview," "theologically consistent," and "thinking like a Christian." He loves the Bible (which is a very good thing), but there are things in John's life that don't seem to fit.

Despite his dedicated study of Christianity, John isn't known for being like Christ! He has a reputation for being proud, critical, and intolerant of anyone who lacks his fine-grained understanding of the faith. John endlessly critiques his pastor's sermons and unnerves Sunday school teachers when he enters the room.

In John's Christianity, communion, dependency, and worship of Christ have been replaced by a drive to master the content of Scripture and systematic theology. John is a theological expert, but he is unable to live by the grace he can define with such technical precision. He has invested a great deal of time and energy mastering the Word, but he does not allow the Word to master him. In Biblicism, the gospel is reduced to a mastery of biblical content and theology.

"Psychology-ism"

Jen always has a group of people ministering to her. She talks a lot about how many "hurting" people are in her congregation, and how the church isn't doing enough to help them. An avid reader of Christian self-help books, she is always recommending the latest one to someone. She often says that Christianity is the only place to find real help and healing, yet she doesn't seem to find that healing herself. Jen spends much of her time discouraged and often leaves church meetings in tears.

Jen is right that our deepest needs are met in Christ, but she sees Christ more as a therapist than as a Savior. Jen is convinced that her deepest needs come out of her experience of neglect and rejection, and so she sees herself more in need of healing than redemption. She is blind to how demanding, critical, and self-absorbed she actually is.

Without realizing it, Jen has redefined the problem that the gospel addresses. Rather than seeing our problem as moral and relational – the result of our willingness to worship and serve ourselves and the things of this world instead of worshiping and serving our Creator (Romans 1) – she sees our problem as a whole catalog of unmet needs. But whenever you view the sin of another against you as a greater problem than your own sin, you will tend to seek Christ as your therapist more than you seek him as your Savior. Christianity becomes more a pursuit of healing than a pursuit of godliness. The gospel is reduced to the healing of emotional needs.

"Social-ism"

George was so thankful for the relationships he had found in the body of Christ. They were unlike any friendships he had experienced before. He was so full of joy for his Christian family that he participated in any activity that put him in contact with other believers. George loved his twenty-something Bible study, but he particularly enjoyed going out with the gang afterward. He loved the retreats, the camping trips, and the short-term missionary projects. For the first time in his life, George felt alive and connected.

George's trouble started when one of his closest friends was transferred out of state and another friend got married. Then his church called a new pastor who decided to de-emphasize ministry to singles. When the small groups at his church were reorganized, George felt like he was stuck with a group of older married people with whom he couldn't relate. Church wasn't the same anymore, so he quit going to his small group. Before long his attendance on Sunday began to wane. Going to church, he said, was like going to someone else's family reunion.

George didn't realize it, but fellowship, acceptance, respect, and position in the body of Christ had replaced his dependence on communion with Christ. The church had become his spiritual social club, and when the club began to break up, he lost his motivation to continue. For George, the grace of friendship replaced Christ as the thing that gives him identity, purpose, and hope. The gospel had been reduced to a network of fulfilling Christian relationships.

Why Are These Replacements So Attractive?

In 2 Corinthians 10:5, Paul talks about "pretensions that set themselves up against the knowledge of God." Remember that a pretense is a plausible lie, with enough truth to be believable. The lies that capture us as Christians usually seem to fit well within the borders of our Christianity. Perhaps postmodernism and sexual immorality are not the greatest threats to the church of Christ in our day. Perhaps we are in more danger from the subtle lies that flow from subtle shifts in how we understand the gospel. We have not forsaken the faith, but we may have redefined it in ways that are fundamentally different from the gospel laid out in Scripture.

This redefinition of the faith does not happen all at once. It may not even surface in the public theological discussions of the church. Rather, the redefinition is a process of subtle steps at the practical level of the church's fellowship, life, and ministry. Hope in Christ gets replaced with Christian activity, emotional experiences, Christian fellowship, or something else, without anyone consciously redefining or forsaking the faith.

All of the "isms" we have considered are attractive because they each emphasize one important aspect of the gospel. The gospel does call me to lead a godly life and to gather with God's people for worship. God will meet me in special ways at certain times. The gospel does call me to influence the world for good, to love truth and to meditate on it. God is a God of comfort who meets us in all our sorrows. We are to be enthusiastic participants in the fellowship of the body of Christ.

The danger occurs when we reduce the gospel to any one of these elements. Whenever I do, my Christianity is no longer motivated by a humble admission of my daily need for Christ and a humble pursuit of his grace. Things that are intended to be the means of this pursuit instead become the ends. For example, the goal of understanding the truths of the gospel is to have a deeper relationship with Christ. But when theological knowledge becomes the goal, Christ is displaced.

There is another, deeper reason why these "isms" are so attractive. Each in some way appeals to spiritual problems we need to address. First, they appeal to our self-righteousness. None of us wants to think that we are as bad off as the gospel says we are! We prefer to think that we just need some minor theological tweaking or more faithful church attendance to function as God intended. Yet the gospel says that no system or activity can provide what we need. Our sin is so great that only Christ's work on the cross can rescue us.

These "isms" also appeal to our selfishness. As sinners, we like to be at the center of the universe. We like being the ones who control the agenda. Yet the gospel makes it clear that the only way to really live is first to die, and that those who strive to live end up dying as a result. When the gospel is reduced to a catalog of "isms" where I choose the one most attractive and comfortable for me, I can participate extensively in Christianity without much personal sacrifice, and with my self, unchallenged, at the center of it all.

These "isms" also appeal to our environmentalism. We tend to believe that the sin that surrounds us is more dangerous than the sin that resides inside us. This is why it is hard for a husband to understand that he can't blame his coldness on his wife, nor can the wife blame her bitterness on her husband, nor can their child blame his rebellion on his parents' failures.

When we forget how desperate our condition really is, Christian activity begins to replace a heartfelt reliance on Christ and his grace. We get more excited about changing the world than we do about the radical changes of heart and life that the gospel promises because of Christ's presence in our hearts.

These "isms" also appeal to our independence. It's hard for us to embrace how weak, blind, and vulnerable sin actually makes us. We don't like to think that we need wisdom and correction daily. We prefer the lie of our own self-sufficiency. Sure, we can recognize the blindness and foolishness in others, but we like to think that we are the exception to the rule. It is uncomfortable to see ourselves as needy and weak, but we are, and that is exactly why Christ is the only answer.

Knowledge of the truth and participation in church activities, when viewed improperly, can give you a distorted view of who you are. Knowledge of doctrine is not the same as Christian maturity and victory over sin. Participation in Christian causes should not mask the sin struggles going on in my heart at the same time.

To the degree that you forget you are a sinner, to that degree you will underestimate your daily need for Christ and the relationships in his body that are his tools of change.

We all know on some level that Christ must be our identity, meaning, purpose, hope, and goal. Yet our self-righteousness dies hard. We want to be at the center of our world, and we think we are capable of more independence than would be spiritually helpful. So we tend to reduce the gospel to comfortable elements, none of which do justice to the message of grace found in Christ.

What Should Fill the Gap?

It's amazing how long it took me to really understand the gospel. Like many Christians, I understood early on that my sins had been forgiven (past grace) and that I was going to spend my eternity with Christ (future grace). But I did not grasp the depth of my need for the benefits of the work of Christ now (present grace). My externalistic Christianity needed to be infused with the present power of the gospel. It is not enough to embrace Christ's promise of life after death. We must also embrace his promise of life before death, which is only possible because of Christ's grace at work in our hearts today. This is what this book is about. It celebrates the grace of forgiveness that is ours because of the life, death, and resurrection of Christ, and it keeps its eye on the hope of eternity. But the primary focus of this book is on present grace.

How does God grow and change us while we live here on earth? What has Christ given to help me with that tough conversation with my spouse last Tuesday night? How does his grace impact a person's struggle with depression or fear? What has Christ given to help me deal with the pressures of parenting or the workplace? What provision has he made for my struggles with lust, fear, or materialism? What do repentance and change actually look like? Why do we struggle with one area of sin more than another, doing the thing we never intended to do?

These are the kinds of practical questions this book will address. Our intention is to take the gospel of Christ's grace into all the specific places where you live your life. We believe that you can know why you do the things you do. You can have a clear sense of where change is needed in your life and what that change should look like. You can understand what God is doing in the present and how you can be part of it.

But let me warn you: There is nothing new in this book – no secrets or magic formulas. We are very excited to offer you something you already know, but may not understand fully and practically. Our goal is to bring the old, old story of the gospel to your heart and life in a way that has been heart- and life-changing for us. Often there has been too much of a separation between the theology we say we believe and the world we struggle in every day. The purpose of this book is to bridge that gap.

Five Gospel Perspectives

Five gospel perspectives give this book its direction.

The Extent and Gravity of our Sin

It has been said that the doctrine of sin is the one doctrine you can prove empirically, yet we all tend to minimize it. Early in our marriage my wife Luella graciously pointed out many failures in my love for her. She wasn't being overly critical; she had seen real areas of sin rooted in wrong attitudes in my heart. I knew she loved me and I knew she wasn't crazy, but I simply couldn't believe that I was as bad as she was making me out to be! I look back and cringe at how self-righteous I was. Self-righteousness is your own personal defense attorney. In a scary moment of self-defense, I said to her, "Ninety-five percent of the women in our church would love to be married to me!" (How's that for humility?) Luella sweetly informed me that she was in the five percent!

I was a pastor at the time. I was regularly counseling married couples, helping them deal with the sin that stood in the way of the loving unity God intended for them. I was good at helping other people see and own their sin. But I was not willing to believe that my need was just as desperate. Maybe I was blinded by my theological knowledge or my pastoral skill. But one thing is sure: I had forgotten who I was, and I was offended that Luella had such a low opinion of me!

I don't think I am alone. The struggle to accept our exceeding sinfulness is everywhere in the church of Christ. We accept the doctrine of total depravity, but when we are approached about our own sin, we wrap our robes of self-righteousness around us and rise to our own defense.

Scripture challenges this self-righteousness with clarity and power: "The LORD saw how great man's wickedness on the earth had become, and that every inclination of the thoughts of his heart was only evil all the time" (Gen. 6:5), and " 'There is no one righteous, not even one' " (Rom. 3:10). The effects of sin twist every thought, motive, desire, word, and action. This disease has infected us all, and the consequences are severe.

Why is this perspective so essential? Only when you accept the bad news of the gospel does the good news make any sense. The grace, restoration, reconciliation, forgiveness, mercy, patience, power, healing, and hope of the gospel are for sinners. They are only meaningful to you if you admit that you have the disease and realize that it is terminal.

The Centrality of the Heart

The average Christian defines sin by talking about behavior. For example, what is the goal of most Christian parents? Is it not to get their children to do the right things? We set up all kinds of relational, motivational, and corrective structures to constrain and direct our children's behavior. These structures are not without value, but if this is your only response to your child's rebellion and sin, you will leave him defenseless against sin once he leaves home and the structures are no longer there.

Beneath the battle for behavior is another, more fundamental battle – the battle for the thoughts and motives of the heart.

The heart is the real or essential you. All of the ways in which the Bible refers to the inner person (mind, emotions, spirit, soul, will, etc.) are summed up with this one term: heart. The heart is the steering wheel of every human being. Everything we do is shaped and controlled by what our hearts desire.

That is why the Bible is very clear that God wants our hearts. Only when God has your heart does he have you. As much as we are affected by our broken world and the sins of others against us, our greatest problem is the sin that resides in our hearts. That is why the message of the gospel is that God transforms our lives by transforming our hearts.

Lasting change always comes through the heart. This is one of Scripture's most thoroughly developed themes, but many of us have missed its profound implications. We need a deeper understanding of Proverbs 4:23, "Above all else, guard your heart, for it is the wellspring of life."

The Present Benefits of Christ

The Christian hope is more than a redemptive system with practical principles that can change your life. The hope of every Christian is a person, the Redeemer, Jesus Christ. He is the wisdom behind every biblical principle and the power we need to live them out. Because Christ lives inside us today, because he rules all things for our sakes (Eph. 2:22-23), and because he is presently putting all his enemies under his feet (1 Cor. 15:25-28), we can live with courage and hope.

Our hope is not in our theological knowledge or our experience within the body of Christ. We are thankful for these things, yet we hold onto one hope: Christ. In him we find everything we need to live a godly life in the here and now. Paul captures it so well: "I have been crucified with Christ and I no longer live, but Christ lives in me. The life I live in the body, I live by faith in the Son of God, who loved me and gave himself for me" (Gal. 2:20).

God's Call to Growth and Change

It is so easy to coast! We have been accepted into God's family, and someday will be with him in eternity. But what goes on in between? From the time we come to Christ until the time we go home to be with him, God calls us to change. We have been changed by his grace, are being changed by his grace, and will be changed by his grace.

What is the goal of this change? It is more than a better marriage, well-adjusted children, professional success, or freedom from a few nagging sins. God's goal is that we would actually become like him. He doesn't just want you to escape the fires of hell – though we praise God that through Christ you can! His goal is to free us from our slavery to sin, our bondage to self, and our functional idolatry, so that we actually take on his character!

Peter summarizes the change this way: "Through these he has given us his very great and precious promises, so that through them you may participate in the divine nature and escape the corruption in the world caused by evil desires" (2 Peter 1:4).

A Lifestyle of Repentance and Faith

God has blessed you with his grace, gifted you with his presence, strengthened you with his power, and made you the object of his eternal love. Because we belong to him, we live for his agenda. And if change is his agenda, then repentance and faith is the lifestyle to which we have been called.

Near the end of his career, Michael Jordan was asked why he always came early to practice before a game, even before the rookies. He was already being called the greatest basketball player of all time. He replied that his shooting percentage was just over fifty percent. That meant that over his career, he had failed almost as much as he had succeeded. He was committed to keep on practicing as long as there was room for him to improve.

There are always new sins for the Christian to address and new enemies to defeat. The Christian life makes God's work of change our paradigm for living, while we celebrate the grace that makes it possible. "For the grace of God that brings salvation has appeared to all men. It teaches us to say 'No' to ungodliness and worldly passions, and to live self-controlled, upright and godly lives in this present age, while we wait for the blessed hope – the glorious appearing of our great God and Savior, Jesus Christ" (Titus 2:11-13).

A Celebration

This book is more than an explanation of the Christian life. It is a celebration of the Lord and his daily provision of grace. We invite you to celebrate with us a grace that not only forgives, but changes us from the deepest, darkest corners of our hearts to the smallest action and every idle word.

No matter what you struggle with now, no matter how successful or stuck you see yourself to be, no matter how young or how old you are in the faith, no matter if you are a man or a woman, a boy or a girl, if you are Christ's child, there is hope for you! It is not based on who you are or what you know. Your hope is Jesus! He lives in you and, because of that, you have a reason to celebrate each new day. You no longer live, but Christ lives in you! We welcome you to a lifestyle of celebrating just what that means.

COUNTERFEIT HOPES

Nothing is more obvious than the need for change. Nothing is less obvious than what needs to change and how that change happens!

In Chapter 1, we looked at the gospel gap in the culture of the church. In this chapter, we will consider how broader cultural influences can lead Christians to look beyond Scripture for alternative pathways to change.

The Crucible of Daily Life

Craig is a single man in his thirties. He deals with the ups and downs of his depression every day. When he was ten, his father left the family and Craig was raised by his mother and her parents. During his childhood the family moved four or five times, so Craig always felt like the "new kid on the block." Then, in his twenties, he met Julie. For the first time, he felt like someone cared for him. His life finally seemed to come together. But two years later, his relationship with Julie fell apart. In the six years since, Craig has hoped and prayed that Julie would come back to him.

Craig grew up learning about the Bible and going to church. He considers himself a believer, but with his life and emotions gone flat, he finds Scripture passages and "Christian" advice boring and at times repellent. "You shouldn't think so much about yourself; start thinking about others." "Why aren't you reading your Bible more and attending church regularly?" "God is sovereign." These responses do not work for Craig. They only breed more bitterness and depression.

Craig wants help. He hates being unable to function. He views his life in terms of Murphy's Law: If something can go wrong, it probably will. If something can go right, it probably won't. If his truck breaks down or he gets a toothache, Craig heaps these normal difficulties onto a bigger pile of self-pity, bitterness, and despair. They seem like clear evidence that his life is a joke and that a distant God only plays games with him.

Craig knows something needs to change. But what – and how?

Cindy and John have been married twenty years. They had five children when a sixth pregnancy caught them by surprise. For the past ten years, they have put all their energy into career and family. John helps with laundry, diapers, and housework. He even gets up in the middle of the night to help Cindy with the newborn!

John and Cindy rarely argue. Their marriage is calm, but it is falling apart on the inside. John feels that Cindy doesn't appreciate his involvement or honor his role as her husband. Cindy feels disrespected by John. He doesn't ask for her input on crucial decisions. She finds out about them after the fact. Recently, John bought a car for their teenage son. Cindy found out about it when father and son drove it up the driveway. This fueled the bitterness she has harbored for most of their marriage.

John and Cindy's pattern has existed for a long time. John thinks the marriage may be over. Though John and Cindy profess faith in Christ, attend church regularly, and pray together as a family, the facade is getting harder to hold together. At any moment it could come tumbling down.

John and Cindy know something needs to change, but when it comes to knowing what should change and how that change can be done, they are stuck.

Closer to Home than We Think

John's, Cindy's, and Craig's stories hit close to home. We understand their confusion and how easily they can be deceived by sin. After all, sin sneaks up on us over time. We are like the proverbial frog in the kettle of slowly boiling water. The water grows warmer and warmer and the frog simply adjusts to the temperature little by little until he is cooked!

Craig didn't wake up one morning and decide that life was overwhelming. It happened over time, though he doesn't understand how. John and Cindy did not think that their marriage was moving towards death. At each stage, they made adjustments and excuses that allowed them to keep functioning. But at a crisis point, their problems rose to the surface and they began to speak out about their frustrations. Silence and ignorance wouldn't work any more. In fact, sidestepping the problems had made matters worse. Now they were too big to ignore any longer.

Craig, John, and Cindy need help. They need to identify the real problem and discover the real solution.

False Hope

We all live on the continuum between slavery and freedom. The Bible warns about the deceitfulness of sin and its bondage. It is full of promises of the freedom we have in Christ. But our culture has its own warnings and promises of freedom, false solutions promised in various theories of change. These alternative theories seem appealing. They promise us that we can avoid chaos, live in freedom, and keep our own agenda and pride intact.

Christians have always faced these problems. We have always had to sift through false promises and theories of change. Even in the first century, Paul had these words for fellow believers:

> So then, just as you received Christ Jesus as Lord, continue to live in him, rooted and built up in him, strengthened in the faith as you were taught, and overflowing with thankfulness. See to it that no one takes you captive through hollow and deceptive philosophy, which depends on human tradition and the basic principles of this world rather than on Christ. (Col. 2:6-8)

Do Not Be Abducted

Paul is concerned that we not allow ourselves to be taken "captive by hollow and deceptive philosophy." The Greek word translated "taken captive" is actually closer to "abducted" or "kidnapped." Paul's point is that we can be abducted by falsehood when we least expect it. He urges us to live with our eyes open to the cultural influences that seek to gain our allegiance when we are not really paying attention. Don't be fooled. Don't think that Paul's advice applies only to big decisions and major doctrines. It is in the little moments of life that battles are lost or won.

I experienced this myself one afternoon when my wife and I were busy doing yard work. Several of our children were playing outside and helping out a bit. It was an encouraging moment for a father until I began wondering where my other child might be. She was not outside helping. She was busy Instant Messaging her friends on the family computer. I started counting up the hours she had spent at the computer over the past several days and I began to get angry. Why isn't she helping with the rest of the family? She's on the computer too much. She rarely does her share around the house. And my anger grew.

What was ironic was that all week I had been praying and preparing for a sermon on humility and patience! But in my back yard, I was quickly taken captive by the idea that my anger was legitimate, that there was nothing wrong with me, but everything was wrong with my child. At that point, I voiced my irritation to my wife. I'm thankful that, in humility and patience, she challenged me. But even then, I justified my irritation and blamed my wife for not holding the line with our child. All this happened in a matter of minutes while I was meditating on a passage about loving difficult people!

I had been given an opportunity to practice what I planned to preach, but I chose to go in the opposite direction. Instead of experiencing change in my own attitudes and behavior, I focused on my circumstances. I conveniently shifted the responsibility for change away from me to my daughter. I kept my agenda intact and, in my heart, moved towards my daughter in sinful ways. The problem, from my selfish point of view, was my daughter. The solution was to change her. I justified my sinful anger in the name of fatherly discipline and accountability. And while this could have been an appropriate time to challenge my daughter's choices, I had started in the wrong place: her behavior, not my own attitudes and emotions.

By Hollow and Deceptive Philosophy

How are we so easily captivated? Paul tells us that we get captivated by hollow and deceptive diagnoses and solutions that present themselves as superior to Christ. Our culture abounds with hollow and deceptive theories of change that masquerade as biblical wisdom, often because they borrow some aspect of biblical truth. Yet they are hollow because they miss the center of biblical wisdom, which is Christ. In some way, they allow the person to live independent of Christ and avoid the deep heart transformation that only Christ can bring about.

What deceptive and hollow alternatives exist in our culture? What presents itself as a plausible alternative to Christ-centered change? These philosophies depend on human tradition and the basic principles of this world rather than on Christ. They might be offered to John, Cindy, and Craig (and you and me) by well-intentioned helpers, but they drag us away from Christ and all of his benefits. Let's consider some of the most common perspectives.

What Needs to Change?

My Circumstances?

The most popular simplistic approach to change focuses on external circumstances. "I need more money." "If I could change my looks, my life would be better." "If I could get married, life would sing." "If I could get out of this marriage and find someone who appreciates me, I wouldn't be so depressed." "If my children respected me the way they should, I would be nicer." This is the kind of thinking I fell prey to with my daughter. It seemed so right to focus on her faults and her need to change. Finger-pointing is the strategy, and the goal is to change my life by changing the circumstances around me.

In the garden, just after the fall, Adam was the first to employ this approach by blaming Eve (and God) for his own sin: "It was the woman you gave me." It's the other person's fault. If it is not another person, it's something else – the hard day at work that leads me to snap at you; the lack of money that leads me to cheat on my taxes. In every difficult situation, temptation abounds to blame others.

This approach to change is not only deceptive, but hollow as well. It misses my need for Christ's redeeming grace, and it places the blame for my sin at God's doorstep! We blame God for placing the problem person or circumstance in our life. We question God's wisdom, goodness, and character. Obviously, with this approach, the grace of God will not be sought or received.

My Behavior?

Sometimes we are willing to acknowledge that the need for change is a little closer to home. "I should be more patient and nicer to my wife." "I have to stop blowing up at my kids and start to give more to my church." "I should reach out to my neighbors and quit visiting those internet sites." "I shouldn't let people's opinions drive me crazy!"

Very likely, all of these statements are true. Your behavior does need to change! But this approach only addresses external actions. It does not go after the reasons why you continue to do these things. Instead, the person simply hopes to replace bad behavior with good. He believes he just needs some skills. He doesn't want to do the time-consuming and painful work of looking at motivation. He just wants to deal with the problem behavior with techniques that will help him navigate life more smoothly.

In John and Cindy's case, this approach might lead them to learn better communication skills – the dos and don'ts of conflict, and some strategies for meeting each other's needs. A "Christian" version of this approach would include some Bible verses to instruct them in new ways to act.

What's wrong with that? John and Cindy do need to learn new skills to live together. The Bible is full of principles and commands to be patient, speak the truth in love, listen well, and speak gently and in edifying ways. Yet a behavioral approach to change is hollow because it ignores the need for Christ and his power to change first the heart and then the behavior. Instead, even the Christian version of this approach separates the commands of Scripture from their Christ-centered, gospel context.

The Bible passages that emphasize the need for new behavior are all built on the foundation of God's grace at work to change our hearts through the power of the Spirit. The Word and Spirit work together, enabling us to see Christ in all his power and mercy. This leads to heart change at the level of what we worship and cherish at any given moment. This kind of radical heart change reorients me vertically – person to God – and I repent of what I have cherished in place of Christ. This vertical change then leads to new behavior on the horizontal, person-to-person, plane. An approach to change that only focuses on external behavior is never enough. Biblical change is so much more!

My Thinking?

You've seen the TV ads. They focus on a social malady like racism or sexually transmitted diseases and end with an upbeat message that education changes people. In this approach to change, your thinking needs to be adjusted so that your behavior will reflect appropriate thoughts about your circumstances. Craig, for example, might be asked to think about the unmet goals in life that cause him to feel disappointment. He might be encouraged to adjust his expectations so that he will be less depressed if they are not met.

This view of change is closer to a truly biblical understanding of change, but it is not sufficient. Our expectations and desires do play an enormous role in determining our actions and responses to life, and the Bible does call us to change the way we think about things. But this approach again omits the person and work of Christ as Savior. Instead, it reduces our relationship to Christ to "think his thoughts" and "act the way Jesus would act." If you have a problem with anger, you are told to memorize certain verses so that you can recite them in moments of anger. If you struggle with fear, you should read Scripture passages that focus on trusting God when you are afraid.

This emphasis on thinking as the solution to our problems fails to introduce the Person who has come not only to change the way we think about life, but to change us as well. We are more than thinkers. We are worshipers who enter into relationship with the person or thing we think will give us life. Jesus comes to transform our entire being, not just our mind. He comes as a person, not as a cognitive concept we insert into a new formula for life.

My Self-Concept?

"Believe in yourself!" "You're a good, gifted person. Go for it." "You can do anything you put your mind to." "Don't be so hard on yourself." This approach to change looks within oneself for the power to change. This seems deeper because it addresses our innermost feelings. It just "feels" more real.

This view begins with a positive view of our innate goodness and the need to affirm our goodness. The more we do, we are told, the more we will be able to love ourselves and others. The great commandment is often cited as biblical proof for this theory of change: "You can't love God or others if you don't first love yourself." It all sounds so biblical! But it makes assumptions about the human heart that the Bible does not. The most important assumption this theory makes is that our hearts are empty and need to be filled. But the Bible does not say that we are empty. Rather, it says that we are a cauldron of desires for everything but the true and living God. This approach says that if we feel hollow, it is because the things we pursue are not enough to satisfy what only God can satisfy. But we are not empty beings! We are rebels against God. This view is deceptive because it seems to capture how we feel inside, but it makes us look far more passive and innocent than we really are. The Bible describes us as defectors and enemies of God who want to fill ourselves with things in creation rather than the Creator (Rom. 1:21-25). This view flatters us far more than we deserve.

Scripture's approach calls us to forsake the things we have sought to fill our emptiness. Before we can be filled with God's grace, we must engage in intelligent, honest repentance. We have to forsake and demolish the god-replacements that have supplanted the true God in our lives. Repentance is a form of emptying the heart. James 4:1 says that we fight with others, not because we are empty, but because we are full of desires that battle within us. Along with deep repentance, Scripture calls us to faith that rests and feeds upon the living Christ. He fills us with himself through the person of the Holy Spirit and our hearts are transformed by faith.

The Bible agrees that guilt and self-loathing can hinder change. On a superficial reading, it would seem plausible that we need lots of affirmation: If I can just deal with this oppressive guilt and increase my self-esteem, then I will be free to live and love. But this approach is hollow because it does not offer good news for the guilty and self-loathing person. Instead of connecting our guilt and shame to our own sin and rebellion against God, this view downplays our guilt and misses a great opportunity to call us to esteem Christ's work on our behalf. It obscures the path to real forgiveness, joy, and peace at the cross. Similarly, the person who labors under a false sense of guilt and shame because of the sins of others against her needs more than affirmation and boosts to her self-esteem. She needs to see that the cross clarifies that she is responsible only for her own sins, not the sins of others that have so deeply wounded her. God's view of sin lifts her shame and self-loathing by giving her an identity that is rooted in Christ, not in the evil she has experienced.

The cross reminds us that though we are made in God's image, we are deeply flawed and bent towards loving ourselves above all. It is this self-love that creates such guilt and shame. Deep down we know we don't measure up. We feel small because we are small, but false teaching encourages us to reject those thoughts of smallness by affirming our own greatness. This may work for awhile, but it rarely lasts. Reminders of our smallness and our failures bring us back to where we started. But the cross of Christ shows me how glorious, merciful, and forgiving God is and how great his love is for me in Christ. This recognition of my guilt and God's glory is the only thing that can eradicate shame and self-loathing. And it is found outside me, not within me. I am called to esteem God, not myself.

Just Trust Jesus More?

Yes! But who is the Jesus I need to trust? In some approaches to change, Jesus is the therapist who meets all my needs. If the self-esteem approach to change is deceptive and hollow, this last one is even more so because it specifically introduces Jesus into the equation. But is Jesus my therapist or my Redeemer? If he is my therapist, then he meets my needs as I define them. If he is my Redeemer, he defines my true needs and addresses them in ways far more glorious than I could have anticipated.

If Jesus is my therapist, he is the One who comes to affirm me. Instead of trying to love ourselves, we think about how much Jesus loves us. This approach is deceptive because it latches onto a very powerful aspect of the gospel: God does shower his love upon us in Christ! Everyone who reads the Bible knows this. But this approach subtly turns Jesus into the one who meets my needs and fills my emptiness – as I define them. It turns God's love into something that only serves me. Repentance for our rebellion and sin against God is minimized or even ignored while God's love for us is maximized. We turn Jesus into someone whose goal in life is to make us feel good about ourselves.

But God's holy love is not like this at all. God's holy love grants forgiveness and cleanses us of our guilt, but it also calls us to admit that we have forsaken his love and settled for things that pale in comparison. C. S. Lewis describes God's love as very different from our shallow, self-centered human love:

> . . . In awful and surprising truth, we are the objects of His love. You asked for a loving God; you have one. The great spirit you so lightly invoked, the "lord of terrible aspect," is present; not a senile

benevolence that drowsily wishes you to be happy in your own way, not the cold philanthropy of a conscientious magistrate, not the care of a host who feels responsible for the comfort of his guests, but the consuming fire Himself, the Love that made the worlds, persistent as the artist's love for his work and despotic as a man's love for a dog, provident and venerable as a father's love for a child, jealous, inexorable, exacting as love between the sexes . . . It is certainly a burden of glory not only beyond our deserts but also, except in rare moments of grace, beyond our desiring.[1]

The holy love of God for sinners is humbling and uplifting at the same time. It calls the sinner to admit his own self-centeredness while cleansing and freeing him from the cage of false love.

Craig, John, and Cindy need so much more than a good feeling about themselves. Yes, they need to see how great God's love is for them in Christ, but they also desperately need to see how often their infatuation for other things replaces God's love in their lives.

Jesus is not a vending machine that dispenses what we want to feel good about ourselves. He is the Holy One who comes to cleanse us, fill us, and change us. He does not do this according to our agendas. He will not serve our wayward needs. He loves us too much to merely make us happy. He comes to make us holy. There will be many occasions when he will not give us what we think we need, but rather, he will give us what he knows we need.

True Hope

In Colossians 2, Paul goes on to argue that we are full in Christ (vv. 9-10), made alive in Christ (v. 11-12) and set free in Christ (vv. 13-15). This changes everything, including the way we struggle against sin.

For in Christ all the fullness of the Deity lives in bodily form, and you have been given fullness in Christ, who is the head over every power and authority. In him, you were also circumcised, in the putting off of the sinful nature, not with a circumcision done by the hands of men but with the circumcision done by Christ, having been buried with him in baptism and raised with him through your faith in the power of God, who raised him from the dead.

When you were dead in your sins and in the uncircumcision of your sinful nature, God made you alive with Christ. He forgave us all our sins, having canceled the written code, with its regulations, that was against us and that stood opposed to us; he took it away, nailing it to the cross. And having disarmed the powers and authorities, he made a public spectacle of them, triumphing over them by the cross. (Col. 2:9-15)

You Are Full In Christ

Everything about God has been revealed in Christ, and when someone becomes a Christian, all that fullness dwells in him. We don't need anything else to fill us up – we have Christ. This is staggering when you consider the greatness of our glorious, mighty, gracious and holy God. Notice, too, that Paul says that this is true of you now. It is who you really are. You are the temple of God. God has chosen to reside in you by the Holy Spirit. You are his and he is yours! Second Peter 1:4 says that believers "participate in the divine nature and escape the corruption in the world caused by evil desires." We do not become divine, but we have the Divine One living in us from the moment we trust in Christ. We have everything we need to live in godly ways. There is no need to be seduced by deceptive and hollow promises of change that lead us away from Christ. These promises will prove to be forms of bondage that enslave us to ourselves and our self-sufficiency. They "protect" us from giving up control and wind up enslaving us to our own agendas.

It is always tempting to find fullness in something other than Christ. Often I opt for peace and comfort rather than Jesus. When I do, I can move in two opposite but equally sinful directions. If I am irritated with you because you get in the way of the things that comfort me, I may lash out at you and keep you from taking what I think I need. But I can also fake "godly" behavior to get the same result. I may choose to "be nice" in order to extract some kindness from you.

On several occasions I have had arguments with my wife, knowing that a good baseball game was about to air on T.V. Watching a game is a time of peace and comfort for me. Because I want that experience, I may apologize to my wife and even ask her to forgive me for the way I sinned against her. From the outside, this may look godly, but on the inside, I was simply faking godliness to get what I wanted. If I consciously live in light of the fact that I am full in Christ, I will ask for forgiveness whether or not I get to watch the game. The most obvious way to determine if my actions were sincere is to look at my behavior when the game comes on and I am interrupted again. If I become agitated, my confession and request for forgiveness were most likely a subtle way of manipulating my wife to get what I wanted.

Paul says that we have been given fullness in Christ. If I act on this truth, nothing can empty me of what is already mine. Baseball game or no baseball game, I can live peaceably with my wife and family. This simple illustration may not be all too impressive, but if the blessings of Christ do not change us in little moments like these, the chances that they will change us in more difficult moments are slim. It is in the everyday details that the grace of Christ must be applied.

New Record and New Power

The fullness of Christ gives us two things: It cleanses us from sin and it raises us to new life! Paul is stressing that the forgiveness of sins brings us freedom over the powers of evil. Our new record and new power are never separated in Scripture and we must keep them together in our lives as well.

The sacrament of baptism depicts these two realities. First, we are cleansed. Sin has been washed away and we have a new standing before God, accepted by him because of what Jesus has done for us.

Baptism also emphasizes that the believer is united to the family of God. Baptism initiates us into the community of faith, where everything Jesus died to give us becomes ours. He died the death we should have died and we escape the condemnation he received. His resurrection is our resurrection. God is satisfied with us because he is satisfied with him. We are raised to new life as the Holy Spirit is given to us.

What does all this mean? It means that we have a new record. Jesus' payment for sin and his righteous life becomes ours. We also have new power. The Holy Spirit that raised Jesus from the dead now lives in us, bringing new life and power to grow in Christ-likeness. Again, notice that the Bible does not separate our new record and new power. One without the other is not true fullness. What if you were given a new record but no new power to live the Christian life? That would be hollow and empty because you would soon fall. What if you were given a new power but no new record? You could change but you would still stand condemned because your past could not be erased. But in Christ, you get it all. You are regenerated, forgiven, and treated as if you had perfectly obeyed the law. The Holy Spirit gives you the power to grow in your sanctification. And you are promised that one day you will be made perfect and live with God forever. No wonder Paul argues that you are full to overflowing! You lack nothing. You don't need Christ plus something else. He is enough. All that he is, we are.

Set Free In Christ

Paul applies the reality of our fullness in Christ even further. With the new record and new power we have received, we are set free from the enslaving power of sin and the condemnation of the law. We are dead to the world and we have power over the Evil One who tempts us with worldly Christ-replacements. We don't have to be controlled by them any more! We are now free to live, act, think, and believe in new and surprising ways.

In Colossians 2:14-15, Christ makes his victory public by subjecting these powers to open ridicule. As one commentator puts it:

> The Roman triumphal procession was the best way to bring home to people that their returning generals had been winning genuine victories. No one in town that day could possibly be ignorant of what had happened as hundreds of weary prisoners of war were paraded, straggling behind the conquering army. Shamed and exposed to public gaze, everyone can see that there is nothing to fear from these once proud soldiers. This splendid illustration is exactly suited to Paul's purpose [in v. 15]. He is intent on showing that true spiritual freedom was won for all God's people through the cross of Christ. Furthermore, this is no secret to be understood and claimed by a favoured few. It is impossible for anyone to know this King and not to know his glorious victory. Freedom from demonic forces is no second or subsequent work of grace to be sought at the hands of God. It is, simply, the gospel privilege for all. For of every true believer it is written that they have already come to fullness of life in Christ, the one who is the head of all rule and authority.[2]

In light of this decisive victory, no wonder the gospel message is called "Good News"!

The Real World

Even more amazing, this news is communicated to believers who lived with persecution, hardship, threats of torture and martyrdom, along with the normal trials of life. The gospel speaks with hope and encouragement against that bleak backdrop. We too have good reason to take heart at these "great and precious promises" that we can "escape the corruption in the world caused by evil desires" (2 Peter 1:4).

In Colossians, our fullness in Christ intersects with the new struggles that emerge when we become Christians. In Colossians 3: 5-11, Paul adds:

> Put to death, therefore, whatever belongs to your earthly nature: sexual immorality, impurity, lust, evil desires and greed, which is idolatry. Because of these, the wrath of God is coming. You used to walk in these ways, in the life you once lived. But now you must rid yourselves of all such things as these: anger, rage, malice, slander, and filthy language from your lips. Do not lie to each other, since you have taken off your old self with its practices and have put on the new self, which is being renewed in knowledge in the image of its Creator. Here there is no Greek or Jew, circumcised or uncircumcised, barbarian, Scythian, slave or free, but Christ is all, and is in all.

Nothing is subtle about the ongoing war that rages throughout the Christian life. Trials and temptations abound, but we respond to them from a new vantage point. J. C. Ryle captures the active reliance upon Christ that is necessary for our sanctification. Holiness must begin with Christ. We must first belong to him.

> Would you be holy? Would you become a new creature? Then you must begin with Christ. You will do nothing at all, and make no progress till you feel your sin and weakness, and flee to Him. He is the root and beginning of all holiness, and the way to be holy is to come to Him by faith and be joined to him . . . Men sometimes try to make themselves holy first of all, and sad work they make of it. They toil and labour, and turn over new leaves, and make many changes; and yet, like the woman with the issue of blood, before she came to

Christ, they feel "nothing bettered, but rather worse" (Mark 5:26). They run in vain, and labour in vain; and little wonder, for they are beginning at the wrong end. They are building up a wall of sand; their work runs down as fast as they throw it up. They are bailing water out of a leaky vessel; the leak gains on them, not they on the leak . . . It is a strong but true saying of Traill's, "Wisdom out of Christ is damning folly – righteousness out of Christ is guilt and condemnation – sanctification out of Christ is filth and sin – redemption out of Christ is bondage and slavery."

Do you want to attain holiness? Do you feel this day a real hearty desire to be holy? Would you be a partaker of the Divine nature? Then go to Christ. Wait for nothing. Wait for nobody. Linger not. Think not to make yourself ready. Go and say to Him, in the words of that beautiful hymn – "Nothing in my hand I bring, Simply to Thy cross I cling; Naked, flee to Thee for dress; Helpless, look to Thee for grace." There is not a brick nor a stone laid in the work of our sanctification till we go to Christ.[3]

This centrality of Christ must continue throughout our Christian life. Ryle continues:

Would you continue holy? Then abide in Christ. He says Himself, "Abide in Me and I in you, – he that abideth in Me and I in him, the same beareth much fruit" (John 15:4-5). It pleased the Father that in Him should all fullness dwell – a full supply for all a believer's wants. He is the Physician to whom you must daily go, if you would keep well. He is the Manna which you must daily eat, and the Rock of which you must daily drink. His arm is the arm on which you must daily lean, as you come up out of the wilderness of this world. You must not only be rooted, you must also be built up in Him.[4]

The blessings that are ours in Christ encourage us to begin fighting the spiritual battle that awaits us. As J. C. Ryle said, "A true Christian is one who has not only peace of conscience, but war within."[5] We are united to Christ for a purpose: "For he chose us in him before the creation of the world to be holy and blameless in his sight" (Eph. 1:4). Our new life in Christ is just that: new life. A glorious fight against the world, the flesh, and the devil is at its heart and one of the clearest signs of our union with him.

Change Is Possible!

The goal of this book is to help you grasp the implications of the good news of Jesus Christ for your identity and the daily trials and temptations you face. Since we are so easily captivated by hollow and deceptive alternatives to the gospel, we need a clearer understanding of what Christ has done. Like Craig, John, and Cindy, we need a clear and specific understanding of how Christ changes us by his grace.

Nothing could be more liberating for Craig as he struggles with depression. Craig has been duped. He thinks of himself primarily as a depressed person and secondarily as a Christian. His depression is the functional identity out of which he acts, reacts, interprets, and responds to life. No wonder he looks at life in terms of Murphy's Law! But Paul says that anyone who belongs to Christ is cleansed and made alive. Craig is not a depressed Christian, but a Christian who struggles with depression. This is more than a semantic nuance. Craig is first and foremost a Christian. His identity in Christ is built on a solid foundation that never shifts, though his emotional state may change from day to day. Craig is not beyond Christ's redemptive power. His Christ-centered identity does not eliminate the ongoing struggle with sin, but Craig is never defined by his particular sin struggle. His identity is bound up in who he is in Christ.

Cindy and John don't have to drift apart, believing that nothing will ever change. They do not have to define themselves in terms of their struggling marriage. Jesus, the true Bridegroom, is with them now and he brings past and future blessings into the center of their marriage. This is true for you too. Christ bridges the gap between struggle and change with the new identity, new record, and new power his salvation brings.

Our world offers many alternative theories of change that lead us away from Christ and his grace. Have these counterfeit hopes affected you? Has your hope in Christ been overshadowed by other promises of freedom that bypass or minimize what Christ has done? Keep reading to grow in your understanding and experience of Jesus and the gifts that are ours through his life, death, resurrection, ascension, and promised return.

HERE'S WHERE GOD IS TAKING YOU

Human beings are "meaning makers." We look for the meaning and purpose in every event, activity, and relationship in our lives. The toddler who asks his mother if God made telephone poles is a meaning maker. The second grade girl who advises her friend on how to get other girls to like her is a meaning maker. The husband and wife who discuss why the husband can't get along with his boss are meaning makers. The elderly woman who wonders why her daughter doesn't visit is a meaning maker.

Meaning making is something we do unconsciously but incessantly. We never stop trying to figure life out. We ask questions. We make assumptions, draw conclusions, make connections, interpret data, and make distinctions. Whether it is the horror of war, a cancer diagnosis, a friend's divorce, a parenting problem, a neighbor's snub, or the state of the economy, we seek to make sense out of everything that happens around us.

Whether we suffer, strive, achieve, or relax, we ask ourselves consciously or subconsciously, What is the point? What does it all mean? And here is the important part: the answers we give ourselves, the meanings we give to our thoughts, circumstances, relationships, and actions, move us in specific directions.

Joan and Bryan married very young. They joked that they would grow up together. Joan grew up, but Bryan didn't. After ten years of marriage, he still approached life like a teenager. He spent too much time with "the guys" and too much money on his "man toys." He took as many hunting and fishing vacations without Joan as he took family vacations with her. He went from job to job because he was never focused on his work. He and Joan were always in debt. Bryan said he was a Christian, but he seemed ready to avoid Christian responsibility whenever he could.

Joan tried everything to turn Bryan into a responsible man. She tried to make their marriage work. She made their home comfortable and even dragged Bryan to counseling on several occasions. Nothing seemed to help. Bryan was immature and self-absorbed. One day, in desperation, Joan packed up, took her two daughters, and drove cross country to her mother's. Six months later, she filed for divorce because she just could not go back to "that selfish man."

Frank was hurt. He had dedicated himself to his downtown church for years, at a time when many believers fled for the ease of suburban Christianity. He did everything he could to contribute his gifts to the ministry he loved. Frank lived with his eyes open to ministry needs and willingly stepped in to fill them. Single with lots of free time, Frank made the church his family, his favorite hobby, and his social network.

Frank was also an avid student of his faith. He took all the discipleship classes the church offered. He read on his own and took evening classes at the local Christian college. He signed up for elder and deacon training every time it was offered. He knew his Bible, but he was always hungry to know more.

But Frank didn't know if he could recover from this blow. For the fifth time, he had been passed over when men were nominated for the office of elder. Frank looked at the list of men: none of them were as active in the church as he was; few of them knew their faith as well as he did. It didn't make sense! He sat on his bed that Sunday night and said to himself, I'm done. Within a few weeks Frank resigned from all ministry involvements and left the church.

Nikki didn't know why she was down, she just was. When she thought about it, she realized she had many more "down" days than "up" days. She hated the way she looked. Her weight made her self-conscious and insecure. She had trouble keeping the house neat and clean. She tried each new diet book, and every new book on the keys to domestic success, but they only left her feeling more defeated. She struggled each day knowing that Rob worked in an office filled with bright, attractive, and successful women. One morning, she looked in the mirror and realized that her motivation for living was slipping away. The twins were still visiting their grandmother, so she took the phone off the hook and climbed back into bed.

Bo knew it might happen some day, but he never thought that it actually would. The year before, he had inherited a huge amount of money. He had always thought of himself as a godly man committed to a simple lifestyle. He didn't need to eat at fine restaurants or buy expensive shirts. His vacations weren't lavish, his house and car were unremarkable. He hadn't expected the money to make that much difference. But it had.

First, he talked himself into a new sports car, telling himself that it was well-made and efficient. He bought a big new house because it would be a great place for ministry. The new wardrobe and country club membership just seemed to go with the package. By the time Bo bought the boat, he no longer needed to argue with himself about the legitimacy of the purchase. He was a man with money and he liked the luxury and prestige it purchased for him.

What Is and What Could Be

Joan, Frank, Nikki, and Bo have some important things in common. Each is dealing with the temptations sinners face in a fallen world. Sometimes these temptations greet us in the little moments of life; at other times we encounter them in times of great significance. Some temptations hit us hardest in times of difficulty and disappointment and others in times of unusual blessing.

In the middle of our own life stories, we try to make sense of what is going on. Instinctively, we sense that things are not the way God designed them. The world we live in is broken, and sometimes it seems so broken that we don't think that there is anything we can do or say to make a difference. Instead, we spend our time dreaming about what could be: If only my boss were more patient. If only my family were closer. If only my living expenses were lower. If only my son would quit arguing. If only we had been able to buy that house. If only our church was more responsive to single parents. If only I had more time.

We all have a personal dream of a better life. We examine our lives, decide where change is needed, and imagine what it would look like. The problem is that our desires don't go deep enough. It is here that the Bible challenges our dreams.

As we saw in Chapter 2, when most people dream of change taking place, we think the change needs to take place outside ourselves. We think, How much better life would be if a certain situation or a relationship were different! Meanwhile, God says that what needs change most is us! He does not just work to fix situations and relationships; he is intent on rescuing us from ourselves. We are the focus of his loving, lifelong work of change.

Conflicting Dreams

Imagination. The ability we have to envision what could be is both wonderful and dangerous. It is wonderful to "see" the unseen, to think ahead and see dreams fulfilled. This motivates human beings.

But dreaming is never morally neutral because the dreamer is never neutral. Herein lies the danger of this intensely human gift. Our ability to dream is easily kidnapped by our sin. While our dreams can reveal our faith, they also expose the lust, greed, selfishness, fear, anger, doubt, hopelessness, and materialism of our hearts. We are fallen dreamers, who dream of better worlds than the one in which we live. But the dreams we envision are often more about our own agenda than they are about our Lord's. Though we may not be aware of it, we are often at odds with our wise and loving Lord. The change he is working on is not the change we dream about. We dream about change in it – a person or circumstance – but God is working in the midst of it to change us. How does he want to change us?

Jesus lived and died so that "those who live should no longer live for themselves but for him who died for them and was raised again" (2 Cor. 5:15). God's love comes into your life to change what you live for.

Peter puts it this way: "That . . . you may participate in the divine nature and escape the corruption in the world caused by evil desires" (2 Peter 1:4). We all want the wrong things, but God is in the business of changing what we want. Everything you ever say or do is the result of some kind of desire. The change Peter talks about is change at the most fundamental level. Peter says that God works to replace my sinful, selfish nature with his divine nature! God reshapes me into his own image. Amid all of life's confusion, he transforms my heart so that I can think, desire, speak, and act in ways consistent with who he is and what he is doing on earth. Positive personal change takes place when my dreams of change line up with God's purposes for change. As I leave behind goals of personal comfort and self-fulfillment, I reach out for Christ. I want to be more like him each day. As I do, I become more prepared for my ultimate destination, eternity with him.

But it doesn't come naturally to connect our desires with God's ultimate purposes. Two realities exist within each Christian: (1) We all have our own instinctive ways of thinking, feeling, acting, and wanting in response to life. (2) Our ultimate purpose is to become like Christ and live with him forever.

It simply does not come naturally for us to connect these two realities. The daily work of the Spirit is what makes this connection. This book is written to help you understand how God meets you and changes you in the middle of life's joys and sorrows. We want you to know how to make God's ultimate dream your purpose for living.

Something Worth Dreaming About

What do you regularly pray about? What kind of "needs" dominate your prayers? As you deal with what is, how do you pray about what could be? Your prayers reveal your dreams. In prayer, we tell God what we think we need. We ask for what we want. Contrast your normal prayers with what Paul prays about in Philippians:

> I thank my God every time I remember you. In all my prayers for all of you, I always pray with joy because of your partnership in the gospel from the first day until now, being confident of this, that he who began a good work in you will carry it on to completion until the day of Christ Jesus.
>
> It is right for me to feel this way about all of you, since I have you in my heart; for whether I am in chains or defending and confirming the gospel, all of you share in God's grace with me. God can testify how I long for all of you with the affection of Christ Jesus.
>
> And this is my prayer: that your love may abound more and more in knowledge and depth of insight, so that you may be able to discern what is best and may be pure and blameless until the day of Christ, filled with the fruit of righteousness that comes through Jesus Christ – to the glory and praise of God. (Phil. 1:3-11)

Can you pick up Paul's excitement? It is quite different from the excitement driving many of the prayers we pray. This prayer is both real and hopeful. Paul knows the people he prays for, with all their weaknesses and challenges. Yet as he thinks about them, he brims with confidence! His confidence is not in his readers' ability to get their act together. Paul's confidence is for these people but not in them. It is completely vertical – man to God – and personal. Paul is confident for the believers in Philippi because his confidence rests on Jesus Christ. Paul is convinced that the good work Jesus began in them will continue until he brings it to completion (vv. 3-5).

As Paul looks at the Philippians, he is also able to pray with joy. He is joyful about their partnership in the gospel. He is joyful about Christ's continued work in their lives. He is joyful in his own love for them, and joyful in their sharing in God's grace with him. Paul wants them to know that they can experience all of these things, and they too can be like him: positive, confident, expectant, and active. The kind of growth Paul desires for the Philippians (vv. 9-11) is rooted in a love for Christ that

- abounds in love and discernment;
- is pure and blameless;
- is filled with the fruit of righteousness.

Paul prays that the Philippian believers' love for God would result in acts of love for others. This is where God wants to take them, and where God wants to take us as well. No matter what you face today, you can be encouraged that God's good work continues in your life, even when you don't see it. God continues his work right in the middle of that tough situation at work, or with your teenager, or that battle with your weight, or your struggle with discouragement. God moves you forward as you submit yourself to him. His presence and faithful work give us confidence. As you have that tough conversation with a friend, you can say to yourself, Christ is working right now to complete what he started in me. As you struggle with your finances, you can say to your spouse, "We can get through this because Christ is working right now to complete what he has begun in us." When it seems that you are in a losing battle with sin, you can say, I have hope for victory because Christ is working in me right now to complete what he has begun.

This Christ-centered confidence moves us toward our ultimate goal, the thing for which we were made, the praise and glory of God (v. 11). Remember that as Paul writes to the Philippians, he is in prison, testing for himself the very truths he is so eager to have them understand!

Life is seldom simple. Growth in God's grace is a process and not an event. Tough things are not going to turn around overnight because you have entrusted them to the Lord. The Bible is honest in its description of how grave and comprehensive our war with sin is. Individuals, friendships, churches, marriages, and neighborhoods don't turn around in a moment. The Bible describes the Christian life as a journey that often takes us through the wilderness. You will get tired and confused. You will have moments when you wonder where God is. You will struggle to see God's promises at work in your life. You will feel that following God has brought you more suffering than blessing. You will go through moments when it seems like the principles of Scripture don't work. It will sometimes seem like the wrong side wins. There will be moments when you feel alone and misunderstood. There will be times when you feel like quitting.

This passage is meant to encourage you to be full of hope in the midst of things you don't fully understand. You don't have to figure everything out. You do need to know and trust the One who does understand, and who knows exactly what he is doing. Do you look at your life as Paul looked at the Philippians' lives and his own? Do you live with Christ-centered confidence? Do you want what God wants for you, or do you hold tightly onto your own agenda?

God will not quit until every bit of his work is complete in each of his children. We can have courage and hope in any situation. God's dream for us will come true.

Seeing with the Eyes of Christ

What you see when you look at yourself will condition your hope and shape your actions. Imagine a house for sale as a "handyman special." One buyer sees the house as it is: the crumbling chimney, the broken windows, the 1930s kitchen, the missing shingles, the outdated wiring, the roof that should have been replaced ten years ago, and the overgrown yard. He is overwhelmed by what it would take to restore the house. His shoulders sag and he drives away. Too much work, not enough hope.

Another buyer sees the same house but looks ahead to what it will be when it is restored. He sees kids playing soccer in the yard, guests laughing together on the wraparound porch, a wonderful meal cooking in the kitchen, the neighborhood being revitalized. Do both buyers look at the same house? Yes. Same possibilities? Yes. But only one buyer has the hope and the courage to believe that he can do what is necessary to make a new reality.

As you look at the "house" that is your life, what do you see? Do you see problems and get overwhelmed? Do you give up and walk away? Does the way you look at your problems cause you to be defensive and angrily pretend they aren't there? Do you speak in biblical platitudes in public, but give way to panic in private? Do you escape into TV, food, busyness, or other distractions? Or do you see the problems through the eyes of Christ, with hope in his presence, his work, and his power to change you? In light of Philippians 1:3-11, how does God welcome you to look at your life in a brand new way? What does God want you to see? As you consider your life in light of this hope-infused passage, how is this moment a step towards the final destination God has planned for you? The process of change – the rehabbing of your house – is going somewhere. Of that you can be confident!

Living with the Destination in View

The Bible contains the world's best and most important story, the story of redemption. You and I live between the first and second coming of Christ in the middle of the story. Sometimes life can seem a lot like reading a novel. You're in the middle of the story and you can't resist scanning the last chapters to see how things turn out. It's only when you know the end that the plot twists begin to make sense.

The biblical story has a clear beginning. Out of nothing whatsoever, God created a beautiful world and placed Adam and Eve in it. They were perfect people, living in a full and complete relationship of love, obedience, and worship with the Creator. They had everything they could ever need or want. Adam and Eve were God's image bearers, appointed by God to be resident managers over the world he had created.

But Adam and Eve were not content to worship and obey God. In a shocking act of disobedience, they stepped outside of God's plan. This

44

defiance opened the floodgates of sin and destruction onto the once perfect earth. The fellowship between God and man was horribly broken. Fear, guilt, and rebellion replaced love, worship, and obedience. All of creation was cursed with weeds, decay, and disease. But God was not content to let things remain broken. He declared war on sin and sent his Son to earth to win the final victory on the cross. He now applies the results of that victory to his sin-scarred children and his sin-marred earth.

When the biblical story ends, God will defeat every last enemy, the final enemy being death. We will become like God and live with him forever. This information is important for three reasons:

1. If you want to go in the right direction, you need to know your final destination.
2. The details of your life only make sense when viewed from the perspective of eternity.
3. Eternity teaches us what is really important in life.

The Bible is a storybook that gives us everything from our origin to our ultimate destiny. God opens up the last chapter of the story for us and invites us to look in, to listen, and then to look back on our lives. The purpose of Scriptures like Revelation is not to provide maps and charts to determine when Christ's return will take place. No, Revelation is in the Bible to help us understand our final destination, and thereby make sense of our lives here and now.

The biblical story makes no sense without eternity. There has to be a better end than what we are living in right now! Sin has to be conquered. People have to be purified. The cosmos has to be restored. Anything less would be a universal defeat. All the suffering, brokenness, trial, sacrifice, and battle would make no sense. Paul says it powerfully in 1 Corinthians 15:19, "If only for this life we have hope in Christ, we are to be pitied more than all men." If God isn't taking us somewhere, following Christ has been a colossal waste of time. There has to be more than this – and there is!

Why would Jed be willing to miss promotion after promotion because he is committed to honesty and integrity? If this life is all there is, Jed is a fool. Why would Andrea be willing to forgive Dana over and over for disloyalty, if there were no eternity? She would be the willing victim of her own foolishness. Why would Pete endure ridicule for his faith from his high school peers, if there is not more than this? If there is no eternity, Pete has made a stupid choice. Why would Michael invest so much time, money, and energy in ministry, if this life is all there is? Why faithfully obey? Why cheerfully give? Why turn the other cheek? Why study God's Word? Why pray without ceasing? Why be committed to what is right? Why seek justice and mercy? Why make personal sacrifices? Why persevere? Why worship?

Everything God does and everything God calls us to only make sense from the perspective of eternity. If there is no end to the story, believers are a bunch of fools who need to be pitied. There is no reason for what we have tried to do.

But there is a final chapter! God has opened it up so that we could look in and then look back to our lives with understanding and hope.

Looking In and Looking Back

One of the most amazing scenes in the Bible is captured in Revelation 7.

> After this I looked and there before me was a great multitude that no one could count, from every nation, tribe, people and language, standing before the throne and in front of the Lamb. They were wearing white robes and were holding palm branches in their hands. And they cried out in a loud voice:
>
> "Salvation belongs to our God, who sits on the throne, and to the Lamb."
>
> All the angels were standing around the throne and around the elders and the four living creatures. They fell down on their faces before the throne and worshiped God, saying:
>
> "Amen!
> Praise and glory and wisdom and thanks and honor and power and strength be to our God for ever and ever.
> Amen!"

Then one of the elders asked me, "These in white robes – who are they, and where did they come from?"

I answered, "Sir, you know."
And he said, "These are they who have come out of the great tribulation; they have washed their robes and made them white in the blood of the Lamb. Therefore,
   "they are before the throne of God
   and serve him day and night in his temple;
and he who sits on the throne
   will spread his tent over them.
Never again will they hunger;
   never again will they thirst.
The sun will not beat upon them,
   nor any scorching heat.
For the Lamb at the center of the throne will be their shepherd;
   he will lead them to springs of living water.
And God will wipe away every tear from their eyes."
(Rev. 7:9-17)

Step into this scene of eternity. Look around, listen carefully, and then look back on your life to understand what cannot be understood any other way. Revelation 7 allows us to see the Lamb on the throne and hear the voices of the saints who have completed their journey. Do you see yourself in the crowd? These saints are people just like you. Like you, they suffered the scorching heat of earthly life. Like you, they went through God's process of radical change. Now they have reached their final destination. They stand before God's throne, purified and free, with a full welcome into the presence of the King of Kings and Lord of Lords, their Savior, their Shepherd Lamb.

Picture yourself there, because in God's story, you are there. This is your destination. This is where God is taking you! You will make it through the heat! Someday you will stand before the throne. There will be a moment when your voice will be heard in the chorus of praise that will never end. Someday you will be convinced that it has all been worth it. Life looks dramatically different when examined through the lens of eternity.

Destination Clarifies Our Values

Listen carefully to the saints who are looking back at earthly life. As they consider all that they experienced, what do they celebrate?

These fellow pilgrims could celebrate a good job, a beautiful house, friendly neighbors, a happy marriage, physical health, and many other things. These are all good things and it is appropriate to be thankful for them. But the saints on the other side are celebrating none of them. As they stand before the Lord, crowned and reigning with him, their restoration is complete. God has finished his work of transforming their lives as he transformed their hearts by his grace. As they stand before him, they are like him in true righteousness and holiness.

And so they rise in a crescendo of worship and celebration saying, "You did it! You did it! You did what we could not do for ourselves. You broke our bondage to sin and restored us to be the willing worshipers you created us to be." The most important thing happening in your life right now is not that new house or new job. It is not your professional success or the love of a friend. The one thing worth celebrating for all eternity is your redemption. By God's grace, you are being progressively delivered from the one thing that can completely destroy you: sin. But God not only delivers you, he restores you. He is making you a partaker of his divine nature.

There will be a day when you stand before God's throne. You won't be anxious with shame or fearful with guilt. As you stand before him, you will be like him because his grace made you a participant in his divine nature. In that moment, you will not be celebrating the physical gifts of earthbound life. Your heart will overflow with the realization that God has been victorious. The battles of change and growth are forever past. The final destination is his presence and throne room. Together, dressed in white robes of righteousness and crowned with glory, we will celebrate the one thing worth living for: the Lamb and his salvation. This is where God is taking you.

Remember Joan, Frank, Nikki, and Bo, who were introduced at the beginning of this chapter? Let's revisit their stories and see the help that looking at life from an eternal perspective would provide each of them.

It is easy to understand why Joan wants to give up. Life with Bryan has been hard. There are days when it all does seem impossible. How will change ever take place? But Joan needs to look at her situation with the eyes of the gospel. The situation with Bryan is not outside of the circle of God's grace. This is exactly the kind of thing for which Christ died. In fact, Christ is at work, in the middle of the messiness and disappointment of Joan's marriage, still working to complete what he has begun.

Eternity reminds us that there is an end, a means to an end, and One who is committed to do what is necessary to bring us to that end. Eternity also is meant to remind Joan that grace is a process. The sturdy strongholds of sin don't come down in a moment. Grace is a process and God is committed to complete the process in each of his children. Eternity stands as a guarantee that what God has begun in Joan, he will continue.

Remember Frank's disappointment with once again being passed over for leadership in his church? In the quiet Sundays that followed, with Frank going nowhere to worship, God was not done with Frank. Frank could not get his mind to stop thinking. He began to wonder if what had happened at church was not so much a failure of God's love, but a sign of it. As Frank sat by himself, feeling a bit old and sad, he began to think of eternity. As he did, things began to get clearer. Frank remembered that God was working on a kingdom; the problem was that it wasn't the one Frank was working on.

Frank was disappointed because his kingdom had not come. His kingdom was about being in the center of power at his local church. But in all of his leadership disappointments, God was working to build his kingdom in Frank's heart. He was preparing Frank to live with joy in his eternal kingdom forever. Frank was shocked to realize that his excitement with church had had little to do with a love for Christ, his gift of grace, and his ongoing work of redemption. Once Frank began to confess that his disappointment and anger were not so much with the church, but with God, he was able to reconcile his relationship to the church.

Nikki simply had her identity all mixed up. Although she was a child of God, that identity, and all the glorious things it meant for her now and in the future, had no impact on the way she thought about herself and her life. When Jesus saves us, he not only changes what we are, but who we are as well. When the saints in heaven look back and celebrate their lives on earth, they celebrate their inclusion in God's work of redemption. They celebrate their identity as his children and the completion of everything God promised to do in and through them. Nikki needed to let eternity clarify her identity as well as her values. She needed to root her identity in lasting spiritual realities, not the fading realities of the physical world. She needed to look at herself from the security of who she was as God's child, and where God was taking her as he worked in the messiness of the here and now. Despite her sins, weaknesses, and flaws, Nikki had a reason to get out of bed and continue living. She was a child of God with a future beyond anything she could ask or imagine. In her current struggles, God was using the things she had not planned to produce in her what she could not achieve on her own.

Bo had always carried around a false and dangerous view of life. Although he was a child of God, Bo had bought the lie of lies. He really did believe that true meaning, purpose, and fulfillment – life – were to be found in material things. The problem was that Bo didn't know this was going on. He thought he had a heart for God. He thought that God was the source of his hope and security. For a long time, Bo's heart had been more ruled by the creation than the Creator, but Bo hadn't seen it because he couldn't afford to go where his heart wanted to go. The inheritance revealed what was really going on in Bo's heart.

This war of desire is why God invites us to step into eternity, look around, and then look back. Like Bo, we all need our values clarified. The physical world around us is attractive and intoxicating. It seems to be able to give life, but it cannot. Eternity reminds Bo and each of us of what is really important and where life can truly be found. When Bo began to look at his life from that perspective, he no longer felt drunk with his new-found riches. He felt rather silly about all the trinkets he had surrounded himself with; they had failed utterly to make him happy.

What about you? Where have you wondered if following the Lord is worth it? Where have you struggled to understand what he is doing? Where have confusion and disappointment weakened your faith? Where have you already let go? Where are you running from the Lord instead of turning to him? How has God's work of change been interrupted by your doubt, confusion, or fear?

As you listen to the saints in eternity, can you see yourself there? If you are one of God's children, you are in that scene. You actually see your future. This is the end of your story. How does the destination encourage you in the middle of your journey? How should the final chapter change the way you respond to the chapters in between? Where are you given new hope even when there doesn't seem to be much hope around you now?

You and I will only be able to understand what is valuable when we examine things from the perspective of eternity. The eyes of eternity alone can tell us what is worth living and dying for. Think very practically and personally for a moment. What are you living for? What is your goal in life? What is the end of your, "If only I had_____"? Every time you confront a friend, raise your voice at your child, or give your spouse the silent treatment, you hope to accomplish something. What is the goal? If you study for hours or work sixty hours a week, you have a purpose in mind. What hopes and promises are giving direction to your life?

Like Joan, Frank, Nikki, and Bo, you always look at your life from the vantage point of your hopes and dreams. You always have some goal or destination in mind, even when you don't fully realize it. The question is whether the hopes, plans, goals, and promises that direct your actions and words are worthy of your calling as a child of God. Do they reflect God's purposes to make you more like Jesus? Do they move you in that direction? Do they draw you closer to the One who will bring you there?

Christianity's change process does not revolve around a system of redemption but around a person who redeems. The Bible calls us to focus on Christ our Redeemer – the Word of God made flesh – who gives us the pattern and power for change. Christ is our hope. He links the forgiveness of the past to the growth of the present to the hope of the future. Hope for the present is rooted in the hope of eternity. It rests on him. The hope of eternity is Christ, and because I have him in my life now, I know he will empower me to complete the journey so that I can see him face to face.

Preparing for the Final Destination

It was one of those late night, concerned parents conversations that come when you get scared about where one of your children is headed. The longer my wife and I talked and brainstormed about worst-case scenarios, the more we felt parental panic. We focused on our fears of all that could go wrong. Our panic did not subside until we began to help each other see the Lord at work in our child's life. We were dedicated Christian parents, but we were still blind to what the Lord was doing before our eyes. We were looking in all the wrong places at all the wrong things. The result was hopeless panic.

We needed to see that our hope was not in the fact that we had everything under control – we obviously didn't. Our confidence could not be in the fact that we had everything tied up in a neat little bow – things were actually quite messy. Our confidence had to be that Christ was carrying us – and our child – through the process he had ordained and would complete. We began to see that this hard moment was a God-given step toward a wonderful destination. This prepared us to deal in a very different way with the issues that had previously produced fear.

Is there someone in your life you are looking at through the lens of pessimistic fear? Is there someone you've given up on? Is there someone you do all you can to avoid? Is there someone in your life you fear? Is there someone you are bitter against? Is there someone you envy? What might God be saying to you about your relationship to this person? How does God's "steps to the destination" perspective change the way you relate to him or her?

You need to make your final destination the lens you use to evaluate your life. We all know that life is sloppy, hard, messy, shameful, and boring. We often deal with things that are out of our control. Good things tend to go bad and bad things tend to seduce us. People leave us hurt and disappointed. Change is often much, much slower than we want it to be. God's Word is full of powerful life principles, but applying them to life is not always an easy task. We tend to encounter the same problems again and again. It is easy to believe that we are powerless to change and that all our effort is meaningless.

The gospel calls us to look at the messiness of life in a radically different way. The good news of the gospel is that Christ has conquered sin and death, and with them every meaningless and destructive end. Our final destination infuses every word, action, desire, and response with meaning and purpose. There are no completely hopeless situations. The gospel welcomes us to a hopeful realism. We can look life in the face and still be hopeful because of who Christ is and where he is taking us. Everything God has brought into your life has been brought with your destination in view. God is moving you on, even when you think you are stuck.

Here's Where God Is Taking You

Your destination is secure. All of the things that are truly worth living for cannot be taken away from you! Yes, you can lose your job, your health, your house, your car, or your friend. The loss of any of these things would be hard. But you cannot lose your identity in Christ. You cannot lose his love and grace. You cannot lose his gift of forgiveness or the place reserved for you in heaven. When you keep your eyes on this destination and pursue the things that move you there, you can live securely in a world where it seems as if nothing is guaranteed. You will not escape the difficulties of life, but you can rest assured that your Savior will use each one to prepare you for the place he is taking you.

Think about it for a moment. You can be at peace even though you do not know how today's drama will end or what tomorrow will bring. You can live with joy even when things make you sad. Christian joy is not about avoiding life while dreaming about heaven. It is about taking an utterly honest look at all earthly life through heaven's lens. There we find real hope.

Help Along the Way

Perhaps you are thinking, I'm glad there is a final destination for me, but I just don't think I'm going to make it. God never expected you to make the journey by yourself! He provides the best possible help all along the way. In Paul's words, "For in Christ all the fullness of the Deity lives in bodily form, and you have been given fullness in Christ, who is the head over every power and authority" (Col. 2:9-10).

This fullness refers to the moment in Christ's life when the Holy Spirit descended on him like a dove. The fullness we have been given by Christ is that same Holy Spirit. God himself comes to live within us and we have everything we need to be transformed into Christ's own image. This "fullness" is not something we have to earn or achieve. It is already within us as a gift of his grace!

This means that spiritually, you are never empty; you are never on your own; you are never left to your own strength, resources or wisdom. Why? You have been given the "fullness" of the Holy Spirit! What God has begun in you, he will complete. Your destiny has already been decided. The One who decided it will give you all you need to get there.

MARRIED TO CHRIST

When I got married, my wife did not know I had liabilities. I'll mention only one here! I was a student who had spent several years on staff with a campus ministry before coming to seminary. I was thousands of dollars in debt with no workable plan to pay it off, and I still had two more years of seminary to go. Fortunately for me, my fiancée had worked steadily and saved a good bit of money. The day we said "I do" was a very significant day for many reasons. Among them was the fact that my debt became her debt and her assets became my assets. It was a great financial deal for me, but not for her. This is what happens when we become Christians. Christ assumes our liabilities and graciously gives us his assets. This is God's amazing grace.

But more happened on our wedding day. Along with this new legal (and financial) arrangement, my wife and I entered into a personal relationship that has grown deeper over the years. We communicate with each another in ways that only two people who have spent decades together can. The same is true of our relationship with Jesus. We not only enjoy legal benefits; we enter into a personal relationship that grows over time as we spend our lives with him.

In Chapter 3, we encouraged you to see the hope for change and the ultimate destiny that is yours because you belong to Christ. In this chapter you will see the person who changes you.

The Person Who Changes You

According to the Bible, change takes place within a deeply personal relationship that is built on a solid legal foundation. We are gradually conformed to the likeness of the One to whom we are married. In the last chapter, we saw a glorious hope to which we are destined. As Philippians 1:6 says, "He who began a good work in you will carry it on to completion until the day of Christ Jesus." That good work begins in relationship to Jesus and is brought to completion within an ever-deepening union with him. This is the most unique aspect of a biblical view of change. It is not less than cognitive change; it is so much more. It is not less than behavioral change; it is so much more. No other secular or religious approach to change comes close to what we find in Scripture. The Bible gives us more than exhortations and rules for change. The great gift Christ gives us is himself!

The metaphor of marriage is used to describe our relationship with God throughout the Old and New Testaments. It rests on the biblical idea of a covenant. A covenant is a relational promise. God binds himself to us. He is our God and we are his people. Ezekiel, in a rather unabashed way, depicts God looking upon Israel as a husband does a wife:

> "Later I passed by, and when I looked at you and saw that you were old enough for love, I spread the corner of my garment over you and covered your nakedness. I gave you my solemn oath and entered into a covenant with you," declares the Sovereign Lord, "and you became mine." (Ezek. 16:8)

Isaiah says, "For your Maker is your husband – the Lord Almighty is his name – the Holy One of Israel is your Redeemer; he is called the God of all the earth" (Isa. 54:5).

Ephesians uses marriage as a metaphor to depict Christ's relationship with his people. After talking about human marriage, Paul says, "This is a profound mystery – but I am talking about Christ and the church" (Eph. 5:32).

While there is a sense in which our marriage to Christ is not yet completed, biblical writers use the marriage metaphor to depict the legal, deeply personal, two-sided nature of the believer's relationship to God. It is the relationship God initiates and in which we participate.

Stay Focused on Christ

As you think about the Christian life as a lifelong process of change, what things stand out as the key ingredients for change? Most of us focus on the "means of grace": Bible study, prayer, fellowship, reading Christian books, the sacraments, service, and witness. God has provided these as means to an end, but they are not the end! All the means of grace are good and necessary for change, but only if they do not become ends in themselves.

The Christian life is not less than these means, but it is much more. Several passages help us think about how wonderful it is to be in union with Christ. In 2 Corinthians 11:1-3, Paul uses the marriage metaphor to talk about being united with Christ. Colossians 1:15-23 gives us a picture of Christ, our bridegroom. In Colossians 2:1-15, we discover the life-changing benefits Christ brings us by faith.

Married to Christ: 2 Corinthians 11:1-3

How central is Christ to the Christian life? That may sound like an obvious question, but not when you read the way Paul speaks to the Corinthians! He says it is easy for Christians to forget that Christ is the center of the Christian life.

> I hope you will put up with a little of my foolishness; but you are already doing that. I am jealous for you with a godly jealousy. I promised you to one husband, to Christ, so that I might present you as a pure virgin to him. But I am afraid that just as Eve was deceived by the serpent's cunning, your minds may somehow be led astray from your sincere and pure devotion to Christ. (2 Cor. 11:1-3)

Paul speaks with the affection of a father. He is jealous for the Corinthians' purity of heart in relation to Christ. He introduces the metaphor of marriage to describe the Christian's relationship to Christ. He speaks of Christ as a "husband" and the Corinthians as pure virgin brides. But Paul worries that they will be seduced by temptation and give their hearts to false lovers instead. While this passage focuses more on the future fulfillment of our marriage to Christ, it captures the idea that we are united to him now.

Engagement in the first century was more significant than it is today. In those days, engagement was as close to marriage as you could get. Notice Matthew's language in the birth accounts of Jesus:

> This is how the birth of Jesus Christ came about: His mother Mary was pledged to be married to Joseph, but before they came together, she was found to be with child through the Holy Spirit. Because Joseph her

husband was a righteous man and did not want to expose her to public disgrace, he had in mind to divorce her quietly.

But after he had considered this, an angel of the Lord appeared to him in a dream and said, "Joseph son of David, do not be afraid to take Mary home as your wife, because what is conceived in her is from the Holy Spirit. She will give birth to a son, and you are to give him the name Jesus, because he will save his people from their sins." (Matt. 1:18-21)

While Joseph and Mary are engaged, Mary becomes pregnant by the Holy Spirit with Jesus. Joseph considered divorcing her but the angel of the Lord instructed him not to do so. Joseph and Mary are engaged, but Joseph is referred to as her husband prior to the formal ceremony and physical union.

In the same way, we are "engaged" or married to Christ, our husband. We await the final consummation when that "engagement" or marriage becomes a full reality. But in the meantime, the biblical writers do not hesitate to talk about the Christian's relationship to Jesus in terms of marriage.

Paul describes the Christian's relationship to Christ in the most intimate terms – so intimate that it is almost embarrassing! But this is what is so amazing about the gospel. God reconciles sinners to himself through Christ and welcomes us into a relationship that is intensely personal. He does not simply tolerate us; he brings us close to himself by giving himself to us. Christ is our husband and we are his bride. We are married to Christ.

What does it mean to be married to Christ? Christ has made us the recipients of his affection and, in turn, we are to make him the ultimate object of ours. Paul speaks to the Corinthians as a jealous father who wants nothing to supplant or compromise this relationship. He urges the Corinthians to shun false saviors and false gospels and to place their hopes and affections solely on Christ.

What false lovers entice you to forget your true husband and the faithfulness he deserves? Why do we worship other things in place of Christ? Quite simply, we worship what we find attractive. We allow many things to eclipse the beauty of Christ. We devote our hearts to our jobs, other people, a state of mind (comfort, security), success, power, peace, or money. We have many options before us, but we cannot get our identity from these things.

I am easily enticed by comfort. After a hard day at work, I am ready for some "down time." I tell myself that I deserve it! Comfort and leisure are good things, but when my personal comfort becomes more important to me than Christ, it impacts my behavior sinfully. If I arrive home to a house full of children who get in the way of my comfort, I rapidly turn into a very harsh person. I have placed myself in the arms of a false lover: my personal comfort. This can happen quickly – even on the heels of counseling someone else to be wary of his own straying heart!

Paul is right on target when he pleads with the Corinthians (and with us) to stay focused on our relationship with Christ in the same way that husbands and wives should focus on their spouses. Remain sincere and pure in your devotion. Guard your heart against anything that intrudes upon that primary relationship. Fight against anything that calls your loyalty into question. Because it is so easy to stray, you must fight the temptation every moment. My marriage to Christ is the most important relationship and circumstance of my life.

The Christian life has been described using many false models. Some approach it as a business: work hard and get a paycheck. Some think of it as a well-planned spiritual workout. Others see it as an educational pursuit: gain more biblical and theological knowledge and equate that with knowing and loving Christ. But Paul reminds us that the Christian life is much more intimate, personal, and comprehensive than all of these. Notice three profound realities that are part of my union with Christ:

If I am married to Christ, the core of my present life is not personal happiness, but spiritual purity.

Like any other marriage, the big issue is my fidelity. Will I remain faithful to Jesus or will I seek fulfillment elsewhere? Spiritual purity, single-minded devotion, and obedience figure more prominently because of my marriage to Christ. Whether good or difficult things happen to me, my attention must remain riveted to my husband, Jesus.

My betrothal to Christ has a "now and then" structure.

My "now" life is preparation for my "then" marriage to Christ, when the marriage supper of the Lamb sets the stage for all eternity. My life now is a time of preparation for that day. The complete fulfillment of this relationship will take place in heaven, though I experience many wonderful aspects now. Since Christ is the prize, anything that could draw me away from him is no longer essential. All of the everyday moments of life are filled with opportunities to be changed into the likeness of the One who married me.

The Christian life is all-inclusive.

The Christian life is far more than having devotions, giving money, participating in ministry, knowing doctrine, or having religious feelings during worship. I can do all of these things without Christ at the center of my life! For Paul, the heart of Christianity is remaining faithful to Christ in a world where many other "lovers" seek my affection.

If Christ is indeed the only prize worth living for, we need to ponder just how wonderful he is. There are many places in the Bible where we could "gaze upon the beauty of the Lord," as the psalmist says in Psalm 27:4, but we will limit ourselves to one passage. Who is our bridegroom and husband? What is attractive about him? What benefits become ours when we are united to him?

Christ the Bridegroom: Colossians 1:15-24

The most obvious and important question that any prospective spouse asks is, "Who is this person I am going to marry?" Most people agonize over this decision because of the level of commitment involved. If I am going to commit to someone for a lifetime, I want to know as much as I can about her before I say "I do." Likewise, Jesus tells us to count the cost before we become his disciples.

In Colossians, Paul gives us a stunning description of our incomparable bridegroom.

> He is the image of the invisible God, the firstborn over all creation. For by him all things were created: things in heaven and on earth, visible

and invisible, whether thrones or powers or rulers or authorities; all things were created by him and for him. He is before all things, and in him all things hold together. And he is the head of the body, the church; he is the beginning and the firstborn from among the dead, so that in everything he might have the supremacy. For God was pleased to have all his fullness dwell in him, and through him to reconcile to himself all things, whether things on earth or things in heaven, by making peace through his blood, shed on the cross.

Once you were alienated from God and were enemies in your minds because of your evil behavior. But now he has reconciled you by Christ's physical body through death to present you holy in his sight, without blemish and free from accusation – if you continue in your faith, established and firm, not moved from the hope held out in the gospel. This is the gospel that you heard and that has been proclaimed to every creature under heaven, and of which I, Paul, have become a servant. (Col. 1: 15-24)

Jesus is more awesome and beautiful than anything else in creation! When we see him as he is, why would we want to give our affection to any other? This portrait of Christ provides a magnificent list of names, character qualities, and roles that help us to see and adore him for all he is worth:

1. He is God. He manifests the glory of God because he is God.
2. He is the Firstborn over all creation. He is the preeminent one.
3. He is the Creator of all things. Everything owes its existence to him.
4. All things were created for him. He is the center of the universe.
5. He is eternal ("before all things"). He is outside of and over creation.
6. He is the Sustainer of all things. He holds everything together.
7. He is the Head of the body. He is the king and life-giver for the church.
8. He is the beginning and firstborn among the dead. Without his resurrection, no other resurrection is possible.
9. He is supreme. Nothing else can compare to him!
10. He is the fullness of God. We need look nowhere else for fullness.
11. He is the reconciler of all things. His redemptive work leaves nothing in the universe beyond his scope.

12. He is the peacemaker. He brings the reign of God to earth and joins sinners to himself so that they can enjoy (and not be crushed) by his glory. This only happened because he set aside his glory to die and be raised for us!

Such an amazing person deserves to be preeminent in your life. He deserves nothing less than your pure and sincere devotion. He is your Creator, Redeemer, Sustainer, your true husband. It may seem strange for Christians of either gender to speak of Christ in this way, but it is a spiritual reality. Human marriage is only an illustration of our union with Christ. God ordained marriage to help us understand what it means to be in relationship with him.

Is Christ the center of your life? Do you demonstrate a sincere and pure devotion to him in your family, career, friendships, marriage, eating, sexuality, ministry, thoughts, pleasures, time, and money?

Jesus is our bridegroom/husband par excellence. What does he bring to this union and what do we bring? Colossians 1:21-23 and 2:1-15 add specifics to this picture.

The Blessings of Our Union with Christ: Colossians 1:21-23 and 2:1-15

When my wife and I got married, we did not fully understand what we were getting ourselves into. Yet we took a step of faith based on what we did know. We entrusted our decision to the grace and mercy of God, believing that he would enable us to grow in our marriage. Over time, we have discovered the strengths each of us brought to the marriage. We also discovered each other's sins and weaknesses.

Our marriage to Christ is different. Christ brings the assets. We bring the liabilities. Yet Christ still joins himself to us!

When couples get married, they sometimes wonder how their new spouse will react when they really get to know each other. Marriage becomes what it is meant to be when your spouse gets to know the real you and loves you anyway! It is the same with our marriage to Christ. We cannot fully appreciate the blessings Christ brings until we see ourselves as we truly are. Then we are amazed at how gracious and merciful Jesus is. In

Colossians 1 and 2, Paul's description of Christ and his gifts to our relationship is set against a sobering description of who we are.

> Once you were alienated from God and were enemies in your minds because of your evil behavior. But now he has reconciled you by Christ's physical body through death to present you holy in his sight, without blemish and free from accusation – if you continue in your faith, established and firm, not moved from the hope held out in the gospel. This is the gospel that you heard and that has been proclaimed to every creature under heaven, and of which I, Paul, have become a servant. (Col. 1:21-23)

Paul continues,

> I want you to know how much I am struggling for you and for those at Laodicea, and for all who have not met me personally. My purpose is that they may be encouraged in heart and united in love, so that they may have the full riches of complete understanding, in order that they may know the mystery of God, namely, Christ, in whom are hidden all the treasures of wisdom and knowledge. I tell you this so that no one may deceive you by fine-sounding arguments. For though I am absent from you in body, I am present with you in spirit and delight to see how orderly you are and how firm your faith in Christ is.

> So then, just as you received Christ Jesus as Lord, continue to live in him, rooted and built up in him, strengthened in the faith as you were taught, and overflowing with thankfulness.

> See to it that no one takes you captive through hollow and deceptive philosophy, which depends on human tradition and the basic principles of this world rather than on Christ.

> For in Christ all the fullness of the Deity lives in bodily form, and you have been given fullness in Christ, who is the head over every power and authority. In him you were also circumcised, in the putting off of the sinful nature, not with a circumcision done by the hands of men but with the circumcision done by Christ, having been buried with him in baptism and raised with him through your faith in the power of God, who raised him from the dead.

> When you were dead in your sins and in the uncircumcision of your sinful nature, God made you alive with Christ. He forgave us all our sins, having canceled the written code, with its regulations, that was against us and that stood opposed to us; he took it away, nailing it to the cross. And having disarmed the powers and authorities, he made a public spectacle of them, triumphing over them by the cross. (Col. 2:1-15)

What a contrast between what Christ brings to the marriage and what we bring! We ought to ask, "What did Christ ever see in us to make us the object of his love and grace?" The obvious answer is, "Nothing!" He showered his mercy on us simply because he chose to!

What do we bring to this marriage?

We are guilty of sin and alienated from God (1:21-23). Two very strong words describe our position before God: we are alienated and enemies of God. Sin alienates us from God and sets us in opposition to him. We dig in our heels and rebel against him.

We are foolish and blind (2:1-5). Sin makes us fools. We are easily deceived, attracted to hollow and deceptive philosophy, and enticed by arguments that lead us away from Christ. Sin blinds us to our sin! We think we are fine. We think we have insight and power to live life. But the opposite is true!

We are powerless and enslaved (2:9-15). Paul uses the word "dead" to describe how trapped and helpless we are. When you are dead, you can't do anything. You cannot improve yourself. Even if we wanted to do what God requires (which we don't because we are alienated enemies), and even if we knew what pleased him (which we don't because we are fools who suppress the truth in unrighteousness), we would do neither because we are incapable of doing anything that is pleasing in God's sight. Yet, despite all this, Christ desires to be in relationship with us. As Paul summarizes it, "While we were still sinners, Christ died for us" (Rom. 5:8).

In a way, this passage functions as a reality check on the eve of your wedding to Christ. If you accept the truth of the way it describes you, you could be filled with guilt and shame toward your future husband. You know you can't be the spouse you need to be! You have two choices: You can run away, overwhelmed by the prospect of failure, or you can comfort yourself because of the character of the person you are about to marry.

Paul wants us to make the second choice. That's why, in the middle of this passage, you are called to live in daily fellowship and friendship with Christ, to celebrate your union with him by pursuing him every day (Col. 2:6-8). What Christ brings to our relationship perfectly meets the deficits, disabilities, and disqualifications we bring to the relationship as sinners.

Jesus justifies us. We are alienated, guilty, and rebellious sinners, but his life, death, and resurrection freed us from the guilt, penalty, shame, and alienation of sin. Paul says that we are holy in his sight, without blemish, and free from accusation (Col. 1:22). This is hard to imagine, but it is past grace!

Jesus is our wisdom. We are foolish and blind. But Jesus gives us all the treasures of wisdom and knowledge. He frees us from captivity to our own foolishness and gives us wisdom. This is present grace.

Jesus is our power. We are powerless and enslaved. He gives us more present grace, a new ability to live as we were intended to live. We also have the promise of future grace as we look forward to the hope to which the marriage metaphor points (Col. 1:5), the hope of heaven and an eternal relationship with Father, Son, and Holy Spirit. We will be together with all the saints, minus the guilt, power, and presence of sin.

Why is it so important to highlight these comparisons? Because the Christian life is built upon the foundation of (1) facing who you really are and (2) trusting who Christ truly is. Everything you do will be shaped by the degree to which you act on the blessings that are yours in Christ.

If you only look at yourself and carry around a load of guilt, you will hide, excuse, blame, rationalize, and cover up your shame rather than enjoy the freedom of confession and the joy of forgiveness. You will not enjoy the lasting fruit that comes from following the wisdom that is already yours in Christ! Instead, you will reduce the Christian life to a simplistic list of rules and behaviors that never touch the real problems, and you will be blind to the gaps in your relationship to Christ.

Imagine a little boy who has been born into a very poor family. He grows up malnourished, poorly dressed, and seldom clean, the object of scorn among his peers. He has little education and few prospects. He leaves home and gets a job as a caddy at a luxurious country club. One day, he meets a young woman from an extremely wealthy family. Much to his surprise, she asks him to be her caddy. This begins a long relationship that, amazingly, culminates in their marriage. At the exact moment he says, "I do," his life changes forever! He is the recipient of new status, wealth, power, and prestige. Yet he has earned none of it. It is simply the result of his new relationship. His marriage changes who he is, what he has, how he experiences life, and how he will live the rest of his life.

This illustration cannot capture everything that is true of our relationship to Christ, our husband. One important element is missing. When you and I come to Christ, it's not just our circumstances, relationships, and status that change. We become different at the deepest spiritual level. Christ's grace transforms our inner spiritual natures. We were once dead, but now we are alive. Our hearts, once hardened by sin, become soft and teachable. We become "new creations" (2 Cor. 5:17).

This change is not simply the product of good theology and disciplined obedience. It is the result of our relationship to Christ. Because I am united to him, I am renewed daily by his Spirit. The evil in my heart is progressively replaced with a growing ability to love, worship, and rejoice. I become a peacemaker. I learn to be patient, kind, good, faithful, gentle, and self-controlled as the Holy Spirit works in my life.

This is what the Christian life is all about. With joy I affirm that I am a new creation in Christ. With humility I confess that sin is still in my heart and I need God's grace today as much as I did when I first believed. The Spirit overpowers the things that once dominated my life. I am in him, though not yet completely like him, so I commit myself to the ongoing heart change that is God's loving focus.

Assets and Liabilities: Ways We Forget Christ

What gets in the way of living out your new relationship to Jesus? What false lovers draw you away from a pure and sincere devotion to Christ? Paul recognized that the things he once considered assets became liabilities when they kept him from seeing his need for Christ.

If anyone else thinks he has reasons to put confidence in the flesh, I have more: circumcised on the eighth day, of the people of Israel, of the tribe of Benjamin, a Hebrew of Hebrews; in regard to the law, a Pharisee; as for zeal, persecuting the church; as for legalistic righteousness, faultless.

But whatever was to my profit I now consider loss for the sake of Christ. What is more, I consider everything a loss compared to the surpassing greatness of knowing Christ Jesus my Lord, for whose sake I have lost all things. I consider them rubbish, that I may gain Christ and be found in him, not having a righteousness of my own that comes from the law, but that which is through faith in Christ – the righteousness that comes from God and is by faith. (Phil. 3:4-9)

Perceived Assets

In human relationships, each person contributes some strengths and gifts, but that is not true in this case. Paul had placed his confidence in the assets of his own achievements, pedigree, and morality. All of these things were blessings, but he wrongly put his confidence in a resume of his own making. We can do the same thing. We can put our confidence in our performance and obedience rather than recognizing them as gifts and strengths that should lead to gratitude.

What strengths and assets pull you away from gratitude to pride? Whatever they are, they can be a liability that keeps you from seeing your constant need for Christ. Let's say you are a parent who faithfully raises your children in a way that pleases God. Could these marks of grace become liabilities? Yes! You may think you are so capable that you lose sight of your dependence on God. You become critical of parents who struggle to raise their children well. When you rely on your gifts instead of Christ, you fail to see them for what they are, and they blind you from seeing Jesus.

Christ's Assets

Meanwhile, Jesus brings assets and no liabilities (Phil. 3:9)! Instead, he pays our debt! When we see this, it changes our perspective on the things that happen to us. If blessings come, they are opportunities to thank God for his goodness. If difficulties come, they are opportunities to grow more dependent upon him.

All of us respond to life based upon who we think we are and what we think we have. Suppose you are a homeless person trying to survive on the street by begging for spare change. One day you learn that a wealthy uncle has died, leaving you a fortune. All that belonged to him has become yours, though you haven't done a thing to deserve it. What would you do? It would be irrational to keep begging on the street! If your mind were clear, you would draw on those financial resources to buy a house. And you would probably find ways to help others you had known on the streets.

Christ brings enormous assets into your relationship. These assets are now yours as much as they are his. He has made you an heir of his assets. You are no longer a beggar on the street. Your bank account is full. You can begin living in a way that reflects who you really are now.

Getting Practical

In 2 Peter 1:3-9, Peter says that many Christians live ineffective and fruitless lives because they have forgotten who they are in Christ. Consider the following examples of how our union to Christ shapes the way we live in difficulty or blessing.

Loss of a Job

In our culture, a well-paying job is important. For some it is the source of security and identity. The loss of a job not only brings financial stress, but it can rock one's entire world when people attach their identity and sense of security to something they have no guarantee will be there tomorrow.

In contrast, a believer can approach his career with a deep appreciation of his identity and security in Christ. The loss of a job may hurt, but the most valuable things in life are not at stake. Because of your marriage to Christ, you have resources that go far beyond your own wisdom, character, and strength. Your husband controls the details of your life and has your good as his goal. This protects you from discouragement and gives you courage and faith in a difficult time.

Working at a Thankless Job

When we look to relationships, circumstances, and accomplishments for a sense of fulfillment, it is difficult to be trapped in an unsatisfying job. But when our fulfillment comes from Christ, we do not approach life feeling needy. We can face each day with a contentment and joy no job could ever give. This does not mean that you will never be discouraged, tired, or bored, but it will mean that you have someone to trust who will help you through the difficulty.

We have been chosen from the mass of humanity to live in an intimate union with Christ. It is amazing even to be tolerated by God. It would be an honor simply to be invited to the wedding! It is beyond comprehension to be the beloved bride of the King of Kings and Lord of Lords! When you understand this, you can't help but live life aware of the honor, privilege, and blessing that are yours. Yes, your job may bore you. Yes, you had hoped to do something more significant. Yes, you wish you could find a way out. But you do not go to work searching for fulfillment. It may give you a sense of dignity, but it does not define you. In Christ you are full, joyful, and satisfied. Although you have a thankless job, you know that Christ never forgets what you do in his name. As part of the bride of Christ, you are connected to the most important things in the universe. Your union with him gives meaning to everything you do and say.

Your Burden as a Single Parent

You panic when you realize you have a job meant for two people: a husband and a wife. Impossible! Unfair! These reactions are rooted in a crucial mistake: We look to ourselves to see if we have the wisdom and strength to do what needs to be done. When we realize that we don't, we get discouraged, angry, and bitter. We have forgotten who we are in Christ. No single (or married) parent has the wisdom and strength needed to care for his or her children, but Christ is the source of all wisdom and strength and he promises to give it to his bride. No single (or married) parent has the godly character the role requires, but Christ has given us his Spirit so that we can do and say what is right and good. You may be a single parent but you are still married to Christ. He will provide for you fully in your admittedly difficult role.

Chronic Physical Suffering

We tend to assume that we will always be healthy and that physical pain will be temporary. Physical suffering is made much harder if health has been a source of security and well-being. In a fallen world our bodies are always wasting away. It is not wise to place our hope in them.

What a difference it makes to know that the most precious things in life are not physical. Although poor health makes life difficult, it cannot rob you of your identity, your meaning and purpose, your joy, or your sense of personal rest. When you respond to physical suffering with an awareness of your eternal union with Christ, you can say with Paul, "Though outwardly we are wasting away, yet inwardly we are being renewed day by day" (2 Cor. 4:16). No matter what our physical condition, we are strengthened by new mercies every morning, encouraged by God's love, and empowered by the Spirit. We would like to retain our strength and avoid chronic pain, but we can fix our eyes on the reality of our union with Christ and the resources he gives.

Earthly Success and Blessing

Just as difficulties are to be experienced through our union to Christ, so too, are good circumstances. They can be as much of a liability as difficulties. When things are going well, we can think we are more favored by God than those who suffer. We can get self-righteous and critical of others as well. God knew the temptation of blessing when he gave Israel a land overflowing with good things. He reminded them not to forget him as they entered the Promised Land:

> When you have eaten and are satisfied, praise the LORD your God for the good land he has given you. Be careful that you do not forget the LORD your God, failing to observe his commands, his laws and his decrees that I am giving you this day. Otherwise, when you eat and are satisfied, when you build fine houses and settle down, and when your herds and flocks grow large and your silver and gold increase and all you have is multiplied, then your heart will become proud and you will forget the LORD your God, who brought you out of Egypt, out of the land of slavery . . .

> You may say to yourself, "My power and the strength of my hands have produced this wealth for me." But remember the LORD your God, for it is he who gives you the ability to produce wealth, and so confirms his covenant, which he swore to your forefathers, as it is today. If you ever forget the LORD your God and follow other gods and worship and bow down to them, I testify against you today that you will surely be destroyed. Like the nations the LORD destroyed before you, so you will be destroyed for not obeying the LORD your God. (Deut. 8: 10-20)

It is tempting to forget God and to grow proud and independent in times of difficulty and blessing. But remembering your union with Christ reminds you that any good thing in your life is the result of his mercy and grace, not your own wisdom, goodness, and effort. Any effort we put into our lives began with the strength he gives us and continues because he is committed to us forever!

Christ gives us all we need to draw nearer to him and enjoy him amid difficulties and blessings. We may get tired, but not despondent. We will be sad, but not hopeless. We will endure pain, but we will not give up. We will enjoy blessings, but not grow proud. We see that our lives do not consist only in what we have, how we feel, or what we have accomplished, but in who we are in Christ. This enables us to stand where we would once have fallen down.

As we think about how change happens, we need to start at the beginning. We have a future because God is committed to finishing what he started in us; we have a Redeemer who has rescued us from our sins, given us his Spirit, and made us his bride. This is true of us as individuals, but we are also part of a much bigger community. We are members of the body of Christ. The bride of Christ consists of everyone who trusts in Christ and is united to him. This community is the context for change we will consider next.

C H A N G E   I S   A   C O M M U N I T Y   P R O J E C T

In the previous chapters, we have focused on individual change and growth in grace. But this process is not simply an individualistic one. It happens best – and primarily – within community.

Let me share one woman's story of her family's involvement in a small group that meets in their home. She speaks frankly about the work involved, along with the deep joy and satisfaction they have experienced over five years in the same group. What she says is central to understanding the importance of relationships if we are going to grow in godliness.

> My husband and I have been a part of the same small group for the past five years. . . . Like many small groups, we regularly share a meal together, love one another practically, and serve together to meet needs outside our small group. We worship, study God's Word, and pray. It has been a rich time to grow in our understanding of God, what Jesus has accomplished for us, God's purposes for us as a part of his kingdom, his power and desire to change us, and many other precious truths. We have grown in our love for God and others, and have been challenged to repent of our sin and trust God in every area of our lives.
>
> It was a new and refreshing experience for us to be in a group where people were willing to share their struggles with temptation and sin and ask for prayer . . . . We have been welcomed by others, challenged to become more vulnerable, held up in prayer, encouraged in specific ongoing struggles, and have developed sweet friendships. I have seen one woman who had one foot in the world and one foot in the church openly share her struggles with us. We prayed that God would show her the way of escape from temptation many times and have seen God's work in delivering her. Her openness has given us a front row seat to see the power of God intersect with her weakness. Her continued vulnerability and growth in godliness encourage us to be humble with one another, and to believe that God is able to change us too.

Because years have now passed in close community, God's work can be seen more clearly than on a week-by-week basis. One man who had some deep struggles and lots of anger has grown through repenting of sin and being vulnerable one-on-one and in the group. He has been willing to hear the encouragement and challenges of others, and to stay in community throughout his struggle . . . . He has become an example in serving others, a better listener, and more gentle with his wife. As a group, we have confronted anxiety, interpersonal strife, the need to forgive, lust, family troubles, unbelief, the fear of man, hypocrisy, unemployment, sickness, lack of love, idolatry, and marital strife. We have been helped, held accountable, and lifted up by one another. We have also grieved together, celebrated together, laughed together, offended one another, reconciled with one another, put up with one another, . . . and sought to love God and one another. As a group we were saddened in the spring when a man who had recently joined us felt that we let him down by not being sensitive to his loneliness. He chose to leave. I say this because, with all the benefits of being in a small group, it is still just a group of sinners. It is Jesus who makes it worth getting together. Apart from our relationship with him . . . , we have nothing to offer. But because our focus is on Jesus, the group has the potential to make a significant and life-changing difference in all our lives.

. . . When 7 o'clock on Monday night comes around, I eagerly look forward to the sound of my brothers and sisters coming in our front door. I never know how the evening will go, what burdens people will be carrying, how I will be challenged, or what laughter or tears we will share. But I always know that the great Shepherd will meet us and that our lives will be richer and fuller because we have been together.

. . . I hope that by hearing my story you will be encouraged to make a commitment to become a part of a small group and experience the blessing of Christian community within the smaller, more intimate setting that it makes possible.[1]

Living in the Tension

In this testimony, we see the importance of redemptive friendships in the process of change. We also see the ongoing tension between what we gain and what we must endure for these relationships to work. The movie

Change Is a Community Project

About a Boy captures this tension well. In it, a single man is trying to come to terms with his freedom as a single person and his longing for a meaningful relationship. As the story begins, his character is musing about his predicament:

> In my opinion, all men are islands. And what's more, now's the time to be one. This is an island age. One hundred years ago, for instance, you had to depend upon other people. . . . Whereas now, you see, you can make yourself a little island paradise. With the right supplies and more importantly, the right attitude, you can be sun-drenched, tropical, a magnet for young Swedish tourists. . . . The sad fact is, like any island dweller, from time to time, I had to visit the mainland.

As the movie unfolds, he moves towards a meaningful relationship, forgoing the freedoms he enjoyed while single. The story portrays humanity's deep longing for relationships, and concludes that they are worth pursuing.

At another level, though, meaningful relationships are often avoided. They require work, sacrifice, humility, and selflessness. While the idea of loving another person taps into something inherently human, it also exposes our sinful self-centeredness. In It Takes a Church to Raise a Christian: How the Community of God Changes Lives, Tod E. Bolsinger observes:

> More than any before us, an American today believes "I must write the script of my own life." The thought that such a script must be subordinated to the grand narrative of the Bible is a foreign one. Still more alarming is the idea that this surrender of our personal story to God's story must be mediated by a community of fallen people we frankly don't want getting in our way and meddling with our own hopes and dreams.[2]

At one level we want friendships. At another level we don't want them! In creation, we were made to live in community, but because of the fall, we tend to run from the very friendships we need. Quite often, our longing for them is tainted by sin. We pursue them only as long as they satisfy our own desires and needs. We have a love-hate relationship with relationships!

The Bible recognizes this profound tension, but still places our individual growth in grace in the context of the body of Christ. The Scriptures call us to be intimately connected to our brothers and sisters in Christ. Our fellowship is an essential ingredient for lasting change. The work of redemption involves our individual relationship with Christ alongside our relationships with others.

Friendships and Personal Change

Have you ever heard someone say, "You've made your bed, now lie in it"? As Christians, we know that nothing could be further from the gospel. This statement says, first, "Your problems are irreversible, so you are stuck in your own mess." And second, "You are totally on your own." In other words, don't expect help from anybody! If things are going to change, you had better find a way to fix them yourself.

Joe was single, lonely, and very angry with people who had been part of his life. He always felt used by others and had become very cynical about the possibility of meaningful friendships. He felt especially betrayed by Christians who shunned him because of several socially unacceptable habits.

Joe was not doing well spiritually. He had cut himself off from other people, and yet he had a deep desire for someone to understand him. Whenever he sought help with his problems, he was given sound biblical counsel about how he needed to think, believe, and respond to his problems – how he needed to change as an individual.

Joe lived within a profound tension. He did not like other people, but he had made human companionship his primary object of worship. He would avoid others and yet complain that others did not care for him. Well-intentioned helpers saw his relationship idolatry, and mistakenly avoided calling him to a community of friends who could help him grow. It was like saying, "Because you have made an idol of food, don't eat!"

Joe was understandably confused and bitter. He needed help. He needed to change and take responsibility for his responses to life's problems. But he also needed a community of friends where he could find hope and encouragement, along with challenging, honest, and loving accountability. Sadly, he was not being encouraged to pursue such redemptive friendships.

What does Joe need? He needs to know that when Christ brings us into the family of God, we are never alone again, no matter how much of a mess we have made of our lives! Yet many Christians latch onto the hope of personal change in a starkly individualistic way. Many helpers fail to move struggling people into the rich context of redemptive relationships. Instead, they cling to the arid individualism of our society. They have a "Jesus and me" mindset as they battle sin and seek to become more like Christ. At first we might think, Why not? After all, getting involved with people is complicated and time-consuming. Who needs it? I could be reading my Bible and praying! Spending time with other people is not very efficient!

But God has a bigger – and, quite frankly, messier and "less efficient" – plan. As we saw in the testimony at the beginning of this chapter, change is something God intends his people to experience together. It's a corporate goal. What God does in individuals is part of a larger story of redemption that involves all of God's people through the ages. You, Joe, and every other believer are already part of the story and part of the family. That is the context in which personal change takes place. Change within community is counterintuitive to the way we often think, but Scripture clearly presents it as God's way of making us more like Christ.

Living in Community Like God Himself

Have you ever wondered why living in community is so important? Your immediate response probably emphasizes the personal benefits of good friendships. While these are valuable, the most important reason for community is the reality that God himself lives in community! Does that sound strange? It shouldn't. God lives in community with himself! Father, Son, and Holy Spirit live in perfect harmony, love, and unity. We begin our discussion about the importance of community where all good theology begins: with God. When we do, it radically alters the way we think about relationships. They become God-centered and not people-centered.

In the last of sixteen sermons on 1 Corinthians 13, Jonathan Edwards says:

> God is the fountain of love, as the sun is the fountain of light. And therefore the glorious presence of God in heaven fills heaven with love, as the sun, placed in the midst of the visible heavens in a clear day, fills the world with light. The apostle tells us that "God is love"; and therefore, seeing he is an infinite being, it follows that he is an infinite fountain of love. Seeing he is an all-sufficient being, it follows that he is a full and overflowing, and inexhaustible fountain of love. And in that he is

an unchangeable and eternal being, he is an unchangeable and eternal fountain of love.

> There, even in heaven, dwells the God from whom every stream of holy love, yea, every drop that is, or ever was, proceeds. There dwells God the Father, God the Son, and God the Spirit, united as one, in infinitely dear, and incomprehensible, and mutual and eternal love . . . . And there this glorious fountain forever flows forth in streams, yea, in rivers of love and delight, and these rivers swell, as it were, to an ocean of love, in which the souls of the ransomed may bathe with the sweetest enjoyment, and their hearts, as it were, be deluged with love![3]

Everything each person of the Trinity is and does is always in union with the others. We were made in the image of this glorious God. Is it any wonder, then, that this deep longing for intimacy and relationship is woven into the fabric of our nature? Human beings long to connect because that is what they were made for. With the entrance of sin, this longing was corrupted and easily becomes idolatrous. Because of sin, we long to find all of our hope for relationship in other human beings. If we don't get what we want out of those relationships, we often do hurtful, sinful things. Our approach to relationships is often self-centered.

But God is a redeeming God who does something utterly amazing to reconcile us to himself and others. The gospel opens the door to friendships where we can be conformed into the very image of Christ. When talking about this new community, the church, Paul clearly has this in view. In Ephesians 4:1-6, Paul turns from talking about our great salvation in chapters 1-3 to the new human community we have been brought into. He begins to instruct the church about the practical outworking of the gospel in everyday life and relationships:

> As a prisoner for the Lord, then, I urge you to live a life worthy of the calling you have received. Be completely humble and gentle; be patient, bearing with one another in love. Make every effort to keep the unity of the Spirit through the bond of peace. There is one body and one Spirit – just as you were called to one hope when you were called – one Lord, one faith, one baptism; one God and Father of all, who is over all and through all and in all. (Eph. 4:1-6)

Change Is a Community Project

In light of the great grace of God, Paul calls members of this new community to enter into relationships with their Christian brothers and sisters in humility, gentleness, patience, and forbearance. He urges the church to be vigilant to keep the unity of the Spirit; he does not tell them to create it, because it is already a fact. When you trust in Christ, you are immediately welcomed into fellowship with the source of love, the triune God, and with his family, the church. In light of that, spare no effort to make sure your relationships reflect the unity and love of Father, Son, and Holy Spirit. It all begins, continues, and will end with God at the center.

Paul grounds this call to community in the redemptive work of the Trinity. Notice how the word one is used in verses 4-6. Each use is attached to a member of the Trinity. There is one Spirit at work in one body. There is one Lord through whom we have one hope, faith, and baptism. There is one Father who is over one family, the church. All of the blessings are ours because of what the Trinity has done in creation and redemption.

Let's reflect on what the Trinity has done to make us one body, united to Father, Son, and Holy Spirit. In Genesis 15, we find an odd story loaded with redemptive significance.

> He also said to him [Abram], "I am the LORD, who brought you out of Ur of the Chaldeans to give you this land to take possession of it." But Abram said, "O Sovereign LORD, how can I know that I will gain possession of it?"
>
> So the LORD said to him, "Bring me a heifer, a goat and a ram, each three years old, along with a dove and a young pigeon."
>
> Abram brought all these to him, cut them in two and arranged the halves opposite each other; the birds, however, he did not cut in half. Then birds of prey came down on the carcasses, but Abram drove them away.
>
> As the sun was setting, Abram fell into a deep sleep, and a thick and dreadful darkness came over him. Then the LORD said to him, "Know for certain that your descendants will be strangers in a country not their own, and they will be enslaved and mistreated four hundred years. But I will punish the nation they serve as slaves, and afterward they will come out with great possessions. You, however, will go to your fathers in peace and be buried at a good old age. In the fourth generation your

descendants will come back here, for the sin of the Amorites has not yet reached its full measure."

When the sun had set and darkness had fallen, a smoking firepot with a blazing torch appeared and passed between the pieces. On that day the LORD made a covenant with Abram and said, "To your descendants I give this land, from the river of Egypt to the great river, the Euphrates – the land of the Kenites, Kenizzites, Kadmonites, Hittites, Perizzites, Rephaites, Amorites, Canaanites, Girgashites and Jebusites."

What is going on in this strange encounter? Abram is struggling to believe God, so God helps him. He tells him to cut some animals in half. That night, a smoking firepot and a blazing torch pass between the animal halves. God was saying, "If I do not keep my promise to you, may what happened to these animals happen to me!" This is called a self-maledictory oath. God is saying, "If I don't keep my end of the bargain, may I be ripped asunder!" Over two thousand years later, God the Son hung on a cross, crying out, "My God! My God! Why have we been ripped asunder?" God allowed what should have happened to us to happen to Jesus. We were the ones who failed, yet the triune God was torn asunder so that we might be united to him and to one another as brothers and sisters in Christ. The perfect love, unity, and joy that existed between the Father, Son, and Spirit were demolished, for a time, for our sake.

This is the ground on which we build all relationships. Every time you are tempted to shun another believer, remember that the Father, Son, and Spirit were torn asunder so that you might be united. When you sin or are sinned against, you are to move towards your sibling in Christ aware that Father, Son, and Spirit were torn asunder so that you might be reconciled! If we approached relationships in the body of Christ with that in view, it would transform our friendships. In Ephesians 4, Paul says that to the degree you do this, you will be "built up" (v. 12), "become mature" (v. 13), "[attain] to the whole measure of the fullness of Christ" (v. 13), and "grow up into him who is the Head, that is, Christ" (v. 15).

Belonging to God's Family

When we place our trust in the work of Father, Son, and Spirit to make us acceptable in his presence and revoke our own attempts to make ourselves acceptable before God, he graciously forgives our sins. He also adopts us as his children. So often, the blessing of adoption is seen only through an individualistic lens: I am a child of God. This is true, but your adoption goes beyond an individual blessing. You have been adopted into a new family. The blessing of adoption is both individual and corporate. When my wife and I adopted our fourth child, he not only got a mother and father, but three older siblings! He became an important part of a larger social group, his family.

When the apostle Paul was discipling new believers, he repeatedly reminded them that there was help in Christ and in Christ's people. This is reflected in Ephesians 2:14-22, where Paul tells them that they are part of something bigger than themselves.

> For he himself is our peace, who has made the two one and has destroyed the barrier, the dividing wall of hostility, by abolishing in his flesh the law with its commandments and regulations. His purpose was to create in himself one new man out of the two, thus making peace, and in this one body to reconcile both of them to God through the cross, by which he put to death their hostility. He came and preached peace to you who were far away and peace to those who were near. For through him we both have access to the Father by one Spirit.

> Consequently, you are no longer foreigners and aliens, but fellow citizens with God's people and members of God's household, built on the foundation of the apostles and prophets, with Christ Jesus himself as the chief cornerstone. In him the whole building is joined together and rises to become a holy temple in the Lord. And in him you too are being built together to become a dwelling in which God lives by his Spirit.

What is God seeking to produce in his people? He intends us to be people who are moving towards each other in community. He removed all the barriers so that we can be people who hope, love, worship, and serve together. It is very important to him.

It is impossible to read this passage and come away with the idea that Christianity is a "just-me-and-God" religion. Have you ever heard someone say, "Yes, I am a Christian, but I don't go to church. Why do I need that when I have the Lord?" Or, "What is most important is my personal devotion to Christ, not the church." The Bible never separates the two. Our salvation connects us to God and his people. It is not an either-or but a both-and arrangement. It is not just in heaven that we will be united around the throne of God. Our personal relationship with Christ unites us to believers now!

Notice how Paul brings this out. He says that God has "destroyed the barrier to create in himself one new man." We are "fellow citizens with God's people and members of God's household." We are "being built together to become a dwelling place in which God lives. . . . " We can't become the Christians we are meant to be by being alone with God. This is not God's intent. What we become, we become together.

We tend to read the Bible through such individualistic lenses that we need to be encouraged to see the strong social themes that are throughout the entire Bible. In the Old Testament, God clearly says, "I will be your God and you will be my people." The "you" is plural. When Paul and other New Testament writers address the body of Christ, their words are most frequently directed to the church as a whole. In Romans 12:1-2, a passage that is often applied only to the individual Christian, Paul urges the church to "present your bodies [somata (plural)] as a living sacrifice [thysian (singular)]." Isn't it interesting that he calls all the individuals who make up the church to present themselves corporately before God as a living sacrifice?

How does this vision impact you? Does it surprise you? Intimidate you? Annoy you? Encourage you? How much does your life currently allow you to develop relationships that are deep enough to help you grow and change? What are some common obstacles that hinder redemptive relationships from developing in our lives? Consider the following list and ask yourself if any of them apply to you:

- The busyness of life, keeping relationships distant and casual.
- A total immersion in friendships that are activity- and happiness-based.
- A conscious avoidance of close relationships as too scary or messy.
- A formal commitment to church activities, with no real connection to people.
- One-way, ministry-driven friendships in which you always minister to others, but never allow others to minister to you.
- Self-centered, "meet my felt needs" relationships that keep you always receiving, but seldom giving.

- A private, independent, "just me and God" approach to the Christian life.
- Theology as a replacement for relationship. Knowing God as a life of study, rather than the pursuit of God and his people.

Do any of these apply? Think about your closest relationships: your spouse, parents, children, or small group. What needs to change so that you can form more meaningful relationships with the people who are already in your life? American culture may idolize the Lone Ranger and Superman as heroes who right wrongs and ride out of town alone, but that solitary approach to life and change is utterly foreign to Scripture. In fact, the Bible sees it as weakness rather than strength! The person of character, according to Scripture, will have genuine friendships and be a genuine friend. After all, isn't that the essence of the second great commandment to "love your neighbor"? When we are adopted into God's family, we have many new brothers and sisters to love!

Yet this is not simple. Being involved with people is time-consuming, messy, and complicated. From our point of view it is inefficient, but from God's point of view it is the best way to encourage growth in grace. Our value system collides with God's, but his means for bringing about change in us is best. That means we will have to make time for these kinds of friendships to emerge and grow. We will have to be realistic, too. Close relationships make it more likely that you will sin against someone or that someone will sin against you. There will need to be times of confession and forgiveness. There will be times when you will need to serve someone, even though you feel you lack the resources. There will also be times when you will be served! That may not sound like a challenge, but if you are proud, it is the last thing you want!

These are the very reasons why community is such a big part of God's plan to transform us into the image of Christ. Living in community pushes us to die to ourselves. There will be times when loving others and allowing others to serve and love us will feel like death, but this is the pathway to real life in Christ. The more we understand our own hearts, the more we see that it takes a work of God's grace to transform self-absorbed individuals into a community of love. Being in redemptive relationships shows us our need for change and helps bring it about!

Being Loved as a Family

Ephesians 3:14-21 highlights God's way of grounding an individual Christian's growth within the body. For years, I read and taught from this passage focusing primarily on individual change and relationship with Christ. I failed to connect the Christian's personal life and sanctification to the larger body of Christ. But Paul is vigilant to see Jew and Gentile living in community, even though there could not have been a more radical notion than the idea of Jew and Gentile being on equal footing with God and each other! The tension that existed between Jew and Gentile in the first century was more profound than the ethnic and racial divisions that exist in America today. In view of this tension, Paul constantly applies the message of grace to individuals, but individuals who are in fellowship with one another. This perspective should keep us from reading Ephesians 3:14-21 through the lens of individualism.

> For this reason I kneel before the Father, from whom his whole family in heaven and on earth derives its name. I pray that out of his glorious riches he may strengthen you with power through his Spirit in your inner being, so that Christ may dwell in your hearts through faith. And I pray that you, being rooted and established in love, may have power, together with all the saints, to grasp how wide and long and high and deep is the love of Christ, and to know this love that surpasses knowledge – that you may be filled to the measure of all the fullness of God.
>
> Now to him who is able to do immeasurably more than all we ask or imagine, according to his power that is at work within us, to him be glory in the church and in Christ Jesus throughout all generations, for ever and ever! Amen.

As Paul prays, he wants the Ephesian believers to grasp the nature of God's love for them in Christ. His prayer certainly reflects his desire for individuals to know God and understand his love, but this knowledge and "power through his Spirit" come to a group of individuals living in communion with God and in community with one another.

Look at the language Paul uses. Do you get a sense of how big the love of Christ is? Can you imagine what it would take to really tap into it? The love of Christ is so wide, long, high, and deep (infinite, in other words) that we cannot see this love or experience it all by our finite selves. We need strength from God to comprehend it and we have to grasp it "together with all the saints" (v. 18). It is much like a jury that relies on twelve different minds to come to a full understanding of the truth. When we are in meaningful relationships with one another, we each bring a unique perspective and experience to our knowledge of Christ's love. One person has been rescued from a menacing addiction. Another has been brought through deep suffering. Still another has been sustained by God's grace in a difficult marriage. The list goes on. When we gather to share our stories, we see a different aspect of the diamond that is the love of Christ. Together, our understanding and experience of God's infinite love becomes fuller, stronger, and deeper. Not only are we strengthened in our individual growth in grace, but the entire body is built up by a fuller sense of the power and hope of God's grace! The Christian life is not less than individual, but it is so much more.

Paul's prayer is that the Ephesians would, together, be rooted and established in love. It is the only way they can be filled with all the fullness and power of God. As isolated individuals, we cannot reach the level of maturity God has designed for us. It only happens as we live in a loving, redemptive community where we celebrate the many facets of the gospel. When we look ahead to Ephesians 4, we see that Paul follows his prayer with all sorts of practical instructions on how to pursue and preserve the unity of this community. Our personal transformation must be worked out within the family of God. The gospel is not only more clearly perceived and experienced within community; it is the basis for the community!

If, as we see in Ephesians 4:4-6, God himself lives in community, could we expect him to want anything different for us? If his redemptive plan caused him to enter our world and get close to us, should we be surprised that he calls his children to do the same with each other (4:1-3)? The things we do to enjoy deep fellowship with God and each other are the very things that make us less self-centered and more like Christ. It is the change he is after!

In the church I pastored, individuals and families always came to a deeper awareness of the grace of Christ when they experienced it through the community of believers. I recall one family that was struggling spiritually. They went through a season of suffering that brought a dozen or more brothers and sisters in Christ to their aid. They were also aware that the church was praying for them on a regular basis. As this family rubbed shoulders with individuals, families, and the entire congregation through their trial, their faith was strengthened. Their presence on Sunday mornings ceased to be routine and their involvement in worship grew. At one time, I had wondered if they would make it through the service without becoming bored. But after their experience of community, they were much more engaged when songs were sung, testimonies were shared, and the Lord's Supper was celebrated. They even started remembering the sermons!

Some time later, I asked them what had made the difference. Without hesitation, they described how they had seen the grace of Christ in those who had helped them. It was a combination of seeing the gospel lived out practically and the personal relationships that had been formed. On several occasions, their friends had shared stories of how God had strengthened them in the midst of a trial. They also prayed with the family. God had caused this family to become dependent upon the body of Christ and, through it, they had come to grasp, together with their fellow Christians, the depth and beauty of the gospel. Such friendships are clearly one of the primary ways God causes us to grow.

Purified as a Family

We have seen that God places us in a redemptive community to change us into the likeness of Christ. We understand the love of Christ more fully when we look at it with other believers. Another component of Christian growth involves saying "no" to what is harmful and "yes" to the things that produce life and godliness. Here, Christian friendships not only help us see something (the love of God); they also help us do something (obey God). Both are important and must be kept together as we think about the Christian life. Christian friendships do not simply help us bask in the sunshine of God's grace; they also help us to roll up our sleeves and strive after holiness.

In Titus 2:11-14, we see the community of faith as a place where we are encouraged to pursue a life pleasing to God.

> For the grace of God that brings salvation has appeared to all men. It teaches us to say "No" to ungodliness and worldly passions, and to live self-controlled, upright and godly lives in this present age, while we wait for the blessed hope – the glorious appearing of our great God and Savior, Jesus Christ, who gave himself for us to redeem us from all

wickedness and to purify for himself a people that are his very own, eager to do what is good.

This is another passage that first appears to present God's grace to individuals, who are then commanded to use that grace as a way to privately "clean up their act." But as the passage describes the final goal of God's grace, it says that Jesus gave himself to us "to purify for himself a people . . . eager to do what is good" (v. 14). The ultimate goal of God's grace is an active, healthy, unified body of believers, a full-fledged family freed from sin and its slavery. It is this people, purified and zealous for good works, that is God's precious inheritance.

Just as in Ephesians, Titus 2 includes instructions for corporate living. We need each other's help as we learn to say "yes" and "no" to the right things! Paul calls believers to live in a way that helps others to be built up as well as built together. We must be built up because divisiveness is a terrible thing. It is damaging when people quarrel and sow seeds of dissension, and Paul warns against it. But the body of Christ must also be built together. It is deformed and disabled when people never fully join and participate in the first place. In a similar way, the apostle Peter, in 1 Peter 2:4-5, 9-10, uses rich Old Testament language to describe the corporate nature of our sanctification:

> As you come to him, the living Stone – rejected by men but chosen by God and precious to him – you also, like living stones, are being built into a spiritual house to be a holy priesthood, offering spiritual sacrifices acceptable to God through Jesus Christ . . . . But you are a chosen people, a royal priesthood, a holy nation, a people belonging to God, that you may declare the praises of him who called you out of darkness into his wonderful light. Once you were not a people, but now you are the people of God; once you had not received mercy, but now you have received mercy.

Peter speaks of individuals as "living stones" who are "being built into a spiritual house to be holy." Like Titus, he issues a corporate call to individuals who have been ransomed by God from a lifestyle of slavery to sin and darkness.

The corporate nature of our growth in grace is highlighted in many places in Scripture. In Romans 12:1-8, 1 Corinthians 12, Ephesians 4:7-16, and

1 Peter 4:10-11, Paul and Peter speak of the diversity of gifts. First Corinthians 12 is especially important, because Paul talks about the many different gifts while using the metaphor of the physical body. Each believer receives gifts from the Holy Spirit to be used "for the common good" (v. 7). We are to live as unique and vital parts of Christ's body, connected to serve, and be served by, the rest of the body (vv. 12, 14). No one part should think of itself as useless, especially when compared to more prominent or "glamorous" parts (vv. 15-27).

Think about the gifts God has given you. How are they meant to serve other members of the body as they seek to honor Christ? What gifts do you need from others to help you do the same thing?

When we don't think about our gifts in this corporate way, the very gifts that are given to bless the community are used to divide it. I remember a situation where a church was located near a trailer park. Over the years, the church had struggled to reach out to this community. In a congregational meeting, the pastor encouraged the congregation to make a new commitment to serve the people there. One person stood up and said that past efforts had failed because the church lacked organization. Another person said that the church had failed due to a lack of knowledge regarding the people's practical needs. Still another said that the church lacked evangelistic zeal.

In each case, the person offering the criticism had the gifts to make the effort succeed! The person who saw a lack of organization had the gift of administration. The person who saw the lack of concern for practical needs had the gift of mercy. And the person who thought the church lacked evangelistic zeal had the gift of evangelism. What should have been a very successful outreach was short-circuited because they had not been using their gifts, the very gifts that were needed most. Instead, they had lapsed into an unhealthy criticism of what others were not doing.

About a month later, these three individuals got together and pooled their gifts of evangelism, mercy, and administration to spearhead a successful ministry to the residents of the trailer park. The lesson is obvious: We are better when we are together. Without a combination of gifts expressing the grace of Christ, that very grace is shrouded in ineptitude and pride. Our gifts are for the common good, not self-aggrandizement. When we fail to see this, we find that our gifts actually create division within the body of Christ, instead of uniting us.

Are there places where your gifts are needed in the body of Christ? A better question is, "Where are your gifts needed?" One good way to determine your gifts is to ask yourself where you see weaknesses in the body. It is highly likely that you see these weaknesses because you are looking at the church through the lens of your gifts. Where you see weakness is probably the very place where God wants you to serve your brothers and sisters.

Have you ever seen what happens in a church when there is a death in a family? The pastor and others seek to comfort the family with the promises of Scripture. Other people bring meals, watch children, make phone calls, run errands, clean the house, drive the grieving family to the funeral home and help them make arrangements. Others give financial resources to cover unexpected expenses. Some assist with banking, budget, and insurance matters. Others simply come to weep with those who mourn. It is the body of Christ using its gifts to corporately express the grace of Christ.

Have you ever experienced the love of Christ in this multiplicity of ways? Wouldn't you agree that God's love and power are more fully revealed when the gifts are used in concert? Doesn't it provide more hope for the future, more encouragement to trust the Lord, more strength to do and be what God calls us to be? Everything is more powerful when combined with the ministries of the rest of the body.

The Sacraments

Much could be said about the sacraments of baptism and the Lord's Supper as means of grace in the Christian life. They are the most tangible ways in which the things we have been discussing are displayed. These visible reminders capture both the individual and corporate nature of the Christian life while simultaneously placing the gospel at the center.

Think about the sacrament of baptism. When Peter preaches to the crowd in Acts 2, they respond to his call to trust in Christ by saying, "Brothers, what shall we do?" Peter responds, "Repent and be baptized!" He calls them to individual repentance and faith in Christ at the same time he calls them to commit to the body of Christ. As we saw in Chapter 2, baptism is a picture of personal regeneration and cleansing as well as a call to enter the body of Christ. It centers on the grace of God while symbolizing individual spiritual cleansing and corporate identification with the church.

In the same way, the Lord's Supper is both individual and corporate. Isn't it ironic that individualism and self-centeredness are evident in both places where the Lord's Supper is set before us? When Jesus was leading his disciples in the Last Supper, Judas was preparing to betray him and Peter would later deny him. James and John wanted prominence as his followers. When Paul gives instructions regarding the Lord's Supper in 1 Corinthians 11, he is responding to incidents in which people are failing to love one another!

Paul's teaching on the Lord's Supper in 1 Corinthians 10 and 11 also emphasizes its individual and corporate dimensions. In 11:28, he urges believers to examine themselves before taking part: "A man ought to examine himself before he eats of the bread or drinks of the cup." This is a call to personal repentance and faith. In 10:17, he says, "Because there is one loaf, we, who are many, are one body, for we all partake of the one loaf." This is the corporate side. The sacraments and our participation in them serve as reminders that the Christian life is both individual and corporate. One without the other is not sufficient. It is not either/or. Though we are not given the option of separating them, we often do.

What is the point of all of this? God's work of change has relationships at the core. They are a necessary means and a wonderful goal. Humble community is not the icing on the cake of the Christian life. In a real way, it is the cake. Relationships of love are a means of personal growth, a mark of God's people being purified, and a clear argument to the world for the truth of the gospel.

When we pursue individual spiritual growth through redemptive relationships, we have a powerful combination that beautifies the bride of Christ as she prepares to meet her bridegroom. As we continue to discuss the specifics of change in the following chapters, remember the relational emphasis that the Bible sets in high relief. It is a reminder of where we need to grow, and how much we need God's grace to see it happen. We must not take the change process out of the context in which God has placed it. We grow together!

THE BIG PICTURE

I have always been a lover of big cities, and my ministry has allowed me to visit many in the world. Whenever I am in a new place, I love to get out and explore. Invariably, I get completely lost. A few years back, I was in Seoul, South Korea. I wandered the back streets for about an hour, and then realized I had no idea how to get back to my hotel. I walked into a little corner bakery. An old man stood behind the counter. I thought that if I spoke slowly, I could bridge the language gap and get help. So I said, "I—m — l—o—s—t." He didn't respond, so I thought that a little more volume might help. I repeated myself, this time more loudly, "I—M — L—O—S—T!" He looked up at me and said, "Where are you from in America, mister?" Not getting the clue, I said slowly and loudly, "PHIL—A—DEL—PHI—A." Together we laughed at what had just happened and he proceeded, in perfect English, to give me directions to my hotel.

Let's imagine that you and I are on the corner of a typical big city street. We have a specific place we need to go, but no idea how to reach it. We need directions! Let's say that as we're deciding what to do, a native of the city asks if we need help. This person gives us very precise directions that take us from where we are standing to where we need to go. Has she totally solved our problem? Not really. If we deviate from her instructions in the slightest, we will be lost again, because we still don't know the city.

We really need what this woman has: an overall, "helicopter" view of the city. In her mind, she can see how every neighborhood connects with the others and how all the streets intersect. She has such a complete, big picture view of the city in her mind that it is virtually impossible for her to get lost. If she could have downloaded that big picture to us, we would not only get to our destination, but we would never get lost in that city again!

One of the mistakes we make in handling God's Word is that we reduce it to a set of directions on how to live. We look for directions about relationships, church life, sex, finances, marriage, happiness, parenting, and so on. We mistakenly think that if we have clear directions we will be all right. But we keep getting lost! All the wise and precise directions given to us in Scripture haven't kept us from getting lost in the middle of our personal "big city."

How People Change

The Bible cannot be reduced to a set of directions for successful living. This does violence to the very nature of the Word of God and robs it of its power. The Bible is the world's most significant story, the story of God's cosmos-restoring work of redemption. The Bible is a "big picture" book. It introduces us to God, defines our identity, lays out the meaning and purpose of life, and shows us where to find help for the one disease that infects us all – sin. If you try to reduce the Bible to a set of directions, not only will you miss its overall wisdom, you will not make sense of the directions. They only make sense in the context of the whole story.

The Bible invites us to fly above the streets of everyday life to get this panoramic view. It invites us to see how, in God's plan, everything connects to everything else, and how God's grace enables us to move from where we are to where he wants us to be. It wants to show us the profound realities we would never understand if we stayed at "street level." And the Bible invites us into relationship with the One who is the ultimate guide. Jesus sees everything from origin to destiny and leads us where we need to go. The Bible imparts to us a wisdom so complete and practical that it can keep us from getting lost again.

Perhaps you are lost in the middle of your marriage and you don't know how to get where you need to be. Maybe you're lost in the middle of parenting. You once had a sense of direction, but not any more. Or maybe you're lost in a friendship that has started down a road of conflict and you don't know how to fix it. Perhaps you're lost in anger, fear, envy, or discouragement. You've asked for directions many times, but the answers haven't helped you find your way. You may feel lost in your relationship to God. Things aren't right spiritually, but you don't know whether they will ever change.

God enters our lostness with the comprehensive and practical wisdom of his Word. The Bible unfolds life as God sees it, inviting us to know God, to know ourselves, to know life, and to know how God works to undo the damage sin has done to each of us. The Bible is the ultimate spiritual compass, able to tell us exactly where we are and where we need to go.

In Chapter 3, we saw that we have a valid reason to hope for change. Christ, in all his power, changes us fundamentally from the moment we first trust him. I am a new creation in Christ and I will enjoy nothing less than total transformation in the future! In Chapter 4, we considered Jesus

Christ, the person who changes us. Marriage to Christ transforms our hearts, and in so doing, transforms our lives. In Chapter 5, we learned that God provides a wonderful context for change in the body of Christ. God knows that we cannot do this alone, so he places us in a ministering community, where daily personal help is available.

We are now ready to examine the process of change. This chapter will start with a big picture look at its various elements.

A God of Grace and a World of Metaphors

When you study your Bible, it doesn't seem to give you a helicopter view of life. When you read the minutiae of historical detail and genealogies or struggle through a theological argument, it may not seem like the Bible applies to your life at all! Scripture can seem like a random collection of stories, poems, teaching, and commands. Yet when you examine the Bible carefully, you see that it does provide an overall picture of life. This is important because only when you have an overall sense of what God is doing can you make sense of the details of your life.

The Bible describes four elements in the change process that God institutes in the lives of his children. If you are interested in personal growth, if you feel stuck in patterns that seem impossible to break, if you have wished to experience a fuller and deeper relationship to Christ, or if you want to help someone else make progress down this road, it will help you to understand how God uses the situations and relationships of daily life to change our hearts.

God's grace and love are revealed in the way he designed his world. His world not only displays his attributes, it functions as a vehicle of truth. In his redemptive love, God created a world that points to him at every turn. The sun, the flower, the rock, the sand, the stream, the ant, the judge, the bride, the sea, the tree, the thorn, the captain, the bird, the sword, the weed, the root, the city, the valley, the fruit, and so on, are common things that are also instruments of truth that reveal God. God knows how spiritually blind we can be. We are much better at seeing physical realities than the spiritual realities behind them. But God uses these familiar things as a lens to help us look at ourselves with new insight and understanding.

How much of your understanding of God, yourself, and life has been illumined by physical creation? God uses a mustard seed to define faith. He uses living water to help us understand the indwelling Holy Spirit. He uses lilies to explain his fatherly care. We wake up every day to a world that illustrates life-transforming truths. God does not want us to stumble through life in terminal blindness. He is not willing for us to be tricked by the enemy's lies and half-truths. He loves us too much to leave us to our own explanations and interpretations. Our God is a God of wisdom and revelation. He is the ultimate source of knowledge and he determined that we too would understand truths we could not understand without him. His world is his instrument to bring spiritual sight.

The Big Picture

When we refer to God's "big picture," we want to acknowledge that the Bible does not explain this model in one specific passage. The "big picture" model we will present in this book organizes the pictures God uses to show us:

- what life in this fallen world is like;
- who we are as fallen human beings;
- who he is as Savior and Lord of all things;
- how he progressively transforms us by his grace.

The elements of this model are found in many passages of Scripture, but they are presented with different language, order, and emphasis. The big picture we present enables us to set forth a vast amount of biblical teaching in a compact visual form. It gives order and understanding to the way God works in our lives. Once you begin to recognize these elements as they occur in Scripture and let them interpret your life, they will enrich your understanding of what the Bible teaches about God, about you, and about life. You will grow in practical wisdom as you walk with your Lord down the road of personal change. This big picture model is the story of every believer. God invites us to enter into the plot!

As you examine the big picture, don't think you are studying theology. For all its theological importance, what you are studying is your own spiritual biography. This biblical picture is meant to be a mirror you use to see yourself as you are. It is a diagnostic tool, telling you what is wrong inside; a map that helps you see where you are and how to get where you need to go. It is meant to be a window to a whole new way of living even when circumstances stay the same. It is a shovel to help you to dig beneath words and actions to understand why you do what you do. It will also remind you that you are never alone in your struggle and that everything you need has been provided in Christ. It teaches you how to tap into the resources of God's grace to become what he first meant you to be. Each element of the picture is about your life in relationship to God.

The biblical passage that gets closest to summarizing the model we are using is Jeremiah 17:5-10.

This is what the LORD says:

> "Cursed is the one who trusts in man,
>   who depends on flesh for his strength
>   and whose heart turns away from the LORD.
>
> He will be like a bush in the wastelands;
>   he will not see prosperity when it comes.
> He will dwell in the parched places of the desert,
>   in a salt land where no one lives.
>
> "But blessed is the man who trusts in the LORD,
>   whose confidence is in him.
> He will be like a tree planted by the water
>   that sends out its roots by the stream.
> It does not fear when heat comes;
>   its leaves are always green.
> It has no worries in a year of drought
>   and never fails to bear fruit."
>
> The heart is deceitful above all things
>   and beyond cure.
>   Who can understand it?
> "I the LORD search the heart and examine the mind,
> to reward a man according to his conduct,
>   according to what his deeds deserve."

Let's examine the main images in this powerful passage. In verse 8, the image of Heat describes life in a fallen world. In verse 6, a Thorn bush in the wasteland represents the ungodly person who turns away from God. Verses 5 and 7 give a clear reference to the Lord as the Redeemer who comforts, cleanses, and empowers those who trust him. We represent this part of the passage by the Cross to summarize all of God's redemptive activity on our behalf. In verses 7 and 8, we see the metaphor of a Fruit tree. It represents the godly person who trusts in the Lord. Verses 9 and 10 show us a God who does not simply focus on our behavior. Though he does not ignore it, his focus is on our hearts. He is the ultimate searcher of hearts, because they are central to the change process he undertakes in us as our Redeemer.

This big picture is not a set of directions, but an aerial view of daily life that informs, motivates, convicts, and guides us. This simple but penetrating view of life involves four elements (see Figure 6.1).

1. **Heat.** This is the person's situation in daily life, with difficulties, blessings, and temptations.
2. **Thorns.** This is the person's ungodly response to the situation. It includes behavior, the heart driving the behavior, and the consequences that result.
3. **Cross.** This focuses on the presence of God in his redemptive glory and love. Through Christ, he brings comfort, cleansing, and the power to change.
4. **Fruit.** This is the person's new godly response to the situation resulting from God's power at work in the heart. It includes behavior, the heart renewed by grace, and the harvest of consequences that follow.

The simple picture in Jeremiah 17: 5-10 summarizes a large body of biblical content. It captures the major elements of change in daily life: Heat-Thorns-Cross-Fruit.

Using the Big Picture

Look at two passages, 1 Corinthians 10:1-13 and 2 Corinthians 1:3-11, through the lens of the big picture (Heat-Thorns-Cross-Fruit). Each passage can be organized in terms of these four elements, though they appear in different ways.

First Corinthians 10:1-13 places the four elements in the context of life's

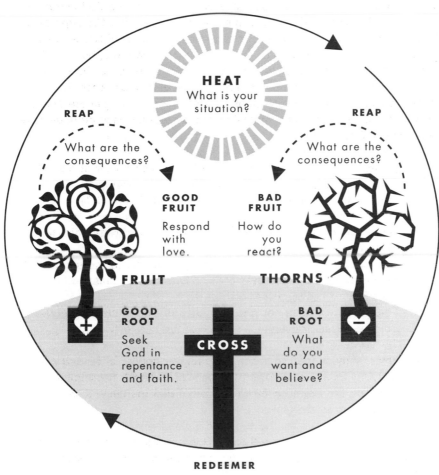

FIGURE 6.1 How Do People Change?

hardships (the big picture model). Second Corinthians 1:3-11 presents them in the context of Paul's personal experience (a case study). As we work through these passages, choose an area of your own life that needs attention and try to see how these elements provide practical personal insight for you.

> For I do not want you to be ignorant of the fact, brothers, that our forefathers were all under the cloud and that they all passed through the sea. They were all baptized into Moses in the cloud and in the sea. They all ate the same spiritual food and drank the same spiritual drink; for they drank from the spiritual rock that accompanied them, and that rock was Christ. Nevertheless, God was not pleased with most of them; their bodies were scattered over the desert.

> Now these things occurred as examples to keep us from setting our hearts on evil things as they did. Do not be idolaters, as some of them were; as it is written: "The people sat down to eat and drink and got up to indulge in pagan revelry." We should not commit sexual immorality, as some of them did – and in one day twenty-three thousand of them died. We should not test the Lord, as some of them did – and were killed by snakes. And do not grumble, as some of them did – and were killed by the destroying angel.

> These things happened to them as examples and were written down as warnings for us, on whom the fulfillment of the ages has come. So, if you think you are standing firm, be careful that you don't fall! No temptation has seized you except what is common to man. And God is faithful; he will not let you be tempted beyond what you can bear. But when you are tempted, he will also provide a way out so that you can stand up under it (1 Cor. 10:1-13).

Paul uses the wilderness experiences of the children of Israel to help the Corinthians understand their own situation. We should be encouraged by Scripture's honesty about the things we experience on earth. God understands what is going on around us and in us. The period in Israel's history mentioned in 1 Corinthians 10 is recorded in Numbers 11-14. These chapters describe the pressures, temptations, and blessings the Israelites faced in the wilderness and their responses. As you read the summaries of these chapters, try to make connections between the Israelites, the Corinthians, and your own life.

- Numbers 11:1: The children of Israel complain to the Lord about their hardships, going so far as to blame him for their plight. If we are honest, we would have to admit that in times of trouble, more complaint comes out of our mouths than praise.
- Numbers 11:4-6: The Israelites complain about the food God provided for them.
- Numbers 11:10-15: Moses complains about the people and the burdens he bears as their leader.
- Numbers 12:1: Miriam and Aaron complain against Moses because they do not like his wife.
- Numbers 13:26-29: The people complain about the battles they must wage to claim the Promised Land.
- Numbers 14:1-14: The entire community of Israel complains about their hardships in the wilderness. They blame Moses and seek a new leader.

Notice how much Israel's response to hardship maps onto ours. We face hard things and we complain about things as mundane as a menu. Before long, our complaining becomes an assessment of blame. Then the blaming goes vertical as it questions God's wisdom and goodness. We too are in the wilderness of a fallen world. We have not yet entered the Promised Land of eternity, so we face hardships like Israel did. Paul tells the Corinthians (and us) that we gain enormous spiritual benefit when we learn from their example.

Let's look for the elements of the big picture model we first saw in Jeremiah 17 (see Figure 6.2 on page 100). First, we see the Heat. In verses 11-14 of 1 Corinthians 10, Paul uses Israel's experiences to help the Corinthians understand their own situation.

On this side of heaven, we all live under the Heat of trial in some way. Mark has a boss who never seems satisfied. Anne's husband is more committed to fishing than their marriage. Sarah endures chronic pain. Tim's teenage son has been in trouble since he turned thirteen. Rachel's church has been through a gut-wrenching split. Jerry struggles with the burdens that accompany his promotion. Brooke lost most of her retirement money in bad investments. Fred is battling heart disease. Jennifer can't control her weight. Bob longs for the simpler days before he got his inheritance. Jason does all he can to avoid his angry father. Old age has ravaged Alex's body.

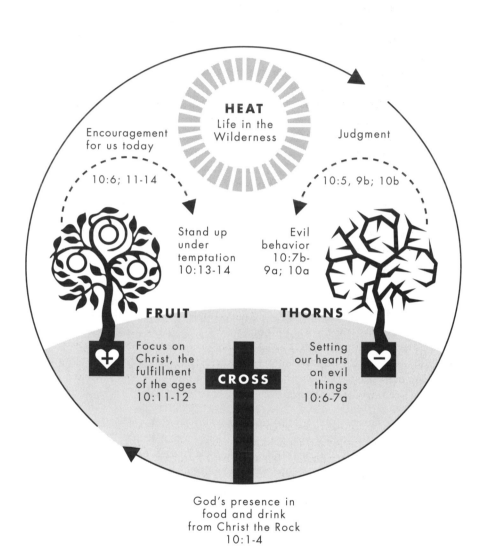

FIGURE 6.2 A Biblical Model for Change (1 Corinthians 10:1-14)

We also see Thorns in 1 Corinthians 10:5-10. Paul details the ungodly ways the Israelites responded to the Heat of temptation (idolatry, pagan revelry, sexual immorality, testing the Lord, grumbling). Don't be fooled by this list. We all have these responses to the Heat in our own lives. Jill complained so much that her friends began to avoid her. Edward handled pressures with too much alcohol. Ted wondered if it was worth going to church when God never answered his prayers. Drew numbed himself nightly with mindless TV. Mike was determined to get his boss's respect if it was the last thing he ever did. Barbara decided to quit her small group because no one took her seriously. Debra was eaten up with envy.

In short, the responses in this passage mirror ours. But the Bible identifies three essential elements in these responses. In verses 7b, 9a, and 10a, Paul emphasizes the specific behavior of the Israelites. In verses 6-7a, he focuses on the heart out of which the behavior grows. In verses 5, 9b, and 10b, he examines the consequences that result.

As we live our lives, we deal with difficulties or blessings every day. Our hearts are always interacting with these situations and relationships. We are always thinking and desiring, trying to make sense of what is happening. There are always things wo want. Those thoughts and desires shape the way we respond to what is going on. And because we are sinners, we tend to respond sinfully. Everything we say and do has some result or consequence. We harvest what we plant and every day we plant seed we will harvest in the future.

Let me give you an example of how it works. Jerry goes to a good church and he took the parenting class when it was offered. But Jerry's teenage son is verbally confrontational (Heat). This disrespect drives Jerry crazy (Thorns in his heart). Jerry gets into his son's face and yells at him, telling him that he is not going to take this disrespect any longer (Thorns in his behavior). This results in a distant and angry relationship with his son (Consequences).

But the Bible's big picture doesn't leave us with the difficulty and the consequences. And neither does 1 Corinthians 10. In verses 1-4 we see the Cross. Paul speaks of God's presence with Israel in the wilderness, his faithful provision, and the exercise of his power on their behalf. "All ate the same spiritual food and drank the same spiritual drink; for they drank from the spiritual rock that accompanied, and that rock was Christ" (1 Cor. 10:3-4).

The hope of the Israelites and the Corinthians is our hope too. The hope Paul talks about is a person. His name is Christ! He is the spiritual food that gives you health and vitality to face difficulties. He is the spiritual drink that quenches the thirst that the Heat in your life produces. Christ sustains me so that I can live with him and for him even when I struggle. His grace not only forgives, it enables and delivers. It endows me with wisdom, character, and strength. And all this is at the heart of what God is seeking to produce in me.

Finally, Paul turns to Fruit in verses 11-14 and calls his readers to embrace Christ. Verse 11 refers to Jesus' first coming as "the fulfillment of the ages." Paul wants his readers to see how privileged they are to be welcomed by God's grace. Paul tells them, "All the promises that gave hope to the people of God have come true for you. In Christ, you have been given more than your heart will ever grasp!" What Paul said to the Corinthians, he says to us.

In verses 11-12, Paul speaks to a believer's new heart, characterized by honest self-examination and humility. This new heart gladly embraces Christ. Take an honest look at your heart and admit your desperate need for him.

Verses 13-14 describe the new behavior that includes a new resolve to stand up under temptation (13) and a new vigilance against the slide toward idolatry so natural to fallen humanity. What Paul envisions here is not just the change that takes place when we come to Christ, but the lifestyle of change that results from an ongoing sense of our need for redemption (progressive sanctification).

That's the big picture – Heat-Thorns-Cross-Fruit. It is an honest, insightful, and humbling view of human beings and why we do the things we do. It is a hope-filled look at the way God enters our world to change our hearts and empower us to do what is right. And it is an encouraging picture of good fruit that results when we respond in faith to God.

A Personal Story

The general outline that 1 Corinthians 10 gives us is illustrated in Paul's personal story in 2 Corinthians 1:3-12. In this passage we see Paul use the Heat-Thorns-Cross-Fruit model to reflect on his own life. Figure 6.3 will guide you through this very personal and practical passage.

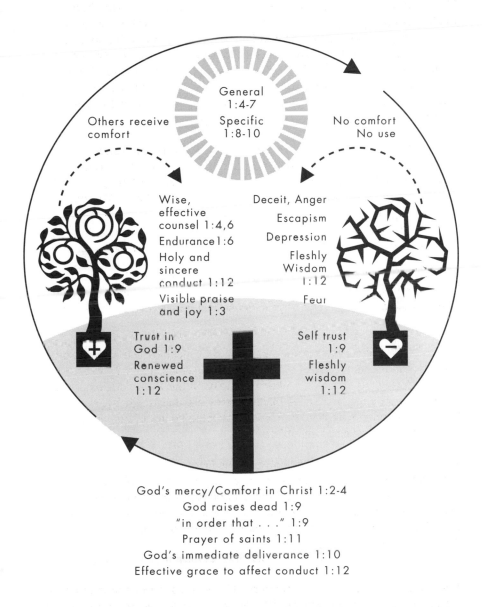

General
1:4-7

Specific
1:8-10

Others receive
comfort

No comfort
No use

Wise,
effective
counsel 1:4,6

Endurance 1:6

Holy and
sincere
conduct 1:12

Visible praise
and joy 1:3

Deceit, Anger

Escapism

Depression

Fleshly
Wisdom
1:12

Fear

Trust in
God 1:9

Renewed
conscience
1:12

Self trust
1:9

Fleshly
wisdom
1:12

God's mercy/Comfort in Christ 1:2-4
God raises dead 1:9
"in order that . . ." 1:9
Prayer of saints 1:11
God's immediate deliverance 1:10
Effective grace to affect conduct 1:12

FIGURE 6.3 A Biblical Model for Change (2 Corinthians 1:3-11)

Praise be to the God and Father of our Lord Jesus Christ, the Father of compassion and the God of all comfort, who comforts us in all our troubles, so that we can comfort those in any trouble with the comfort we ourselves have received from God. For just as the sufferings of Christ flow over into our lives, so also through Christ our comfort overflows. If we are distressed, it is for your comfort and salvation; if we are comforted, it is for your comfort, which produces in you patient endurance of the same sufferings we suffer.

. . . We do not want you to be uninformed, brothers, about the hardships we suffered in the province of Asia. We were under great pressure, far beyond our ability to endure, so that we despaired even of life. Indeed, in our hearts we felt the sentence of death. But this happened that we might not rely on ourselves, but on God, who raises the dead. He has delivered us from such a deadly peril, and he will deliver us. On him we have set our hope that he will continue to deliver us, as you help us by your prayers. Then many will give thanks on our behalf for the gracious favor granted us in answer to the prayers of many.

Now this is our boast: Our conscience testifies that we have conducted ourselves in the world, and especially in our relations with you, in the holiness and sincerity that are from God. We have done so not according to worldly wisdom, but according to God's grace.

Paul is very candid as he talks about the Heat in this time of his life: "hardship suffered in the province of Asia," and "under great pressure." Although we only have one descriptive phrase here, it has a real-life intensity to it. He is humbly honest about his response: "despaired even of life" and "in our hearts we felt the sentence of death." The words capture the experience of overwhelming fear. Paul talks about the Thorns of self-reliance (v. 9) and worldly wisdom (v.12) that so often shape our responses to this kind of situation. He powerfully points to the Cross: God's compassion and comfort (v.1), God's presence (vv. 8, 9), his power – "who raises the dead," his deliverance (v.10), and his provision of the body of Christ, "as you help us by your prayers." Paul also describes the Fruit of faith as he shares his story: visible joy and praise (v. 3), endurance (v. 6), trust in God (v. 9), right behavior (v.12), and ministry (vv. 5-7).

Like the apostle Paul, we too will find ourselves in situations that seem far beyond our ability to endure. Maybe problems in our church have left us overwhelmed. Perhaps finances are a trial. Maybe parenting has left you feeling exhausted and inadequate. Maybe living a godly life in a godless workplace seems like an impossible calling. Or maybe you feel defeated by soured family relationships.

Where do you feel like you are beyond your ability to endure? The Bible speaks into just that kind of experience. God enters our stories with the hope of Christ and shows us where we are and where we need to go.

Although Israel's and Paul's struggles took place in different eras and circumstances, the same four elements are found in each. They form a picture that helps us understand our own lives from God's perspective as well. You and I do not have to be lost in the middle of our own stories. We do not have to wonder how we got where we are and how we will get where we need to be. You can know exactly what Christ has provided so that you can live as he has called you to live. As he did in these passages, God meets us and changes us in the middle of life's challenges. The Heat may not go away. In fact, it may get hotter! Yet we are never alone. God is with us to provide the grace we need to face what he calls us to face.

In the chapters to come, we will take a more detailed look at the four elements and their part in God's change process. If you are willing to use each of them as a mirror, you will grow in wisdom about the world, in knowledge about yourself, and in friendship with your Lord. Our prayer is that this book will help you identify areas where you need to grow as a person and in your relationship with the Lord. Our prayer is that this will provide a foundation for you to minister the same help to others.

Life as God Sees It, Change as God Does It

Lost? There is hope. Near someone who is lost? There is help. Let God's view of life and change give you personal hope and ministry courage. Let God's simple metaphors light your way.

Heat (What is your situation?)

You and I always react to things that happen around us. Whether it is the scorching Heat of difficulty or the unexpected Rain of blessing, you always respond to whatever comes down on you. The Bible is honest about the things that happen here. You will recognize the world of the Bible because it is the world you live in every day.

Thorns (How do you react? What do you want and believe?)

You and I are never passive. We always respond to the Heat (or Rain) in our lives. Maybe it's a tough boss or a crazy extended family, a rebellious child or a chronic sickness. Maybe it's a new career opportunity or a newly acquired inheritance. Whatever it is, the Bible helps us to see how we react to the Heat in our hearts and our outward behavior. It reminds us that sinners respond to the fallen world sinfully, and each reaction yields a harvest of consequences.

Thorns are about the biblical category of "fleshly wisdom," those foolish responses that come all too naturally to us when hard things happen. Someone speaks unkindly to us, so we let our bitterness grow. Something unexpected happens and we respond by denying, avoiding, blaming, or seeking to take control. Negative things come our way and we allow ourselves to doubt God and let our participation in worship and ministry wane. We are blessed with unexpected money and we spend it on ourselves. We don't get the raise we thought we deserve, so we work halfheartedly.

Scripture makes it clear that these responses are not forced upon us by the pressures of the situation. What I do comes from inside me. The things that happen to me will influence my responses but never determine them. Rather, these responses flow out of the thoughts and motives of my heart. This is why you can have five people in the same situation with five different responses!

Cross (Who is God and what does he say and do in Christ?)

It should be a tremendous encouragement to us that the God of the Bible presents himself as "an ever present help in trouble" (Ps. 46:1). The ultimate example is Christ, who took the name Emmanuel and came to a fallen world to live, die, and rise again. He continues to be "God with us" as he indwells us with his Spirit. He gives us everything we need to respond to life in godly ways. The promise of the Cross extends beyond renewed strength or enhanced wisdom. Christ gives us himself and in so doing remakes us from the inside out. If you are a believer, you are in the process of being remade to reflect the character of Jesus himself. And your Lord is employing every circumstance and relationship in your life to accomplish that goal.

Fruit (How is God calling me to seek him in repentance and faith?)

Because of what Christ has done for us, we can respond to the same old pressures in a brand new way. When blessed, we look for ways to bless others. In trouble, we run to God and not away from him. We don't seek to avoid life, but move toward it with courage and faith. We don't take vengeance but entrust ourselves to the only wise Judge. This is the life the presence of God and the grace of Christ make possible. These new responses produce good Fruit in our lives and in the lives of others.
Look at your life through the eyes of your Redeemer. Let him reveal your behavior and your heart as well. The courage of self-examination leads to the hope of lasting personal change when God is involved. Emmanuel has entered your story and nothing will ever be the same again!

H E A T   1 :
G O D   I N   T H E
R E A L   W O R L D

When he was summoned to his boss's office that morning, he thought it was for a raise. His plan had worked! He'd wanted to establish his career, save some money, and then think about getting married and having a family. He had been very successful; in fact, he was the youngest person ever to run a design team. There had been talk of a bonus and even being named director of the design department. He had always had a good relationship with his boss, so he looked forward to talking about his future with the company.

As he entered the office, his boss was more serious than usual. That was odd. His design team had just completed work on a cutting-edge product. It had cost a lot of personnel time and company money, but they were about to roll out the prototype.

"I've got bad news," his boss began. The product they thought was unique had just been introduced by another company. They had been so focused on design that they had neglected market research. It was a costly error that threatened the entire company's survival. He heard words he never thought he would hear: "I'm going to have to let you go, and frankly, I don't know if you'll work in this industry again."

His life was over; his carefully laid plans shattered by one conversation. It didn't seem possible, and it surely didn't feel real. But the months to come would demonstrate just how real it was.

The Morphing of Emotions

Very few people wake up one morning and decide to change their theology. Changes in a person's belief system are seldom that self-conscious. The person you just read about had a very painful experience. In ways we don't often recognize, these experiences are hermeneutical; that is, they become lenses we use to interpret life. Unfortunately, we are seldom aware that this is happening.

The emotions we feel as we first go through difficult experiences are not static. They morph into subtle but extremely influential conclusions about God, ourselves, others, and life. Yet these major changes in what we believe have not been well thought out. We have not put ourselves through a careful theological re-evaluation. Rather, our unresolved feelings become our interpretations of life. Emotions morph into conclusions, and we end up not believing the things we say we believe.

The person you just read about felt discouraged and alone. He wondered why these things had happened to him. He questioned where God was and why he would allow such devastation. At times, he questioned the value of his faith. Yet he was largely unaware of the spiritual battle going on inside.

Have you ever felt alone, wondering if anybody would understand what you were going through? Have you ever hidden a struggle because you were afraid of what people would think? Have you ever thought a problem was too big to be solved? Has this ever led you to question whether God understood or cared? Think about your own faith. Has it really only been shaped by teaching, preaching, and personal Bible study? Or is there a gap between what you profess to believe and what you actually believe when the rubber meets the road? Perhaps you are close to someone who is going through a hard time and finding it difficult to hold onto her faith. If any of this sounds familiar, this chapter on the Heat of everyday life is for you.

The Heat: God's View of My World

We've seen that the Bible says that we are always living under the scorching Heat of trouble or the cool Rain of blessing. In either case, we are always responding to what is happening to us. The Bible doesn't offer a sanitized version of life or our reactions to it. Dark, shocking, and painful stories abound. Scripture shows us people who think, act, plan, decide, and speak just like we do. If the Bible left out these real-life stories of murder, rape, famine, disease, judgment, depression, war, adultery, theft, corruption, and overwhelming fear, how likely would we be to believe that God's Word could help us?

It is incredibly encouraging to realize that the Bible addresses the world as we know it. God makes it very clear that he understands the Heat we face every day. It isn't always pleasant to read the honest stories of Scripture, but it is comforting. We realize that we will never face an experience, no matter how dark or difficult, that would be a shock to our God. The hope and help God offers his children reflect his knowledge of the full range of human experience.

That's why some of the most comforting passages of Scripture may not even have the word "comfort" in them. They may not be neatly tied together with a happy ending or say much about God's promises, love, and grace. Yet they give hope in their accurate depiction of the things we face. Psalm 88 is one of those passages.

O LORD, the God who saves me,
    day and night I cry out before you.
May my prayer come before you;
    turn your ear to my cry.
For my soul is full of trouble
    and my life draws near the grave.
I am counted among those who go down to the pit;
    I am like a man without strength.
I am set apart with the dead,
    like the slain who lie in the grave,
whom you remember no more,
    who are cut off from your care.
You have put me in the lowest pit,
    in the darkest depths.
Your wrath lies heavily upon me;
    you have overwhelmed me with all your waves.
You have taken from me my closest friends
    and have made me repulsive to them.
I am confined and cannot escape;
    my eyes are dim with grief.
I call to you, O LORD, every day;
    I spread out my hands to you.
Do you show your wonders to the dead?
    Do those who are dead rise up and praise you?
Is your love declared in the grave,
    your faithfulness in Destruction?
Are your wonders known in the place of darkness,
    or your righteous deeds in the land of oblivion?
But I cry out to you for help, O LORD;
    in the morning my prayer comes before you.

Why, O LORD, do you reject me
  and hide your face from me?
From my youth I have been afflicted and
      close to death;
  I have suffered your terrors and am in despair.
Your wrath has swept over me;
  your terrors have destroyed me.
All day long they surround me like a flood;
  they have completely engulfed me.
You have taken my companions and loved
      ones from me;
  the darkness is my closest friend.

Alone in the Darkness?

What did you feel when you read Psalm 88? Read it again and put yourself
in the writer's place.

Vv. 3-5: you are in deep inner despair.

Vv. 6-7: you feel forsaken by God.

V. 8a: you have lost your friends.

V. 8b: you feel trapped and helpless.

Vv. 9-12: you feel like you are dying, crying out for help, but none comes.

Vv. 13-14: you feel as though God has turned his back on you.

Vv. 15-17: you feel like bad things always happen and nothing ever changes.

V. 18: you feel like you wake up every morning to a very dark world.

Did it bother you that the psalm did not end on a positive note? Does it
unsettle you that this dark psalm is in the Bible? Do you wonder what good
we are supposed to get from reading it? Let me suggest some things we
can gain from it.

1. God understands the full range of human experience, from supreme
    joy to crushing sorrows.
2. The promises of the Redeemer come to people who live in a world
    where such things take place.
3. God's honesty about these experiences invites me to be honest
    about the things I face. Biblical Christianity is never blind or stoic in
    its reaction to life.
4. Going to God with my despair, doubt, and fear is an act of faith.

Psalm 88 reminds me to run to God in desperate moments, not away from him.

5. The Bible is not about an idyllic world full of noble people who always make the right choice. The Bible describes a world we recognize, where very good and very bad things happen, and where people make wonderful and horrible choices. The Bible describes a world that sometimes makes us laugh, but often makes us cry.

As you examine your own life, are you like the psalmist? Can you be honest with God? Are you afraid to face how you are responding to the Heat of your life? Do you wonder if God really welcomes your honesty, so you hesitate to bring the cries of your heart to him? Do you feel like you have to put on a good front of unwavering faith before God and people? Does your faith genuinely impact your daily life?

I had an epiphany one Wednesday evening in the middle of our small group meeting. People were sharing prayer requests, but it was the same old grocery list of situational, self-protective prayer requests masquerading as openness and self-disclosure. I found myself thinking, Why did we all feel the need to clean up our prayer requests before giving them? Why were we all so skilled at editing ourselves out of our prayer requests? Why were we so good at sharing the difficult circumstances we faced, yet so afraid of talking about our struggles in the middle of them? Did we really care more about what people thought than we did about getting help? Did we really think that God would be repulsed by our sins and weakness? I wondered who we thought we were fooling. It was as if we had all agreed upon an unspoken set of rules, a conspiracy of silence.

I looked around the room. These were people I thought I knew well. I did know what many of them were facing, yet I knew little of the wars going on inside them.

I brought my thoughts back to the discussion, determined to break the silence. I didn't think I was better than the others. I had been a willing part of the conspiracy too, but I was determined to be so no longer. That night I prayed that God would break down the walls of fear that kept us from sharing our hearts with one another and bringing to God the things that were really going on. I asked God to give us the hope, faith, and courage to put our struggles into words that would reach his ears, the ultimate source of compassion, forgiveness, wisdom, and power. To my surprise, others followed with similar prayers, confessing their fears, doubts, and struggles. God began to change our group that night.

Psalm 88 is an invitation to that kind of honesty. It calls us to an open and authentic faith in the face of chronic sickness, the burden of wealth, the rejection of friends, trauma and abuse, the loss of a job, the temptations of success, a child's rebellion, a loved one's death, a church split, perverted justice, the cloud of depression, and a host of other things that are part of life. In Psalm 88, God welcomes us to come out of the shadows, to honestly express our struggles. When we do, we will find that God already knows and understands!

Even More Encouraging

The title to this psalm says it is a song. Why would God ever want his people to sing such a discouraging dirge? What would be the point of putting, "The darkness is my closest friend" to music? This is where the psalm becomes most encouraging!

Psalm 88 is a song of the sons of Korah. The Korahites were the doorkeepers of the tabernacle, those who led Israel in procession to the tent of worship and sacrifice. This mournful song was one of the songs they would sing! Do you see what this means? God intended the darkest human laments to be brought together with the brightest human hopes. Honest expressions of fear, pain, and doubt were welcome in the place of worship, atonement, and forgiveness. The mess of human misery was welcomed into the place of mysterious, glorious grace.

No psalm more powerfully communicates, "Come to me as you are, with all your doubt and fear, pain and discouragement. Hold before me your shattered hopes and dreams, and find redemption and rest when it seems there is none to be found. Don't hesitate because your heart is weak and your mind confused. Don't hesitate because you have questioned my goodness and love. Come as you are, for my sacrifice is for you, just as you are." This kind of honesty before God is meant to be part of our worship. What a helpful and hopeful invitation! We do not have to put on spiritual masks to approach God. We can come as we are. His love is sturdy and his grace is sufficient.

Biblical Realism

Another passage that breathes biblical realism is James 1:1-15.

[1]James, a servant of God and of the Lord Jesus Christ, to the twelve tribes scattered among the nations: Greetings.

[2]Consider it pure joy, my brothers, whenever you face trials of many kinds, [3]because you know that the testing of your faith develops perseverance. [4]Perseverance must finish its work so that you may be mature and complete, not lacking anything. [5]If any of you lacks wisdom, he should ask God, who gives generously to all without finding fault, and it will be given to him. [6]But when he asks, he must believe and not doubt, because he who doubts is like a wave of the sea, blown and tossed by the wind. [7]That man should not think he will receive anything from the Lord; [8]he is a double-minded man, unstable in all he does.

[9]The brother in humble circumstances ought to take pride in his high position. [10]But the one who is rich should take pride in his low position, because he will pass away like a wild flower. [11]For the sun rises with scorching heat and withers the plant; its blossom falls and its beauty is destroyed. In the same way, the rich man will fade away even while he goes about his business.

[12]Blessed is the man who perseveres under trial, because when he has stood the test, he will receive the crown of life that God has promised to those who love him.

[13]When tempted, no one should say, "God is tempting me." For God cannot be tempted by evil, nor does he tempt anyone; [14]but each one is tempted when, by his own evil desire, he is dragged away and enticed. [15]Then, after desire has conceived, it gives birth to sin; and sin, when it is full-grown, gives birth to death."

Every passage of Scripture was written in an historical context and this passage, like the others, loses its impact when it is wrenched out of its setting. In fact, it can sound superficial until you understand the writer and his audience. James was a prominent pastor in Jerusalem. His congregation was in the middle of severe persecution that probably took place around the time Stephen was stoned in Acts 7 and 8. That background helps us to see James's words not as the platitudinous preaching of a detached theologian, but as the wise and caring advice of a seasoned and loving pastor. James takes what he knows to be true about God's wisdom and comfort and applies it to friends who are suffering greatly. Let's look at what he shares with them.

In verse 2, James gently reminds his congregation that trials are inevitable. Notice his use of the word "whenever" – not "if." James is saying that trials will come. He knows that difficulties become more difficult when we naively assume that troubles won't come our way. God never promised that his children would escape a fallen world. In his wisdom, he has chosen for us to live in the middle of its brokenness. Whether it is weeds or disease, rejection or corruption, war or pollution, disappointment or danger, we are all somehow touched every day by the fall. We shouldn't be surprised when suffering and difficulty come our way; in fact, we should probably be surprised when they don't.

James wants to protect his congregation from the painful shock of surprise. He wants them to live with a healthy biblical realism. Similarly, in Philippians 1:29 and 1 Peter 4:12, Paul and Peter urge us to recognize that we live in a world where trials are a normal part of life. They are not an exception to the order of things; they are the rule.

In verses 2 through 4, James emphasizes the blessings of trials. Does that phrase seem like a contradiction? James has a very strange way of talking about trials – he suggests that they are something we need. Most of us don't say to God, "You know, Lord, my life has been all too easy lately. I would really appreciate it if you could send some suffering my way." Our instincts are exactly the opposite. We see trials as things we should do everything in our power to avoid. But James says that rather than being an interruption to God's work, trials are part of his plan.

Without the trials we so dislike, James says we would remain immature, incomplete, and deficient as Christians. Trials help us! Through them we become more mature and more complete, until finally we lack nothing!

In verses 5 through 8, James assures us that he does not think that this makes the trials easy. He does not endorse a superficial happy face to mask inner struggle or a Christian stoicism. Instead, James urges us to run to God for help and wisdom. When we do, we will find that God gives generously to those who are humble in heart. James's model for responding to trial is not "gut it out," but "cry out." When we cry out to the all-sufficient God, we will receive all the wisdom we need.

In verses 9 through 12, James continues to surprise us with the way he looks at trials. He reminds us that a trial can come in the form of difficulty or blessing. Riches can be as much a trial as poverty! Losing a job or getting a promotion, being rejected or receiving the praise of others, failure or success, physical illness or perfect health – each is a form of trial according to James (and the rest of Scripture). Both present opportunities for temptation and sin, as well as testing and growth.

Look at your own life. Have all your trials been times of suffering? What about that raise that made you selfish with your money? What about good health that tempted you to be undisciplined with eating and exercise? What about the pride that accompanied success in ministry? We don't just struggle with want; we struggle with blessing as well. James's warning is wise and timely for us all.

In verses 13-15, James shifts his focus from trial to temptation. For James (and the rest of Scripture), a trial is an external situation (Heat) that reveals what is happening in the heart (either Thorns or Fruit). A trial can lead to significant personal growth at the heart level or it can lead to temptation and sin. In others words, the soil of trial can produce a harvest of either Fruit or Thorns. What makes the difference?

James says that the harvest depends on what is happening inside a person. If the trial leads to temptation and sin, it is because the person has been "dragged away and enticed" by the "evil desires" of his own heart. It is very humbling and important to admit that trials do not cause you to sin. God does not tempt you to sin by sending trials your way. If we respond sinfully to the trials he sends, it is not because we have been forced to sin, but because our hearts have chosen to do so.

Do we really believe what James is saying about trials and how we respond to them? For example, someone might say, "Jim makes me so angry!" In that statement, Jim is responsible for the anger the person is expressing. Or we say, "This traffic makes me nuts!" Does traffic have some moral power that causes us to act contrary to the true character of our hearts? Here is the humbling truth: Trials do not cause us to be what we have not been; rather, they reveal what we have been all along. The harvest the trial produces is the result of the roots already in our hearts.

Finally, in verses 16 through 18 James reminds his congregation of the goodness, grace, love, and mercy of God in times of suffering.

> Don't be deceived, my dear brothers. Every good and perfect gift is from above, coming down from the Father of the heavenly lights, who does not change like shifting shadows. He chose to give us birth through the word of truth, that we might be a kind of first fruits of all he created. (James 1:16-18)

God is the giver of good gifts. The greatest blessing of all is Jesus Christ, our Redeemer and Friend. Through him we have been given the one thing every sinner desperately needs – new life!

What sweet, amazing and comforting advice! James's words are full of grace and truth. He does not flinch at the reality of suffering, but calls us to run in honesty and humility to God. He also warns us of patterns of cynicism and sin that are often excused because of our circumstances. He points us to the God who loves us and came to redeem us. Consider what this passage has to say as you face trials of your own.

1. The certainty of trials (v. 2). What trial has caught you by surprise? How did the surprise impact your response?
2. The benefit of trials (vv. 2-4). How can you see God using this situation to make you spiritually complete? How would you not have grown without this trial?
3. The need for wisdom (vv. 5-8). How has your prayer life changed through this trial? Does knowing that God truly understands your experience change the way you handle the situation?
4. Two kinds of trials (vv. 9-12). How has it helped you to see that difficulty and blessing are both forms of trial? Can you identify both in your life?
5. Temptation and trials (vv. 13-15). What temptations do you tend to face in the middle of trials? How does this passage, with its focus on the individual and the heart, affect the way you think about your situation (Heat)?
6. Avoiding cynicism (vv. 16-18). What has become clearer to you about the goodness and grace of God as you have gone through trials? Has your love for Christ increased or decreased?

Heat 1: God in the Real World

Psalm 88 and James 1 remind us that the Bible speaks of a God who comforts people in the middle of genuine difficulties in a sin-stained world. Psalm 88 emphasizes that God understands what we are going through. James 1 provides an example of a pastor applying this truth to the lives of people he dearly loves. In both passages, the reality of the Heat is acknowledged and responded to in ways that are truly liberating. We are not alone. God does understand!

You, Your Lord, and Trials

Take an opportunity to examine yourself in light of these things. Think first about why suffering tends to surprise us. Ask yourself, What assumptions do I tend to make about suffering, and how do they increase the pain I experience? Here are some common false assumptions:

Do you tend to minimize how painful life can be?

Do you expect life to be free of trouble? (This often happens when we think we lead a good life compared to others.)

Do you tend to think of good things and bad things as completely separate experiences? In reality, difficulty is often hidden in blessing, and blessing is found in difficulty.

Do you expect the good things you have to be permanent?

Do you live as if you are invincible, thinking that you will have the wisdom and strength to avoid or endure suffering? Are you surprised when you don't?

Are you trusting your life to modern technology's apparent ability to protect or rescue us?

Do you place undue confidence in your ability to control your life, mistakenly assuming that you can manage your way out of suffering?

Now take some time to think about your life. Where is the Heat in your current situation? Use the following questions to make your responses concrete and practical.

What pressures do you regularly face?

What are your God-given opportunities?

What are your everyday responsibilities?

Where are you facing difficult circumstances?

What temptations are you facing?

Who are the difficult people in your life?

What unexpected blessings have you received?

In what situations do you feel alone or misunderstood?

What challenges does the value system of modern culture present?

In what areas do you feel overwhelmed by the things "assigned" to you (blessing or difficulty)?

What are the places you are tempted to hide from or avoid?

What situations tempt you to say you are okay when you are not?

What is the hardest experience of your past?

What is your greatest fear about the future?

As you answer these questions, remember that you are actively loved by a God who has entered into relationship with you. He understands every pressure you face and he is with you in them all. He invites you to bring your concerns, disappointments, fears, doubts, and regrets to him. When life doesn't seem to be working because the Heat is too great, run to your Lord and not away from him. You will find comfort, wisdom, and strength that cannot be found anywhere else.

CHAPTER 8

HEAT 2: YOU IN THE REAL WORLD

What do you expect life to be like?

Do you expect an ordered, predictable calm where your plans are unobstructed? Do you assume that people will agree with you and affirm your choices? Do you think you will be able to avoid sickness, accident, and injury? Do you believe you can plan your way out of stress and avoid situations where you feel overwhelmed?

Our experiences become more difficult when we carry unbiblical, and therefore unrealistic, expectations into them. We are shocked when we find ourselves in stressful situations. We question God's goodness and wonder what has gone wrong with our faith. We think that God has changed the rules on us.

That's why Josh was so disappointed. He was one of the good guys. He played by God's rules. He worked hard, made wise choices, and exercised lots of discipline. He was serious about his relationship with God and active in his church. He was a faithful husband to Judy and an involved father. Given all this, Josh assumed that God would continue to give him the "good life."

He didn't want something extravagant. He just wanted his life of work, Christian friends, and family to go on without a hitch. But now Josh stood at what once had been the doorway of his dream home. Josh had built it with his own hands, and Judy had decorated it. It was their place. But now there was no house. A hurricane had blown it all away. Except for a few photo albums, everything was gone. Josh could not calculate the loss.

Where was God? Why would he let this happen? Why had Josh bothered to work hard, only to lose it all? Josh knew he should pray, but he didn't want to. He was shocked, angry, and disappointed. It wasn't supposed to be this way.

The Real World: The Details

What words or phrases do you use to describe the world? In Romans 8, Paul captures the essence of life on earth this way:

> For the creation was subjected to frustration, not by its own choice, but by the will of the one who subjected it, in hope that the creation itself will be liberated from its bondage to decay and brought into the glorious freedom of the children of God. We know that the whole creation has been groaning as in the pains of childbirth right up to the present time. (Rom. 8:20-22)

Paul uses three phrases to describe earthly life between the fall and Christ's second coming.

Subjected to Frustration

We face futility in this broken world. Nothing seems to work out. Nothing seems to change. It seems like your efforts count for nothing. You wake up in the morning with a knot in your stomach because you know the problem is still there. This frustration exists in little irritations like traffic and disasters like hurricanes. You see it when squabbling children spoil another family dinner and when money-hungry executives bankrupt your company and leave you without a job. Sin has frustrated the cosmos and none of us will escape it. Where do you encounter futility and frustration in your life?

Bondage to Decay

Everything living is dying in some way. The bondage lies in our inability to reverse the process. It is as close to us as our physical bodies. From the second we are conceived, the dying process begins. You see it in other places too. The great new car will someday succumb to rust and mechanical failure. The beautiful bouquet will wilt and die. Our homes deteriorate and relationships disintegrate. Even our spiritual lives drift into coldness and deadness. God, who once seemed so close, now seems distant. The Bible that once evoked spiritual excitement in us now seems dry and boring.

In God's original plan, life was to give way to life, on into eternity. But sin has inflicted decay on our world and none of us will escape. Where do you encounter its reality in your life?

Groaning as in Pains of Childbirth

No woman who has given birth can read this phrase dispassionately! Paul's first two phrases describe what life is like; this phrase focuses on our experience in the midst of it. Life is filled with struggle and pain. The image of childbirth reminds us that this pain is a part of a process. Now is painful because then won't be. It is only because a child will be born then that a mother experiences pain now. The example of childbirth reminds us that there is a redemptive purpose at work in the pain, but that does not make the pain go away! Understanding the hope of the gospel doesn't produce stoicism or denial. You don't deal with pain by minimizing it. Paul is clear: there is pain and we shouldn't be shocked when it comes our way. Where are you experiencing it right now?

As you consider these verses, notice that Paul uses a similar phrase in each one. Frustration, decay, and pain are true of "the creation," an all-encompassing category that includes everything but God. Everything else has been touched by sin and the fall. Nothing I am involved with, nothing that surrounds me, functions the way it was originally intended. Everything is broken in some way. You see it everywhere

- in nature, with storms, pollution, natural disasters, vicious animals;
- in our physical bodies, with disease, weakness, old age;
- in relationships, with conflict, division, violence;
- in the mechanical world and its plane crashes, train wrecks, and appliance breakdowns;
- in human culture, with distorted values, racism, corrupt government, ethnic cleansing, and perverted justice;
- in work, where "weeds and thorns" and all the matters mentioned above make labor more burdensome.

The Bible adds an even more sobering dimension of reality: the existence of personal evil. It is not enough to say that the entrance of sin into the world has made it a harder place to live. The Bible alerts us to an even more troubling reality – a spiritual enemy named Satan. He lives to tempt, trap, and torment humanity, using all the results of the fall as tools of his evil trade. He engages in direct attacks and subtle, indirect ones to thwart

God's purposes for us and the world. While God works to restore all that the fall damaged, Satan seeks to use the damage to his advantage. He uses the frustrating and painful things as weapons against us, to damage our hearts and cripple our faith. He is our enemy, prowling "around like a roaring lion looking for someone to devour" (1 Peter 5:8). In the next verse, Peter includes the Devil's evil activity in the category of hardship (Heat) when he says, ". . . you know that your brothers throughout the world are undergoing the same kind of suffering" (5:9).

You wake up each morning to brokenness. The frustration, decay, and pain you experience are not signs that you have been forgotten, forsaken, or singled out by God. They are normal for everyone who lives on this earth. As you encounter environmental brokenness, the sinful brokenness within you, and the presence of a real enemy, Satan, how should you deal with them?

Lessons from the Wilderness

If you film a video, you won't be in it. You can see everyone and everything else, but you won't see yourself because you are behind the camera.

We often tell the stories of our lives in the same way. We can make ourselves conspicuously absent from our summaries of our own lives. For example, a child tells his parents about an incident at school with little or no reference to himself. The parents learn a lot about the circumstances and the behavior of others, but very little about their child.

The Bible is very different in the way it looks at life. It always finds the person in the middle of the situation and focuses on what the person does. Scripture wants more than an accurate picture of my circumstances. It calls me to focus on what I am doing in the middle of it all.

The Bible uses many physical images to convey truth to us. One of the Old Testament's prominent images is "wilderness." It describes life in a hard place, where people struggle with difficult circumstances. The exodus wanderings of the nation of Israel are the chief example, as we saw in Chapter 6. In 1 Corinthians 10, Paul told us that the lessons from those wilderness wanderings are "examples written down as warnings" to help us recognize ourselves and the typical ways we respond to the Heat in our lives. Paul's point is that it is not enough to recognize the Heat and suffering in our world; we need to think about how we respond to it as well.

Let's look in more detail at three vignettes in the book of Numbers and one explanation in Deuteronomy that are particularly helpful warnings.

The Bane of Boring Food

The rabble with them began to crave other food, and again the Israelites started wailing and said, 'If only we had meat to eat! We remember the fish we ate in Egypt at no cost – also the cucumbers, melons, leeks, onions, and garlic. But now we have lost our appetite; we never see anything but this manna!"

The manna was like coriander seed and looked like resin. The people went around gathering it, and then ground it in a handmill or crushed it in a mortar. They cooked it in a pot or made it into cakes. And it tasted like something made with olive oil. When the dew settled on the camp at night, the manna also came down.

Moses heard the people of every family wailing, each at the entrance to his tent. The LORD became exceedingly angry, and Moses was troubled. He asked the LORD, "Why have you brought this trouble on your servant? What have I done to displease you that you put the burden of all these people on me? Did I conceive all these people? Did I give them birth? Why do you tell me to carry them in my arms, as a nurse carries an infant, to the land you promised on oath to their forefathers? Where can I get meat for all these people? They keep wailing to me, 'Give us meat to eat!' I cannot carry all these people by myself; the burden is too heavy for me. If this is how you are going to treat me, put me to death right now – if I have found favor in your eyes – and do not let me face my own ruin."

The LORD said to Moses: "Bring me seventy of Israel's elders who are known to you as leaders and officials among the people. Have them come to the Tent of Meeting, that they may stand there with you. I will come down and speak with you there, and I will take of the Spirit that is on you and put the Spirit on them. They will help you carry the burden of the people so that you will not have to carry it alone.

"Tell the people: 'Consecrate yourselves in preparation for tomorrow, when you will eat meat. The LORD heard you when you wailed, "If only we had meat to eat! We were better off in Egypt!" Now the LORD will give you meat, and you will eat it. You will not eat it for just one day, or two days, or five, ten or twenty days, but for a whole month – until it comes out of your nostrils and you loathe it – because you have rejected the LORD, who is among you, and have wailed before him, saying, "Why did we ever leave Egypt?" ' "

But Moses said, "Here I am among six hundred thousand men on foot, and you say, 'I will give them meat to eat for a whole month!' Would they have enough if flocks and herds were slaughtered for them? Would they have enough if all the fish in the sea were caught for them?"

The LORD answered Moses, "Is the LORD's arm too short? You will now see whether or not what I say will come true for you." (Num. 11:4-23)

The startling thing in this passage is that the "trial" is relatively minor. It centers on a monotonous menu: manna. But the Bible doesn't focus on the trial. It examines how the people responded to it. What were some of their reactions? They complained, wailed, longed for an idyllic past, criticized their leader, rejected the Lord, and questioned God's plan. When we face difficulty, don't we tend to do the same things?

- We long for life the way it was before.
- We look for someone to blame.
- We question God's goodness, faithfulness, love, and wisdom.

Look carefully at these responses. Who is glaringly absent? We are! We so easily remove ourselves from the picture and blame our circumstances, God, or other people, forgetting that our hardship has been made harder by our response to it.

The Fear of Threatening Circumstances

That night all the people of the community raised their voices and wept aloud. All the Israelites grumbled against Moses and Aaron, and the whole assembly said to them, "If only we had died in Egypt! Or in this desert! Why is the LORD bringing us to this land only to let us fall by the sword? Our wives and children will be taken as plunder. Wouldn't it be better for us to go back to Egypt?" And they said to each other, "We should choose a leader and go back to Egypt." (Num. 14:1-4)

This passage moves a step further. If the struggles within the wilderness are overwhelming, the prospects of entering the Promised Land seem even worse. In Numbers 13, spies entered Canaan to assess what would be required to take possession of it. The people panicked when they learned that even in the place they looked forward to for so long, they would not be free of trials. They realized that they would face huge obstacles in the Promised Land. In Numbers 14, they are in an all-out panic. They ask themselves, "Why did we ever leave Egypt? Why is the Lord bringing this on us? What's going to happen to our wives and children? Wouldn't it be better to go back to Egypt?" And if we are honest, we have to admit that we do the very same thing. We ask:

- "How in the world did I get here?"
- "Where is the Lord in all of this?"
- "What will happen to me now?"
- "What am I going to do?"

Have you ever asked these questions? They reveal a level of fear, doubt, and panic that further complicate a difficult situation.

The Blame Game

In the first month the whole Israelite community arrived at the Desert of Zin, and they stayed at Kadesh. There Miriam died and was buried.

Now there was no water for the community, and the people gathered in opposition to Moses and Aaron. They quarreled with Moses and said, "If only we had died when our brothers fell dead before the Lord! Why did you bring the Lord's community into this desert, that we and our livestock should die here? Why did you bring us up out of Egypt to this terrible place? It has no grain or figs, grapevines or pomegranates. And there is no water to drink!" (Num. 20:1-5)

As the Israelites continue their journey, things deteriorate further. They are tired of difficulty, and, as is so often the case with sinful human beings, they start looking for someone to blame. Moses is an easy target, but Moses was not responsible for the situation Israel was in. God (through the pillar of fire and the cloud) had led them to this exact location. He had done so because he had a specific purpose in mind. This would be another occasion for God to demonstrate his power to the doubting Israelites. Yet this is not how they interpret the situation at all!

This passage shows us how quickly pain morphs into anger. It calls us to humbly admit that, as sinners, we tend to respond sinfully to whatever difficulty we encounter. The agitated hospital patient yells at his nurse. The husband who feels neglected by his wife becomes bossy and demanding. The salesman who gets stuck in traffic blares his horn at the car in front of him. The stressed-out mom is harsh and critical with her children.

This passage makes one thing clear: the anger we reveal in the middle of trial says more about us than it does about the trial. The Bible keeps the focus on us! It confronts the self-righteousness and spiritual blindness that make us think that our greatest problems are outside us, not inside. We maintain that changes in situation, location, and relationship would allow us to respond differently. We say that the difficulty causes us to respond in sinful ways. But the Bible teaches again and again that our circumstances don't cause us to act as we do. They only expose the true condition of our hearts, revealed in our words and actions.

What God Does in the Wilderness

Remember how the LORD your God led you all the way in the desert these forty years, to humble you and to test you in order to know what was in your heart, whether or not you would keep his commands. He humbled you, causing you to hunger and then feeding you with manna, which neither you or your fathers had known, to teach you that man does not live on bread alone but on every word that comes from the mouth of the LORD. Your clothes did not wear out and your feet did not swell during these forty years. Know then in your heart that as a man disciplines his son, so the LORD your God disciplines you.

Observe the commands of the LORD your God, walking in his ways and revering him. For the LORD your God is bringing you into a good land – a land with streams and pools of water, with springs flowing in the valleys and hills; a land with wheat and barley, vines and fig trees, pomegranates, olive oil and honey; a land where bread will not be scarce and you will lack nothing; a land where the rocks are iron and you can dig copper out of the hills.

When you have eaten and are satisfied, praise the LORD your God for the good land he has given you. Be careful that you do not forget the LORD your God, failing to observe his commands, his laws and his decrees that I am giving you this day. Otherwise, when you eat and are satisfied, when you build fine houses and settle down, and when your herds and flocks grow large and your silver and gold increase and all you have is multiplied, then your heart will become proud and you will forget the LORD your God, who brought you out of Egypt, out of the land of slavery. (Deut 8:2-14)

The wilderness wanderings were not a sign of Moses's poor leadership. They were not a sign of God's forgetfulness, faithlessness, or weakness. Yet this was how the children of Israel interpreted their circumstances. They doubted God so intensely that they actually considered returning to Egypt! Deuteronomy 8 tells us that God had a purpose for each trial. In each one, God sought to do three things for the Israelites: to teach, humble, and discipline them. Why?

First, God was preparing them for the spiritual obstacles they would face in the sufferings and blessings of the Promised Land. They needed to experience trials in order to understand that no matter what things looked like, God's hand would sustain them. Like all sinners, the Israelites could easily drift into autonomy and self-sufficiency.

Second, they needed to see the propensity of their own hearts to drift away from trusting God and obeying his commands.

Third, they needed to see regular demonstrations of God's power, so that they would not fear the things they could not defeat on their own.

These trials did not call God's character into question; rather, they stand as signs of his covenant-keeping love. God knows exactly what he is doing! His eyes are on each of his children and his ears are attentive to each cry. But God will turn up the Heat to give his children what they need to face the challenges ahead.

The problem with the Israelites was not that they faced trials, but what they did with them. Israel's troubles were in the thoughts and desires of their hearts. They interpreted their trials incorrectly and saw them as reasons to doubt God's goodness, not as proof of it. They preferred comfort and ease over spiritual readiness for the trials that awaited them in the Promised Land.

In that way, the people of Israel are just like us. If you are humbly honest, you will admit that their responses are familiar. You've done the same things in moments of trial. You've become irritable and angry. You've looked for someone to blame. You've even questioned the goodness of the God you say you love. That is why Paul says that these incidents were recorded for us (1 Cor. 10) as warnings, to keep us from falling into the same patterns of doubt and sin.

We're Still in the Wilderness

Life on earth is a wilderness. Each day we face unexpected difficulties, and even blessings knock us off our path! In it all, God works to expose, change, and mature us. He has not forgotten you or the promises he made to you. He has not left you to the limits of your power and wisdom. In ways that are glorious, yet often hard to understand, God is in your Heat. He calls you to turn from questioning him to examining yourself. Where do you question his goodness, grace, and love? Where do you toy with the idea of going back to "Egypt"? When do you neglect daily Bible study and worship? Where do you struggle with anger, envy, disappointment, and blame?

Think of a situation or relationship that is a regular source of struggle for you. What do you think about God, others, and yourself as you wrestle through it? What do you crave ("If only I had . . .")? How do you respond to the situation, to others, and to God? What have you learned about yourself as you've thought about your responses to the Heat in your life?

What tends to get at you the most?

> Problems in relationships?
> Difficulty at work?
> Disappointment in your marriage?
> Problems in your church?
> Extended family relations?
> Problems with health?
> The stresses of parenting?
> An overbooked schedule?

The pressures of the culture?
Financial stress?
The expectations of others?
The temptations of a promotion?
The temptation of affluence?
The difficulties of ministry?

God is not absent from your Heat. Psalm 46:1 reminds us that he is an "ever-present help in trouble." When you are in the middle of the Heat, you haven't somehow gotten yourself outside the circle of God's love and care. God is simply taking you where you do not want to go to produce in you what you could not achieve on your own. As you rest in his love, you will learn about the heart behind your responses so that you can grow in the faith, hope, and love to which you were called. The Heat will remain because it's a fallen world and we still need to change. But in it all, his grace is always present and always sufficient.

T H O R N S   1 :
W H A T   E N T A N G L E S
Y O U ?

It's embarrassing to admit, but maybe you can relate. She was supposed to pick me up at 6:00 PM. At 6:15 I called her. She assured me that she was only five minutes away, but she arrived at 6:30. I was mad. Didn't she know I had been at work for twelve hours? Didn't she know I would be dead tired? She knew she had left too late to pick me up in time, I thought. She tried to make conversation during the ride home, but I didn't want to talk. I wanted her to know she had upset me.

Fortunately, that only lasted a couple of minutes. Then I dealt with myself and things were okay. But that silly interlude illustrates important things about our struggles as sinners. It is true that Christ's death for us and his presence within us change who we are. We are new creatures in Christ even in a world full of Heat! But we all know that it is easy to forget the wonderful things that are ours as children of God. It is easy to give way to thoughts, emotions, and desires that should no longer rule us, and easy to be more defined by our problems than by the grace of Christ. That is why it is so important to remember the new character qualities and behavior patterns that are in your life because of Jesus. You already have a new heart. You have been radically changed by his grace and are being progressively restored day by day. That is the focus of God's work in your life right now.

The only way to properly celebrate these realities is to humbly ask, "God, where are you calling me to further change? What qualities that you promised to your children are still not active in my heart? What do you want me to see about you?"

My struggle with the late pick-up from work demonstrates the importance of these questions. There is evidence of God's grace in my life. That is why I was convicted of my wrong attitude. But there is also still a need for growth, as evidenced by my struggle with anger in the first place. This leads us to look at the Thorn bush of Figure 6.1 (see page 97).

The Thorn bush represents the fact that, as sinners, we tend to respond sinfully to circumstances of life. We bend and twist the truth: "The check is in the mail." We harbor anger and bitterness: "I can't believe that after all I've done for her, she would do this to me!" We shift blame: "I wanted to do it, but he talked me out of it." We manipulate others to get what we want: "You are clearly the most qualified person to get this job done." We communicate in harsh, judgmental ways: "I would have never done such a thing. I can't believe you would be so dumb!" We numb ourselves with busyness, substances, or material possessions: "I would like to talk to you about last night, but I am simply too busy." We attempt to get our identity from other people or our performance: "No one in our church has been involved in more ministries than I have." We give in to lust. We mete out our own vengeance: "I want her to hurt the way she hurt me." We get defensive and self-protective: "I would really rather not talk about it!" We respond selfishly and thoughtlessly: "I don't care what she needs! I need one evening to myself." We talk unkindly about others and envy what they have. We seek to consolidate power or gain control. We curse one another with silence or rejection. The list goes on and on.

Do you find yourself anywhere on this list? Do you recognize patterns or tendencies in your life? Where are you more the Thorn bush than the Fruit tree? None of us is fully restored to the likeness of Jesus Christ; there are shadows of all these Thorns in our lives. As we compare the Thorn bush to the Fruit tree, we will understand the specific ways God calls each of us to growth and change. In other words, facing the way we are like a Thorn bush is one of God's chief ways of transforming us into Fruit trees.

God's Call to Discontent

In John's case, the problem was that he was simply too content. He had reached a plateau in his relationship with God. He had a strong faith and was involved in his church, but there were Thorns in his life that just weren't going away. For example, John had an explosive temper. He regularly blew up in traffic and got mad at his wife when they worked together around the house. He could barely control his anger at the officials at his children's athletic events.

John also struggled with debt. He always had his eye on the next new tool or "man-toy." He drove a late model luxury car and lived in a house he couldn't afford. Despite several raises and a reasonable budget, John's materialism had led him into debt.

Thorns 1: What Entangles You?

John had problems in his relationship with his wife, Meg. Rather than a relationship of servant love, tenderness, and unity, their marriage had the feel of military détente. They didn't fight a lot; they just lived separate lives and ended each day sleeping in the same bed. Meg didn't feel close to John, so she surrounded herself with friends with whom she shared her joys and sorrows.

There are many Johns in our churches – people who know the Lord but whose lives clearly need change. Yet they live in the Christian community with no sense of urgency or evidence of a personal agenda for growth. As Christians, they are far too easily satisfied.

God calls you to be dissatisfied. You should be discontent, restless, and hungry! The Christian life is a state of thankful discontent or joyful dissatisfaction. That is, I live every day thankful for the grace that has changed my life, but I am not satisfied. Why not? Because, when I look at myself honestly, I have to admit that I am not all I can be in Christ. I am thankful for the many things in my life that would not be there without his grace, but I will not settle for a partial inheritance!

In this sense, it is right for me to be discontent. It is right for me to want nothing less than all that is mine in Christ. He does not want us to enjoy only a small portion of the riches he has given us. He calls us to wrestle, meditate, watch, examine, fight, run, persevere, confess, resist, submit, follow, and pray until we have been transformed into his likeness.

This life of self-examination and joyful discontent should not be confused with a life of paralyzing self-condemnation. God does not call us to self-loathing, but to a willingness to examine our lives in light of our hope as new creatures in Christ. That hope is not only based on the promise of forgiveness, but on his promise of personal deliverance and restoration as well. The same grace that has forgiven me is now in the process of radically changing me. I should not be satisfied until that transformation is complete. A passage in Hebrews is helpful in this regard.

> Therefore, since we have a great high priest who has gone through the heavens, Jesus the Son of God, let us hold firmly to the faith we profess. For we do not have a high priest who is unable to sympathize with our weaknesses, but we have one who has been tempted in every way, just as we are – yet was without sin. Let us then approach the

throne of grace with confidence, so that we may receive mercy and find grace to help us in our time of need. Every high priest is selected from among men and is appointed to represent them in matters related to God, to offer gifts and sacrifices for sins. He is able to deal gently with those who are ignorant and are going astray, since he himself is subject to weakness. This is why he has to offer sacrifices for his own sins, as well as for the sins of the people. No one takes this honor upon himself; he must be called by God, just as Aaron was. So Christ also did not take upon himself the glory of becoming a high priest. But God said to him,

> "You are my Son;
> today I have become your Father."

And he says in another place,

> "You are a priest forever,
> in the order of Melchizedek."

During the days of Jesus' life on earth, he offered up prayers and petitions with loud cries and tears to the one who could save him from death, and he was heard because of his reverent submission. Although he was a son, he learned obedience from what he suffered and, once made perfect, he became the source of eternal salvation for all who obey him and was designated by God to be high priest in the order of Melchizedek. (Heb. 4:14 - 5:10)

As I face crucial spiritual struggles in my life and see where I still need to change, what is my hope? The writer of Hebrews points to six things:

1. God is not surprised by my struggle. He already sees the whole problem. He will never be shocked or caught off guard. This is precisely why he sent Christ to earth.
2. The Bible is for people just like you and me. When the writer says that Christ was tempted "in every way, just as we are" (Heb. 4:15), he is reminding me that the Bible speaks to ordinary people with all the familiar struggles of faith and character.
3. Christ enters into my struggle. He has been there. He faced the full range of temptations I do. He knows what it is like to face them.

4. Christ will help. I can be confident that I am not alone in my
    struggles. Jesus gives mercy and grace appropriate to my need
    just when I need it.
5. Christ pleads my case to the Father. In all of my struggles I have an
    advocate. He pleads to the Father on my behalf until I have been
    fully delivered from every temptation!
6. I can come to God with confidence. I do not have to clean myself up
    or minimize my struggles. I can come as I am and receive what I
    need. In my times of struggle, I do not have to run from the Lord. I
    can run to him to receive what he alone can give.

Real hope is not rooted in my performance, my maturity, my theological
knowledge, or my personal perfection. It is not rooted in the quality of my
character, my reputation, or my success in ministry. My hope is Christ! He
is in my life forever, looking on me with tenderness and compassion. He
will progressively transform me until the job is complete. That is the hope
that helps us to persevere with the Thorns in our lives.

Don't Live Like a Gentile

Ephesians 4:17 - 6:18 is one of Scripture's passages on trusting
restlessness and joyful discontent. Its contrast between the old and new
ways of living is based on a celebration of the love of Christ (Eph. 3:14-
19), the reality of God's power indwelling us through the Holy Spirit (Eph.
3:20 - 21), the offices Christ has established, and the gifts he has given
his church (Eph. 4:11-16). How do we celebrate all these wonderful gifts?
By being committed to a life where self-examination and commitment to
personal change are the norm. This is what Ephesians 4 is about.

> So I tell you this, and insist on it in the Lord, that you must no longer
> live as the Gentiles do, in the futility of their thinking. They are darkened
> in their understanding and separated from the life of God because of
> the ignorance that is in them due to the hardening of their hearts.
> Having lost all sensitivity, they have given themselves over to sensuality
> so as to indulge in every kind of impurity, with a continual lust for more.
>
> You, however, did not come to know Christ that way. Surely you heard of
> him and were taught in him in accordance with the truth that is in
> Jesus. You were taught, with regard to your former way of life, to put
> off your old self, which is being corrupted by its deceitful desires; to be

made new in the attitude of your minds; and to put on the new self, created to be like God in true righteousness and holiness.

Therefore each of you must put off falsehood and speak truthfully to his neighbor, for we are all members of one body. "In your anger do not sin." Do not let the sun go down while you are still angry, and do not give the devil a foothold. He who has been stealing must steal no longer, but must work, doing something useful with his own hands, that he may have something to share with those in need.

Do not let any unwholesome talk come out of your mouths, but only what is helpful for building others up according to their needs, that It may benefit those who listen. And do not grieve the Holy Spirit of God, with whom you were sealed for the day of redemption. Get rid of all bitterness, rage and anger, brawling and slander, along with every form of malice. Be kind and compassionate to one another, forgiving each other, just as in Christ God forgave you. (Eph. 4:17-32)

In verses 17 through 24, Paul sets up the contrast. The Gentile (old way, Thorn bush) way of living is rooted in wrong thinking (v.17) and wrong desires (v.19) and results in wrong responses to life. Notice the catalog of responses: indulging in every kind of impurity (v.19), lying (v. 25), destructive anger (v. 26), stealing (v. 28), unwholesome communication (v. 29), fighting, slander, and an unforgiving spirit (vv. 31- 32). You cannot celebrate the wonderful things Christ has given you and be content with sin in your life.

We know it's still there when we're at the beach and plagued with impure thoughts. Under pressure, we still can avoid the truth, fudge on our taxes, or "borrow" office supplies. We allow ourselves to get angry at friends, parents, spouses, and children and tolerate too much conflict in our lives. We slander reputations in gossip and withhold from others the forgiveness we so often need ourselves. We all need to ask, "Where is the old Gentile way (Thorn bush) still evident in my life?"

In verses 20-24, Paul contrasts the old Gentile (Thorn bush) way with the new "know Christ" (Fruit tree) way. It is rooted in a new way of thinking (vv. 20-22) and a new set of desires (vv. 22-24) that result in new responses: speaking the truth (v. 25), being angry without sinning (vv. 26-27), a lifestyle of giving (v. 29), kind, compassionate, and forgiving relationships (vv. 30-31). If you take time to examine yourself, you will see that many of these good Fruit responses are present in your life. We should never take this for granted, because it is a sure sign of Christ's presence. God has changed you! You are not what you once were! Yet the transformation process is ongoing. We need to be committed to new growth and change.

As our transformed hearts bear Fruit in godly new responses, Paul shows us that change will come to a catalog of human situations (Eph. 5 and 6): everyday relationships (5:3-7); interactions with the world (5:8-14) and in the body of Christ (5:15-21); marriage (5:22-33); parenting (6:2-4); and the workplace (6:5-9) – in short, all of life!

Finally, Paul reminds us that this is what spiritual warfare is all about.

> Finally, be strong in the Lord and in his mighty power. Put on the full armor of God so that you can take your stand against the devil's schemes. For our struggle is not against flesh and blood, but against the rulers, against the authorities, against the powers of this dark world and against the spiritual forces of evil in the heavenly realms. Therefore put on the full armor of God, so that when the day of evil comes, you may be able to stand your ground, and after you have done everything, to stand. Stand firm then, with the belt of truth buckled around your waist, with the breastplate of righteousness in place, and with your feet fitted with the readiness that comes from the gospel of peace.
>
> In addition to all this, take up the shield of faith, with which you can extinguish all the flaming arrows of the evil one. Take the helmet of salvation and the sword of the Spirit, which is the word of God. And pray in the Spirit on all occasions with all kinds of prayers and requests. With this in mind, be alert and always keep on praying for all the saints. (Eph. 6:10-18)

Often when we hear the words "spiritual warfare," our minds think "demonic possession" and "exorcist deliverance." But Paul normalizes the term for us. Where does spiritual war take place? In all the normal situations and relationships of life. The greatest war is not between nations or peoples. It is the war for our hearts. But Christ my Redeemer has already won this war by his life, death, and resurrection. I now have the right to apply that victory to my heart and life. I can come out of hiding, confess my need, and believe that there is hope and help for me.

The Christian life is a war. We cannot live with a peacetime mentality, pursuing rest, retreat, and spiritual relaxation. None of us has reached our destination yet, so with hope in Christ, we follow, fight, watch, and pray, believing that we can be better tomorrow than we are today.

Getting Personal

A lifestyle of joyful discontent involves looking at yourself in terms of the Fruit tree and the Thorn bush in Figure 6.1 (see page 97). Consider your responses to the following questions:

- What are your Thorns? (Complaining, laziness, anger, envy, lust, bitterness, avoidance, pride, indifference, hard words, blame, judgmental spirit, greed, lack of self-control, and so on.)
- Where do your actions and responses fail to demonstrate the Fruit of faith?
- In your current situation and relationships, how are you responding sinfully?
- Where are you experiencing the consequences of your responses?
- Where have you slacked off?
- When have you given in to anger or envy?
- Where have you quit doing what God says is good?
- To whom have you spoken unkindly?
- Where have you blamed others?
- When have you accused God?
- Are you dealing with your feelings by doing unhealthy things (too much eating, spending, or working; escaping with too much TV or too many novels; too much emphasis on things like clothing, appearance, houses, cars)?

God calls you to humbly take a close look at yourself. He calls you to believe and act upon the gospel promises of forgiveness, restoration, wisdom, strength, deliverance, and power by acknowledging your responsibility for the Thorns in your life. Getting to the Fruit tree always starts there! The first step in planting a healthy, beautiful garden is to remove the weeds.

Thorns 1: What Entangles You?

Thorn Bush Responses

If you look around, you soon realize that we do not all respond to obstacles, temptation, suffering, and difficulty in the same way. We do not all respond to blessing, abundance, and success in the same way either. Our responses are not shaped by the situation but by the thoughts and desires our hearts bring to those situations. Nevertheless, it can still be helpful to look at some of the typical ways people respond to life. Do you see yourself in these Thorn bush categories?

1. Deny, avoid, and escape. Here we pretend that things are okay when they aren't. We pretend that we are okay when we aren't. We avoid anything that brings us close to grief and we look for ways to escape. This escape may involve drugs and alcohol, people, community service, gardening, work, TV, overspending, or overeating. Whatever we choose, we are refusing to deal with what has happened in our lives, and we fail to see how our responses expose the true cravings of our hearts.

Andy is overwhelmed by problems in his marriage to Joyce and the burden of parenting four young children. Although he maintains the appearance of a happy Christian family, he finds it increasingly hard to face his responsibilities at home. Work has become his refuge. Since he owns his business, he can justify the early mornings and late nights that keep him away from the pressures he feels at home.

2. Magnify, expand, and catastrophize. Here we give in to thinking that our life is defined by one painful moment; that there is no good, truth, or beauty to make life worth living. We use suffering as the lens through which we view our entire world, and only see pain, loss, and want. We convince ourselves that no one has gone through what we are going through. The larger our suffering looms, the more blind we are to the blessings we enjoy every day.

Although there is much she could be thankful for, Lisa thinks her life is one problem after another. Lisa has not borne unusual suffering, but she considers her life to be filled with much more pain than blessing. She carries this negative worldview into each new experience.

3. Become prickly and hypersensitive. When we go through a difficult time, it is easy to see suffering where it doesn't exist. We allow our hearts to marinate in anger and bitterness, and become overly sensitive and prickly: "I've been hurt once and it won't happen to me again." When we haven't taken the Lord as our refuge, we become hyper-vigilant, scanning our surroundings for possible disrespect or mistreatment. We live defensively and self-protectively, always keeping our guard up.

Joan is always on the lookout for potential disrespect. Recently, her boss asked all the women in her department to lunch – everyone except Joan. Joan was hurt and angry to be so publicly disregarded. The next day, Joan confronted her boss, only to learn that she had not been asked to attend because the boss was happy with her performance, but he did have concerns about the rest of her department.

4. Return evil for evil. Here a person is swallowed up in malice, control, self-pity, fear, self-righteousness, brooding, anger, envy, and vengeance. We meditate on how someone has wronged us and what we would like to do in return. Bitterness and returning evil for evil complicate the problem. We damage our relationships with others and God.

Bill says it clearly as he talks about his unfaithful wife: "I'd like to see her hurt the way she hurt me." He is unaware that this thought shapes all his responses to Jenny. The constant criticism and the lack of cooperation that now make their marriage difficult are really forms of vengeance.

5. Bogged down, paralyzed, captured. This person quits in the face of suffering. He no longer pursues Christian friends, reads his Bible, or prays. His attendance at worship services drops off. He stops volunteering for ministry. Nothing seems worth his investment. So he withdraws from godly pursuits, exposing himself to even greater temptation.

Asaph said it best in Psalm 73, "Surely in vain have I kept my heart pure." Essentially, he is saying, "God, I've obeyed you and this is what I get?" Sometimes you look at life and the bad guys seem to win. You wonder if it is really worth going on. There are times when we are paralyzed because what we face seems insurmountable.

6. Self-excusing self-righteousness. In subtle ways I quit viewing myself as a sinner and blame my sins on others. As I lose sight of my own sinful heart, I become intolerant and judgmental of others and blame them for my failure.

Thorns 1: What Entangles You?

Tom's cold and distant dad has made life tough at home, but Tom's life has been made even tougher by his own anger and rebellion. He probably won't finish high school. He has already had his driver's license revoked. But when Tom looks at the trouble in his life, he lays all of his failures at his dad's feet, making what is already hard even more difficult.

Each of us needs to confess that we have all of these reactions in us to some degree, if only for a moment. When we examine ourselves in the light of Scripture and look for Thorns that may be growing, growth in Christ results. There is an abundant supply of grace for every Thorn you identify in your life, so that your Thorns may be turned into sweet and beautiful Fruit!

Every negative reaction flows out of our hearts. They reveal what our hearts really think, what we really trust and love, and where we have placed our hope. In other words, these reactions help us to locate our particular God-replacements, the things we serve instead of God.

Fruit Tree Responses

As we face our Thorn bush responses, God does not intend us to stop there. He calls us to repent, to receive Christ's forgiveness, and to rely on his power to replace Thorn bush responses with Fruit tree responses like these:

1. Face reality. It is right to experience the grief, sorrow, anguish, and pain that accompany suffering. Honest sorrow is the Fruit of righteousness. Jesus himself did not live a life without feelings. He wept. He felt anguish. It is never a lack of faith to feel sorrow when it is the appropriate reaction to the Heat we face.

Betty does not have a "Praise the Lord anyway" response to her divorce. Her days are punctuated with tears in an appropriate mix of deep sorrow over the destruction of her marriage and a righteous anger over the offenses that led to it. She does not indulge in paralyzing self-pity or vengeful anger, but she isn't being stoic either. Her mourning is part of an appropriate biblical response to what she has suffered.

2. Respond with appropriate intensity. Sorrow, anguish, and grief must be expressed, but with the appropriate intensity. There is always something bigger than the heartache of the moment. Even if I have been betrayed or lost something precious, my relationship with God, my identity in Christ, the truths of God's Word, and the glory of eternity all remain secure and unchallenged. (See 2 Corinthians 4:7-5:10, where Paul compares today's suffering to present and future redemptive realities.)

George suddenly lost his job. His firing was unexpected and unfair. He was shocked, saddened, and angered, yet he also experienced an unusual calm and self-control. George understands that his employers can take his job, but they cannot take the most precious things in his life. Although he feels betrayed, he also recognizes that even now there are many things for which to be thankful.

3. Be alert. Suffering is meant to wake us up from spiritual complacency. It is God's workroom, where he sculpts us into his image. Thus, it is a time for action, discipline, and perseverance. It is a time to experience in new ways all of the truths we have professed are our hope.

It was amazing to hear Tamara say, "I am so thankful for this experience! I thought I knew God, but now I really know him. I thought I knew myself, but I realize I really didn't. I thought I trusted God's promises, but the things God took away from me were what I really trusted. I hope I do not have to go through this kind of thing again, but if I do, I know it will be for a purpose. I was asleep and God awakened me into action. I'm living with a purpose I did not have before."

4. Engage in constructive activity. Actions taken in moments of grief and pain are often actions we live to regret. We panic and run away. We break a relationship. We forsake a commitment. We doubt God. We hurt ourselves. God calls us to do what is good. Seek God. Run to the body of Christ. Find comfort in the Word. Do the normal things God calls you to do. What governs the actions you are taking? Are your responses shaped by a heart ruled by the Lord or by the sheer panic of loss?

Through his suffering, Jim learned the value of the good things God calls us to do. Though he was tempted to give up, Jim got active. God's Word was his comfort. The body of Christ became his source of wisdom and strength. Times of prayer fueled every day. Jim took what people said about him seriously and became committed to personal change. He looked for solid Christian books and tried to fit regular reading into his daily schedule. He refused to be overcome and not only grew himself, but ministered to others.

5. Remember. All of the hope and promise of the gospel belongs to you. In Christ, you have been made new. Because he loves you, God does not want you to experience just a portion of the inheritance he sent his Son to give us. He works in every situation to finish the transformation he has begun in our hearts.

Each day we should remind ourselves of the utter simplicity of God's comfort and call. First, God comforts us with his presence and power and calls us to trust him. We are to entrust to God the things we cannot control. Second, God calls us to obey, and promises to bless us as we do. In good and bad circumstances, we must ask, "What has God called me to do and what has he provided in Christ to enable me to do it?"

I can admit my faults with no need to minimize, hide, or give way to paralyzing guilt. I can confess that I need to grow without beating myself up. I can cry out when life is hard but accept responsibility for the way I deal with it. I don't have to cover my sin, polish my reputation, and keep a record of my successes. I can look at my tomorrows with enthusiasm and hope. Yes, I am still a flawed person in a broken world. But my view of myself is not dark and depressed because the gospel has infused it with hope. Christ is with me and in me, and I will never be in a situation where he isn't redemptively active. Though change is needed in many ways, I am not discouraged. I am in the middle of a work of personal transformation. This process is often painful, but always beneficial.

When you examine yourself and expose the Thorns still in your life, believe that you can bear good Fruit even though you live under the burning Heat of difficulty. In your surprise, pain, and disappointment, don't run away from your Redeemer! He cares and understands. And he offers mercy and grace in a form fit for the changes that need to take place in you.

T H O R N S   2 :
W H Y   D O   Y O U   G E T
E N T A N G L E D ?

Why do I sin? If you are a Christian, you can't avoid this question, nor can you settle for simple answers. Why does a parent get so upset when a child won't do a few household chores? Why does a man or woman succumb to the sexual overtures of a co-worker? Why do teenagers become depressed when their so-called friends snub them? Why do you do the things you do? It seems like a simple question, but it really isn't!

Your task is like a medical doctor's: your diagnosis of what is wrong will determine what you think the cure is. If a doctor diagnoses an infection, she will prescribe an antibiotic. If she diagnoses cancer, she'll prescribe radiation or chemotherapy. The cure only works if the diagnosis is correct. If the diagnosis is wrong, the cure may lead to painful, even deadly, consequences. When it comes to soul care, misdiagnosing a personal problem can also have deadly consequences. In the early stages things may go well, but over time the situation worsens.

In the last chapter, we looked at the many ways we are entangled by sin. In this chapter, we want to consider why we sin. Your answer to this question will determine what your cure will be. The Bible has a way of cutting through the superficial diagnoses of secular (and even many Christian) theories. We need Scripture's clarity and insight into why we do the things we do if we are to find the lasting cure.

We need answers that have the power and wisdom to help people like Joe and Mary. They have been married for twenty-two years. During that time, Mary has become increasingly overwhelmed and exhausted. As they told their story, it became obvious that Mary was married to an angry man. He did not exhibit any anger before they were married, but something changed almost immediately. On their honeymoon, Joe blew up at Mary for the first time. It was not pleasant, but Mary wrote it off as a momentary lapse due to the pressure of the wedding. A few weeks later, Joe did the same thing, becoming loud and nasty when he came home one night to a cold dinner. This was the beginning of twenty-two years of Joe "losing it" on a regular basis. The children had grown to anticipate these blow-ups. They had also grown fearful and bitter. Twenty-two years later, despite the intervention of many pastors and counselors, their family was in shambles and Joe and Mary were at the end of their ropes. By God's grace, they continued to seek help, but the marriage was now suffering from an angry husband and a fearful, bitter wife. The situation seemed grim.

To Joe's credit, he had sought help over the years. But sadly, the diagnoses he had received did not go deep enough. Not surprisingly, that made the suggested solutions insufficient for any lasting change. There were times when Joe could be patient, but it never lasted. Now he had pretty much given up and resigned himself to where he was. However, this didn't change the fact that his sin hurt others. Thorny responses to life are that way. The diagnoses and cures offered to Joe over the years had proven ineffective in bringing any real change. Let's consider some of the diagnoses and cures that are popular in our society.

Diagnosing the "Real" Problem

Other People

Over the years, Joe had reached his own conclusion about his problem: he had simply married the wrong person. Mary was cool; she avoided talking to him. He never felt like she was in the marriage 100 percent. She was also spontaneous and unorganized. Joe had concluded that if Mary would stop avoiding him and do a better job of keeping the house in order, it would eliminate his problem with anger. That is what Mary had tried to do for two decades. There were times when the demands of parenting kept her from getting the housework done. Joe would get agitated and eventually complain to Mary about her lack of organization. And it was true; Mary was not as organized as Joe. Even she began to think she was the problem. She lived with a gnawing sense of guilt and failure whenever Joe got angry. She redoubled her efforts to be conscientious about the housework, especially when Joe told her that he would be a nicer person if she would stay on top of things. He also told her that she needed to get better at resolving conflict. Joe didn't see that he wasn't someone you wanted to spend a lot of time talking to. He was someone who could win any argument by the sheer volume of his words.

Thorns 2: Why Do You Get Entangled?

Their pastor suggested that Mary get help from others to keep the house more organized. He thought that this would relieve pressure on both of them and improve the tone of the relationship. Housecleaning teams from the church came to their house weekly to help Mary straighten up, vacuum, and dust. They also helped Mary plan a menu for the week. This seemed to help for awhile. But Joe became even more demanding and hostile. He had the uncanny ability to find things around the house that were not cleaned and organized to his liking. On a few occasions, he called the pastor to complain that the people helping Mary were not doing an adequate job. He suggested that the church select a different group of people to help, and even supplied a list of wives he thought were competent housekeepers. Surprisingly, the church did just that! At first this seemed to help, but soon Joe was dissatisfied with this group of women as well. Mary once again became the focus of attention. "If you would be more organized and take care of things, we wouldn't need all of these other people in our house who don't know what they are doing anyway," he would say.

As that solution wore thin, their pastor suggested finding someone to help them communicate better. The first time they met with the counselor, Joe was amazingly articulate about Mary's failings. He dominated the entire session detailing Mary's problems with communication and conflict. Predictably, Mary received a lot of advice about how to communicate better. "A gentle answer turns away wrath," she was told. She began to open up and express her concerns and opinions to Joe as gently as possible. This only made Joe angrier! He started complaining about how argumentative Mary had become; she was not following his lead as her husband. These efforts failed within the first month.

Joe's problem is as old as Genesis 3. When Adam was called to account by the Lord, his first line of defense was, "It was the woman you gave me." Blame-shifting is the most natural and comfortable explanation for our sin and it has been in use for thousands of years. "My problem is you, therefore you need to change. If you change, then I will change." Clearly, this diagnosis does not go deep enough.

Family of Origin

Another common explanation for our sin is to blame it on our past: "I act this way because I grew up in a dysfunctional family." If that reasoning is true, we can all use it, since we all grew up in homes full of sinners who sinned against us to some degree. In Joe's case, he had been physically and sexually abused as a young boy. It had never been dealt with. His family was loud and confrontational, while Mary's family quietly avoided conflict. Joe was quick to point out the sin patterns in Mary's family that made her afraid to deal with things in a straightforward way. Joe also blamed his behavior on his childhood experiences. "My father was loud and angry. It's what I grew up with and it's hard for me to not do the same things."

With barely a pause, he would then put the onus back on Mary. "She is just like her mother. She is disorganized and she avoided her husband just like Mary does me." Joe had mastered the art of blaming others for his problems. These things did not just explain his anger, they were excuses for it. "At least I don't treat you like I was treated." "I'm not as bad as my father." "At least I am trying to get help." These statements were used to make him look better and point the finger back at others.

When Joe mentioned his family of origin, he would usually get emotional and sometimes even cry. Mary was encouraged to empathize with Joe's childhood suffering and to avoid pushing the sensitive buttons that provoked anger. Mary made many attempts to be more kind and patient, but when she was quiet, Joe would complain about her silence. When she was more communicative, he said she was stubborn. Blaming their respective upbringings for their problems was another simplistic diagnosis, and as a solution to Joe's anger, it was short-lived.

I've Had a Bad Day

This diagnosis simply puts a different spin on our propensity to blame our problems on others. In this case, my real problem is the difficulties of life. Joe often complained about a bad day at work, a lack of money, and so on. One night he complained about the traffic on his way home. "Someone cut me off at a turn and it just set me off!" When he saw Mary, he began yelling at her for things she had done three weeks before. When he finally admitted that he was being too harsh, he said it was because of the other driver. He apologized to Mary, but never really owned his sinful behavior.

Thorns 2: Why Do You Get Entangled?

My Body Made Me Do It!

An explanation that has become increasingly popular under the guise of medical science is the idea that physical weakness can cause you to sin. Joe often blamed his anger on a lack of sleep. If he had not been taking his medication faithfully, he would say that was the real cause of his anger. While a physical ailment can make us more prone to sinful responses, the Bible never allows us to blame our sin on our bodies. The scientific evidence for the "disease" model is conjectural at best. Even if science were to prove a certain physiological predisposition to anger or some other sin, it would not excuse the behavior. At most, it could help us understand why certain individuals are more prone to certain struggles.

There are many more examples of false, Heat-oriented diagnoses and solutions. The ones we've chosen are the ones most commonly employed to explain and excuse behavior. While external conditions can be very influential in our lives and should not be ignored, the Bible says that they are only the occasion for sin, not the cause. Difficulties in life do not cause sin. Our background, relationships, situation, and physical condition only provide the opportunity for our thoughts, words, and actions to reveal whatever is already in our hearts. Our hearts are always the ultimate cause of our responses, and where the true spiritual battle is fought.

A Word of Caution

You may have noticed a common thread in these explanations for our sinful responses: they all focus on externals. All of Joe's ineffective diagnoses pointed to the Heat as the cause of his sin. Not surprisingly, the solutions all pointed to somehow changing those external circumstances. If my real problem is other people, then I need to change them or avoid them. If my real problem is my family of origin, I need to steer clear of those family members and find someone to re-parent me. If my real problem is suffering, I need to find people who will supply endless comfort. If my real problem is unmet needs, the solution is to fill up what is lacking in me. If my real problem is my body, I need to get more sleep or find the right pill to even me out.

We do not minimize the significance of the things that influence us, or the suffering we all experience. This is why we talked so extensively about suffering in Chapters 7 and 8. The Bible is filled with examples of people in difficult circumstances, many of whom were sinned against brutally. Scripture constantly reminds us that we must never take suffering lightly because God does not. The Bible's central message is that God did not gloss over suffering, but took costly measures to end it. He sent us a Redeemer, his Son Jesus Christ, who suffered alongside us to give us hope, meaning, and endurance amid life's struggles. But Jesus is more than the Great Empathizer. He has promised to return and put an end to the injustices, hurts, and corruption of this world once and for all. As believers who live in the midst of these difficulties and are called to serve others in his name, we are never to minimize the brokenness of this world. C. S. Lewis said it this way:

> Christianity does not want us to reduce by one atom the hatred we feel for cruelty and treachery. We ought to hate them . . . But it does want us to hate them in the same way in which we hate things in ourselves.[1]

As we talk about the heart as the wellspring for all of our responses to life, we must never minimize suffering – ours or anyone else's. Nevertheless, we must make the important distinction between the occasion for sin and the ultimate cause of sin. This will determine what you think the solution to your problem will be. It will also determine who will receive glory . . . you or Christ! If your problem is ultimately outside you, Christ is not needed. The opportunity to experience the love, grace, and power of Christ is replaced by something else.

Occasions and Causes

As we distinguish between the occasion and cause of sin, it is important to acknowledge that some of the "solutions" we have discussed may be wise ways to help someone deal with difficulty – even though they are not ultimate solutions. For example, if someone's well-being is being threatened, it may be appropriate to separate her from the other person for a season. It is very appropriate to comfort someone who has been seriously abused, even though comfort alone will not be enough. You are not pandering to someone's self-centered needs. Jesus provided food on many occasions to people who were suffering. He spoke words of comfort and performed many miracles. This was not just a way to authenticate his deity. It was because he had compassion for the hurting.

Thorns 2: Why Do You Get Entangled?

But at the end of the day, Jesus knew that there was a deeper issue to be addressed. He never bypassed a person's heart (Luke 6:43-45). Taking someone's suffering seriously and ministering to them with Christ's compassion will never, by itself, be enough. It will fall short of helping someone change in a significant, lasting way because it fails to address the heart. These external solutions also bypass the centrality of the gospel. Christ is either unnecessary or just one part of the solution.

What Is Your Biggest Problem?

When we rightly identify the source of our problem, we are on our way to a solution that celebrates the grace of Christ. But we must first acknowledge that the problem is us! It is inside us, deep in the recesses of our hearts. How do you react to this news? Are you shocked? Disappointed? Offended? Angry? It's certainly not what we want to hear. When I am impatient with my children, the last thing I want to admit is that it is my fault. I want to blame my child and justify my sin! But if we don't face our own sins, we will never get to the real solution. We will minimize the redeeming love of Father, Son, and Spirit or bypass it completely. This is deadly. There is nothing more serious!

The Bible says that my real problem is not psychological (low self-esteem or unmet needs), social (bad relationships and influences), historical (my past), or physiological (my body). They are significant influences, but my real problem is spiritual (my straying heart and my need for Christ). I have replaced Christ with something else, and as a consequence, my heart is hopeless and powerless. Its responses reflect its bondage to whatever it is serving instead of Christ. Ultimately, my real problem is a worship disorder. The following passages stress the centrality of the heart to our sinful responses to life.

The Law and the Heart

The Ten Commandments may not be where you would expect to find an emphasis on the centrality of the heart, but it is there if you look carefully.

"I am the LORD your God, who brought you out of Egypt, out of the land of slavery.

"You shall have no other gods before me.

"You shall not make for yourself an idol in the form of anything in heaven above or on the earth beneath or in the waters below. You shall not bow down to them or worship them; for I, the LORD your God, am a jealous God, punishing the children for the sin of the fathers to the third and fourth generation of those who hate me, but showing love to a thousand generations of those who love me and keep my commandments.

"You shall not misuse the name of the LORD your God, for the LORD will not hold anyone guiltless who misuses his name.

"Observe the Sabbath day by keeping it holy, as the LORD your God has commanded you. Six days you shall labor and do all your work, but the seventh day is a Sabbath to the LORD your God. On it you shall not do any work, neither you, nor your son or daughter, nor your manservant or maidservant, nor your ox, your donkey or any of your animals, nor the alien within your gates, so that your manservant and maidservant may rest, as you do. Remember that you were slaves in Egypt and that the LORD your God brought you out of there with a mighty hand and an outstretched arm. Therefore the LORD your God has commanded you to observe the Sabbath day.

"Honor your father and your mother, as the LORD your God has commanded you, so that you may live long and that it may go well with you in the land the LORD your God is giving you.

"You shall not murder.

"You shall not commit adultery.

"You shall not steal.

"You shall not give false testimony against your neighbor.

"You shall not covet your neighbor's wife. You shall not set your desire on your neighbor's house or land, his manservant or maidservant, his ox or donkey, or anything that belongs to your neighbor." (Deut. 5:6-21)

Thorns 2: Why Do You Get Entangled?

The first three commands focus on what or whom you worship. They command us to make the one true God our God, and condemn making a god of anything else. The order of the commands is important, because the commands begin by focusing on our heart tendency toward idolatry. That is why, in Deuteronomy 6:4-5, the centrality of worship is emphasized. These two verses capture the essence of the first three commands:

> Hear, O Israel: The LORD our God, the LORD is one. Love the LORD your God with all your heart and with all your soul and with all your strength.

The reason we fail to keep commands 4-10 is because we have failed to keep the first three. If you break commands 1-3, you will break commands 4-10. Your Thorny, sinful responses to life grow out of a heart that has defected to worship something else.

Consider the Israelites' situation. They had been freed from bondage in Egypt and had wandered in the wilderness on their way to Canaan. Their journey to the Promised Land had been filled with trials, temptations, enemies, and suffering. Still, God's greatest concern was not what they had encountered (or would encounter in the future), but who they would worship! He knew that the greatest battle would be for their hearts. Even after they had seen the great miracles of Moses and experienced the love of their God, they would still be tempted to worship and treasure other things over him. God knew that if they did not remain loyal and faithful to him, their entrance into the Promised Land would give rise to temptations that would lead to sin.

Look at commands 4-10. Why did the Israelites so often fail to keep them? Why do you and I fail to keep them?

- Commandment 4: Remember the Sabbath. At the heart of the fourth commandment is the call to honor and obey God in your worship, work, and rest. But when commands 1-3 are broken, I worship and serve myself and use my time for my own self-interest. I make work my god and define myself through my career. I elevate personal peace and comfort above God.
- Commandment 5: Honor your father and your mother. At the heart of the fifth commandment is the call to honor and obey God by respecting those in authority. But when commands 1-3 are broken, my will and honor become primary.

- Commandment 6: Do not murder. At the heart of the sixth commandment is the call to honor and obey God by loving, serving, and forgiving others. But when commands 1-3 are broken, I demand to be loved and served by others. When I am wronged, I demand revenge.
- Commandment 7: Do not commit adultery. At the heart of the seventh commandment is a call to honor and obey God by remaining sexually pure and by keeping my promises to others. But when commands 1-3 are broken, my pleasures rule.
- Commandment 8: Do not steal. At the heart of the eighth commandment is the call to honor and obey God by freely and joyfully sharing my resources with others. But when commands 1-3 are broken, I want things for myself.
- Commandment 9: Do not bear false witness. At the heart of the ninth commandment is a call to honor and obey God by speaking truthfully, in ways that build others up. But when commands 1-3 are broken, my words are used to make me look good and you look bad.
- Commandment 10: Do not covet. At the heart of the tenth commandment is the call to honor and obey God by rejoicing in the blessings of others. But when commands 1-3 are broken, I want what you have, and I don't want you to have it!

The structure of the Ten Commandments teaches us that we fail to keep commands 4-10 because something has gone wrong inside us. We wrap our hearts around something other than the living God and we believe the lie that without it, life is meaningless.

As we look at Joe's life from this perspective, we have a better understanding of why he is angry. Something has replaced the worship of the true God in his heart. Joe says he wants his wife to "respect" him. This desire has become more important to him than God. He treasures and cherishes "respect" more than his Redeemer. When he does this, he has broken commands 1-3, and when he does not get the respect he lives for, he breaks the sixth commandment. Instead of being patient, kind, and loving, he verbally "murders" Mary. If she sins against him and disrespects him, he refuses to forgive her. Instead, he holds a grudge and makes her pay by harassing her and pointing out all her faults. Mary is not perfect, but she is not the cause for Joe's breaking the sixth commandment. He broke the sixth commandment because he had already broken commandments 1-3. He made a choice, whether consciously or not, to set his hopes on something other than God to bring meaning, purpose, and value to his life.

Certainly, the external circumstances of Joe's life have shaped these sinful responses. We do not gloss over the fact that Joe was sexually abused and otherwise sinned against. At the same time, we must point out that Joe did not become a sinner after the abuse. He was a sinner before it took place and he has gone on to respond to it in sinful ways. As we comfort him with God's compassion and remind him that God hates the sin committed against him, we must also help Joe see how these experiences – and his responses to them – have led him down a particular sinful path in his relationship with his wife.

The "respect" Joe demands from Mary is really a desire for control and Mary's complete subjection to his will. It has little to do with the biblical model of a wife's respect for a husband who sacrificially loves her. Instead, this "respect" (control and subjection) is something Joe cares more about than anything else. Thoughts about his life glorifying the Lord are on the far edges of his life. How has this happened?

Joe needs to see that he has never brought his early experiences to the Lord in a way that would allow the gospel's transforming power to heal the broken places of his life. Instead, he has decided to handle it himself. He has promised himself that he would never allow anyone to hurt him again. This defensive, self-protecting response has created a person bent on controlling his world, never to be rejected or taken advantage of again. Whenever Joe feels threatened by Mary in any way, he regains control by verbally pummeling her into a place of submission. Displaced from the center of Joe's heart, God has no room to work in situations where Joe needs to listen to Mary, admit his own sin, and seek forgiveness. His fears of rejection, along with his craving for respect and constant affirmation, have enslaved Joe. His godless solutions have trapped him in the place he has spent his life trying to escape. They have made the lives of his family a misery as well. Joe is not a free, peaceful, and humble person who loves God and others. These realities cannot be overlooked if we want to help Joe grow and change. Rather, they are at the heart of his hope, because they point his heart to Christ.

Good Things Morphing Into Ultimate Things

At this point, some people say, "What is wrong with Joe wanting his wife to respect him? Isn't that what a wife is supposed to do?"

Respect is a good thing. It's not a sin to desire it. But Joe's pursuit of it illustrates the deceitfulness of sin and the waywardness of the human heart. Romans 1:25 helps us understand what has gone wrong. We'll look at it in its broader context.

> [21]For although they knew God, they neither glorified him as God nor gave thanks to him, but their thinking became futile and their foolish hearts were darkened. [22]Although they claimed to be wise, they became fools [23]and exchanged the glory of the immortal God for images made to look like mortal man and birds and animals and reptiles. [24]Therefore God gave them over in the sinful desires of their hearts to sexual impurity for the degrading of their bodies with one another. [25]They exchanged the truth of God for a lie, and worshiped and served created things rather than the Creator – who is forever praised. Amen.

This last verse is essential for a proper understanding of the slippery dynamics of sin and the propensity of the human heart to worship something other than God. Human beings are always tempted to love and serve things in the creation rather than the Creator. So often, we think of false worship and idolatry only in terms of things that are obviously sinful. While this can be the case, Romans 1:25 indicates that idolatry is often the result of taking good things in creation and making them ultimate things. They usurp the supreme place that only the Creator should have in our hearts and lives.

When God created all things, he pronounced them "good." Created things are not sinful in themselves. They become idols when we exalt them to the place only God should occupy. Consider the following examples:

- A father wants his child to honor and obey him so that when he grows up, he will not be hostile to those in authority. This is a good desire and something God commands. But when this desire for respectful children becomes this father's ultimate goal, it becomes his functional god. It leads him to manipulate his son to get him to obey. The father may become very controlling, exploding in anger when the child steps out of line. He may become depressed by any failure in his son, or self-righteous, proud, and condescending toward parents whose children are less obedient. He relates to his son like Joe relates to Mary.

- A young man longs to find a spouse. He reasons that marriage is something God created, and is therefore a good desire. But he goes to extremes in his relationships with women. When they ignore him, he becomes depressed and susceptible to sexual temptation. When he does attract a woman's interest, he destroys the relationship by smothering her with too much attention.

- A woman is gifted and successful in her job. She recognizes work as a good thing God has made, a way to use her gifts and experience a sense of dignity in the service of others. In time, however, this woman finds herself increasingly anxious about whether she is doing everything she needs to do. She starts taking work home, assumes too many responsibilities, and soon has trouble sleeping.

These individuals have taken something good – like obedient children, marriage, and work – and built their lives around them. God the Creator has been replaced by something in creation. When these good things become functional gods, they become idols. The worship of these God-replacements leads to Thorny attitudes, thoughts, emotions, and actions. Ultimately, each of these individuals has taken God's good gifts and allowed them to become more important than the Giver. Blessings have usurped the Giver of those blessings. Creation has usurped the Creator. When this happens, sinful responses will inevitably emerge in a person's life.

Looking at Joe's life from this perspective, we see that he has turned something good into something that usurps God's rightful place in his life. While it might appear to be harmless for him to crave respect and affirmation, it is really a form of treason. When these things are reigning supreme in his life, he defects from his allegiance to his Redeemer and gives his loyalty and devotion to something else. When respect and affirmation are seen properly, they are blessings to be given and received with thanks. But when they become ultimate goals, they become very destructive. Joe sees respect from Mary as something more precious and vital than God. He has also concluded that God cannot be trusted to protect him from harm, so he must control his own universe.

For Joe to grow in grace and relinquish his attempts at god-like control over people and circumstances, he must see how he has exchanged the truth about God for a lie. The lie is that respect is more valuable than God! The lie is that God is not good, wise, or loving, and therefore cannot be trusted. Joe has concluded that only he can make his world safe.

Commandments 1-3 have been broken. Joe worships and treasures respect more than God and then breaks the other commands. He treasures his own ability to run his life over God's and becomes a tyrant in his home. Someone who truly wants to help Joe would be foolish to counsel Mary to support and encourage him without also calling Joe to repent for his angry, controlling behavior. With Joe excused and Mary accused, it would be like pouring gasoline on a roaring fire. It would only deepen the rift in their marriage and allow Joe to continue his ungodly ways.

Counseling Joe would certainly offer the hope and comfort of the gospel, but this would include showing him how his sinful heart has responded to his painful past. A godly view of change requires Joe to face how serious his controlling behavior has been. He needs to bring the Heat of his past sexual abuse before the Lord. He needs to recognize that he is not responsible for the sins committed against him, but he does need to own his sinful responses to the abuse. This will not be easy for Joe, but it is the gateway to another kind of life. Wise and humble brothers in Christ need to surround Joe with love, godly counsel, and prayer. They need to call him to repent when he craves affirmation and uses anger to manipulate his family.

Mary also needs the help of her Christian community to respond to Joe with grace and strength. She needs help to renounce revenge and practice forgiveness. She needs to know that her church's spiritual leaders will be her advocates as she challenges Joe's anger. To offer anything less is not love for Joe and Mary in the fullest biblical sense.

An Example from James

The book of James offers a candid yet loving discussion about the cause and cure for anger and conflict. In chapter 4, James does not mince words because he is driven by love. His words combine truth and love simultaneously. If any of us is going to change, we need the same combination to recognize when something good has become our functional god.

> [1]What causes fights and quarrels among you? Don't they come from your desires that battle within you? [2]You want something but don't get it. You kill and covet, but you cannot have what you want. You quarrel and fight. You do not have, because you do not ask God. [3]When you ask, you do not receive, because you ask with wrong motives, that you may spend what you get on your pleasures.
>
> [4]You adulterous people, don't you know that friendship with the world is hatred toward God? Anyone who chooses to be a friend of the world becomes an enemy of God.

When two people have conflict, it's easy to see the war on the outside. But James points out that this war is an outgrowth of a war inside each person's heart. Desires are not being met, so people lash out in an attempt to satisfy those desires. In verse 4, James goes even further. He says that people engaging in ungodly conflict have already begun to worship someone or something other than God. They are guilty of spiritual adultery, which is another way to describe idolatry. The person is giving himself to a false lover.

This simple yet profound explanation of why we do what we do can have a radical impact on a person's life. It is radical because understanding our heart's idolatry opens the door for us to appropriate and apply the gospel. We have finally gotten to the root of things; we are no longer floating on the surface. We know that God is committed to reclaiming our hearts through the work of Christ and the Holy Spirit. When we see our Thorns, they help us detect our idols, our specific God-replacements, and our ruling desires. We see where our hearts need transformation, and we are led to hunger and thirst for grace. This is exactly where James goes in verses 5-10.

> [5]Or do you think Scripture says without reason that the spirit he caused to live in us envies intensely? [6]But he gives us more grace. That is why Scripture says:
>> 'God opposes the proud but gives grace to the humble."
>
> [7]Submit yourselves, then, to God. Resist the devil, and he will flee from you. [8]Come near to God and he will come near to you. Wash your

hands, you sinners, and purify your hearts, you double-minded. [9]Grieve, mourn and wail. Change your laughter to mourning and your joy to gloom. [10]Humble yourselves before the Lord, and he will lift you up.

In verses 5 and 6, James says that God is a jealous lover who will not let you share your affection with anyone but him. The word jealous has negative connotations when used in reference to human beings, but it is only positive when it refers to God. When we talk about God's love, we could appropriately replace the word jealous with the word zealous. God is zealous to recapture our affections, so the Holy Spirit works to reclaim our hearts. Isn't this amazing? Most spurned lovers would not pursue the unfaithful spouse, but God pursues you. If you are his bride, he will not let you wander forever. He may allow difficult things in your life to regain your attention, but he is willing to do it to be foremost in your life again.

In verses 5 and 6, God moves toward you and in verses 7-10, he invites you to move toward him. God gives you grace at the very moment you are straying, and promises to give you even more when you repent and humble yourself before him. He loves to shower his mercy upon the humble.

An essential element of growing in grace is a willingness to look at what fuels the ungodly responses in your life. "Purify your hearts," says James. Look at what you've allowed to become more attractive to you than the Lord. "Wash your hands," he continues. Exchange your sinful responses for godly ones. It is all by grace, but that does not mean we are passive! Christian growth is warfare. It is worth doing the hard work of discovering what leads us away from this glorious God.

The questions that follow can help you do this more effectively. Repentance is not true repentance unless it is specific and intelligent. We don't sin in the abstract; we sin in concrete, particular ways. Since that is true, we need to take an honest look at our lives – both heart and behavior. Spiritual awareness is a blessing. Through it, we can experience change. Use these questions to turn away from idols and turn to the mercy and power of Christ. As you do, don't forget that you are married to Christ. His assets are your assets. Your sin has been dealt with at the Cross and you don't have to be afraid to take a good look at yourself!

Thorns 2: Why Do You Get Entangled?

X-Ray Questions[2]

1. What do you love? Is there something you love more than God or your neighbor?
2. What do you want? What do you desire? What do you crave, long for, wish? Whose desires do you obey?
3. What do you seek? What are your personal expectations and goals? What are your intentions? What are you working for?
4. Where do you bank your hopes? What hope are you working toward or building your life around?
5. What do you fear? Fear is the flip side of desire. For example, if I desire your acceptance, then I fear your rejection.
6. What do you feel like doing? This is a synonym for desire. Sometimes we feel like eating a gallon of ice cream, or staying in bed, or refusing to talk, etc.
7. What do you think you need? In most cases a person's felt needs picture his or her idol cravings. Often what we have called necessities are actually deceptive masters that rule our hearts. They control us because they seem plausible. They don't seem so bad on the surface and it isn't sin to want them. However, I must not be ruled by the "need" to feel good about myself, to feel loved and accepted, to feel some sense of accomplishment, to have financial security, to experience good health, to live a life that is organized, pain-free, and happy.
8. What are your plans, agendas, strategies, and intentions designed to accomplish? What are you really going after in the situations and relationships of life? What are you really working to get?
9. What makes you tick? What sun does your planet revolve around? Where do you find your garden of delight? What lights up your world? What food sustains your life? What really matters to you? What are you living for?
10. Where do you find refuge, safety, comfort, and escape? When you are fearful, discouraged, and upset, where do you run? Do you run to God for comfort and safety or to something else? (To food, to others, to work, to solitude?)
11. What do you trust? Do you functionally rest in the Lord? Do you find your sense of well-being in his presence and promises? Or do you rest in something or someone else?
12. Whose performance matters to you? This question digs out self-reliance or self-righteousness. It digs out living through another. Do

you get depressed when you are wrong or when you fail? Have you pinned your hopes on another person? Are you too dependent on the performance of your husband, wife, children, or friends?

13. Whom must you please? Whose opinion counts? From whom do you desire approval or fear rejection? Whose value system do you measure yourself against? In whose eyes are you living?

14. Who are your role models? Who are the people you respect? Who do you want to be like? Who is your "idol?" (In our culture, this word is used for role model.)

15. What do you desperately hope will last in your life? What do you feel must always be there? What can't you live without?

16. How do you define success or failure in any particular situation? Are your standards God's standards? Do you define success as the ability to reach your goals? The respect and approval of others? Is it defined by a certain position or the ability to maintain a certain lifestyle? By affluence? By appearance? By acceptance? By location? By accomplishment?

17. What makes you feel rich, secure, and prosperous? The possession, experience, and enjoyment of what would make you happy? The Bible uses the metaphor of treasure here.

18. What would bring you the greatest pleasure? The greatest misery?

19. Whose political power would make everything better for you? Don't just think in a national sense. Think about the workplace and the church. Whose agenda would you like to see succeed and why?

20. Whose victory and success would make your life happy? How do you define victory and success?

21. What do you see as your rights? What do you feel entitled to? What do you feel is your right to expect, seek, require, or demand?

22. In what situations do you feel pressured or tense? When do you feel confident and relaxed? When you are pressured, where do you turn? What do you think about? What do you fear? What do you seek to escape from? What do you escape to?

23. What do you really want out of life? What payoff are you seeking from the things you do? What is the return you are working for?

24. What do you pray for? The fact that we pray does not necessarily mean we are where we should be spiritually. On the contrary, prayer can be a key revealer of the idols of our hearts. Prayer can reveal patterns of self-centeredness, self-righteousness, materialism, fear of man, etc.

25. What do you think about most often? In the morning, to what does your mind drift instinctively? When you are doing a menial task or driving alone in the car, what captures your mind? What is your mindset?

26. What do you talk about? What occupies your conversations with others? What subjects do you tend to discuss over and over with your friends? The Bible says that it is out of the heart that our mouths speak.

27. How do you spend your time? What are your daily priorities? What things do you invest time in every day?

28. What are your fantasies? What are your dreams at night? What do you daydream about?

29. What is your belief system? What beliefs do you hold about life, God, yourself, others? What is your worldview? What is the personal "mythology" that structures the way you interpret things? What are your specific beliefs about your present situation? What do you value?

30. What are your idols or false gods? In what do you place your trust or set your hopes? What do you consistently turn to or regularly seek? Where do you take refuge? Who is the savior, judge, controller of your world? Whom do you serve? What voice controls you?

31. In what ways do you live for yourself?

32. In what ways do you live as a slave to the Devil? Where are you susceptible to his lies? Where do you give in to his deceit?

33. When do you say, "If only. . ."? Our "if onlys" actually define our vision of paradise. They picture our biggest fears and greatest disappointments. They can reveal where we tend to envy others. They picture where we wish we could rewrite our life story. They picture where we are dissatisfied and what we crave.

34. What instinctively feels right to you? What are your opinions – those things that you feel are true?

These questions can help you to think more clearly and deeply about why you do the things you do. They can give you a better idea of which things typically morph from good to god in your life. These discoveries are a blessing because they help you to see how truly lavish the grace of God is.

The model of change we are considering in this book calls each of us to honest self-examination. In Joe's and Mary's case, they need clarity on the

Heat in their lives and their sinful, Thorn bush responses before they can experience the transforming power of the Cross. If Joe does not do this, his bondage to anger will continue, likely destroying his marriage. His life will be an example of the apparent powerlessness of the gospel. If Mary does not do this, she will move down a path of fear and intimidation or quiet, bitter hopelessness.

But there is another way: the way of Spirit-wrought wisdom and power that brings liberating change when we are honest before God about our sin. The fact that we can turn good things into idols must be faced. Most of the time, it requires help to see it and repent. It is frightening to let go of something we are convinced is our life – even when the alternative is Jesus! Our hearts are so often captivated by paltry God-replacements that matter to us more than the true God. When we start to see this, it is the beginning of change and the pathway to freedom.

The good news of the gospel shines brightest against the backdrop of our sin, so don't be afraid to look at these things. Take time to pray as you work through these questions. Don't lose sight of your union with Christ and God's promise to patiently love you and change you! If you engage in this kind of godly examination, you will be ready to experience the good news of the Cross that we will focus on in the next two chapters.

CROSS 1: NEW IDENTITY AND NEW POTENTIAL

We all hate problems. We all want solutions. I am the kind of person who hates to read the instruction manuals that come with items requiring assembly. Whenever I see "No assembly required" on an item, I get a rush of calm and joy! But my failure to read the instructions is often disastrous. I can be halfway through a complicated process of putting something together, only to find that the pieces aren't fitting properly. Repeated efforts to force a piece into place end with anger and frustration. Only then do I search for the instructions and begin to read them step by step. Sometimes I wind up taking the whole thing apart and starting from the very beginning. I hate that! What could have been thirty minutes of work becomes two hours or more because I chose not to slow down and follow the instructions word for word.

If you are like me, you tend to do the same thing when it comes to personal and interpersonal problems. I don't want to take the time to patiently walk through the issue with wise, biblical counsel. I find myself forcing an issue, thinking I am saving time and work, only to be reminded later that I have made some serious blunders. When you are putting together an inanimate object like a bicycle, it's no big deal. There is little harm done. But when you take the same approach to human beings, the results can be devastating.

Throughout this book, we have slowed down to think deeply about a serious issue of life: change. At times, we as authors were tempted to skip the groundwork and begin the book here! But if we had done that, we would have set you up for failure and misunderstanding. The grace of Christ and the dynamics of biblical change need to be understood within the framework of our circumstances and our sinful responses. We've needed to look at specific kinds of Heat, potential sinful responses, and questions about motivation. Without those things, this book would ring hollow. Jesus would still have been the solution, but you wouldn't have had a clue about how grand a solution he is, because we had skipped over the serious nature of our problems. It has been said that if you don't take time to face the bad news, the good news looks less good. But when you take a long, honest look at your real problem, the grace of Christ really shines!

In Chapters 9 and 10, we saw that our Thorny responses to life are the fruit of issues rooted in the heart. Even though life is hard, it is not the hardships that cause us to respond as we do. Our responses are shaped by the thoughts and motives of our hearts (Heb. 4:12). When our love for something in creation replaces our love for our Creator and Redeemer, we will have Thorny (sinful) responses to both blessing and hardship.

In this chapter, we begin to consider the resources we have in Christ to deal with our heart struggles. What does Christ give us as we battle subtle yet powerful idols? Why is the Cross the only place of hope if our greatest problems are within us? How will our lives change as we step out with Cross-centered hope? Second Corinthians 5:15 says that Jesus came so that "those who live should no longer live for themselves, but for him who died for them ...." Our focus in the next two chapters is how this promise of new life in Christ delivers us from life-controlling idolatry.

The Holy Spirit and a New Heart

Every person lives with a sense of potential – or lack of it. Every time my wife and I had a new baby, it was exciting to see him take his first steps. At a certain age, every one of our children learned to use a sofa or a chair to pull himself up to a standing position. After a few weeks, the children would ponder the possibility of letting go, to move around without the need for props! You could see it in their eyes. It was as if they were asking themselves, Do I have the potential to let go and roam free? When they did let go, their faces showed awe and fear at the same time. They would shake their arms up and down as they took a step or two before falling down. Then they would pick themselves up again and start over. What is going on in children as they learn to walk? In their own simple way, they are sizing up their potential. Based on their confidence in that potential, they let go of the chair and begin to move their feet. Their confidence would override their fears and the challenge of walking.

Cross 1: New Identity and New Potential

Adults are always measuring their potential too. When your boss, coach, or teacher gives you a new assignment, inwardly you begin assessing your ability to complete the task. As you drive to the home improvement store, you think about whether you can handle the repair job you have decided to begin. As you enter your last months of pregnancy, you start wondering about what kind of mother you will be. As you prepare to ask your girlfriend to be your wife, you ask yourself if you have what it takes to be a good husband. We do this all the time as we face life's challenges, both big and small. Do we have what it takes? Our answer shapes the decisions we go on to make. If we think we don't have what we need to succeed, we will probably decide not to do the thing that is before us.

As you face your life today, with all of its blessings and difficulties, you are assessing whether or not you have the potential to succeed. What things lead you to say, "I am doomed to failure; there is no way I can pull this off"? What leads you to say, "I think I am ready to do what I have been assigned to do"? What do you use to measure your potential? Do you say, "Well, I came from a good family with good models"? "I've gotten a solid education." "I have the talents necessary for this task." "I have learned from past experience." "My past successes indicate that I will be successful again."

For you, as a Christian, each of these things has value because you know that your Lord has been sovereign over every experience and relationship in your life. Through each of them, he has been preparing you for what he has called you to do. Yet, at the same time, this standard of self-evaluation misses the core of your potential as a Christian. For example, it misses how a Christian can feel unprepared and ready at the same time. It misses how you can recognize past failures and present weaknesses and still step forward to do things you have never done. It misses how you can do things in a brand new way even if you have failed in the past. It misses why some of us can admit that we have neither good family models nor a successful track record, yet still have the potential to do genuine good in our circumstances and relationships. It misses why Christians can have hope and courage to face the things they failed at yesterday. Family, education, talents, experience, and success all have value, but they miss the core of our potential as children of God. In light of that, let's consider the new potential we have because of who we are in Christ.

Your Potential: The Indwelling Christ

In Galatians, Paul is trying to explain the gospel to people who had a corrupted understanding of it at best. Early on, he says something so wonderful that it is almost impossible to take in: "I have been crucified with Christ and I no longer live, but Christ lives in me. The life I live in the body, I live by faith in the Son of God, who loved me and gave himself for me" (Gal. 2:20). Let these words sink in, and try to grasp what Paul is saying. The Cross of Christ determines our potential in ways far greater and deeper than the things we usually rely on.

In this verse, Paul is not focusing on the fact that the Cross enables me to be accepted by God and adopted into his family (though this is very important, as we will see in the next chapter). Here Paul wants us to see the new life we have in Christ through the gift of the Spirit. It's important to recognize this because many believers tend to think of the Cross only in terms of a doorway into relationship with God. Paul is saying that the Cross is that doorway, but it is so much more! Notice also that Paul's focus is not on eternity. Yes, the Cross guarantees us an eternity free of sin and suffering with our Lord. But, again, many believers tend to think of the Cross as an escape route from eternal punishment to eternal paradise. Again, Paul would agree that the Cross certainly is that, but it is so much more!

What is Paul's focus? He wants us to know that the Cross defines our identity and potential right here and now because we are alive in Christ. We have the very Spirit of Christ living in us. A passage that is important to keep together with Galatians 2:20 is Romans 8:9-10. In these verses, Paul says:

> You, however, are controlled not by the sinful nature but by the Spirit, if the Spirit of God lives in you. And if anyone does not have the Spirit of Christ, he does not belong to Christ. But if Christ is in you, your body is dead because of sin, yet your spirit is alive because of righteousness.

According to Paul, Christ indwells us through the person of the Holy Spirit. He gives us a new heart and new power to live out of an entirely new potential. Let's consider the three main elements of Paul's statement.

Cross 1: New Identity and New Potential

Three Redemptive Truths

The Redemptive Fact: "I have been crucified with Christ and I no longer live."

Paul is saying something more than that Christ was crucified for him or that the Cross of Christ benefits him. He is saying that when Christ was crucified, he (Paul) was crucified as well. When Jesus died physically, Paul (and all believers) died spiritually. Paul sees himself so united to the death of Christ that he can say, "I no longer live." What does this mean?

From birth, each of us was under the control and dominion of sin. The death of Christ was not a defeat, but a triumph (see Col. 2:13-15). In his physical death, Christ broke the spiritual power and authority sin had over us. Look again at the words, "I have been crucified." The verb tense points to a definitive action in the past, with a continuing and permanent result. What Christ did then on the Cross permanently alters who you are now and who you will continue to be. But Paul goes even further. He says, "I no longer live." Paul is saying that the changes inside him are so basic to who he is as a human being that it is as if he no longer lives! Yes, he is still Paul, but because of his death in Christ, he is a Paul who is utterly different at his core.

When you grasp the fundamental nature of this change within you as a believer, you will begin to grasp your true potential. You are not the same as you once were. You have been forever changed. You no longer live under the weight of the law or the domination of sin. Christ's death fulfilled the law's requirements and broke the power of sin. You do not have to give in to sin. You can live in new ways amid the same old situations, because when Christ died physically, you died spiritually. This constitutional change is permanent! Do you view yourself with this kind of potential for a new life in Christ?

The Present Reality: "But Christ lives in me."

It is not enough for Paul to say that the death of Christ made him new. He says that when he died, the old Paul was not replaced with a new and improved version of Paul, but with Christ himself! He's not simply saying that the new Paul is better at controlling the sin in his heart. He is saying that where sin once controlled, Christ now rules! Our hearts, once under the domination of sin, are now the dwelling place of Christ, the ultimate source of righteousness, wisdom, grace, power, and love.

Here is the gospel of our potential. It was necessary for us to die with Christ so that he could live forever in our hearts. The old sinful me has died. But it has not been replaced with a better me. The replacement is Christ! My heart is new, because Christ lives there. My heart is alive, because Christ lives there to give it life. My heart can respond to life in new ways because it is no longer dominated by sin, but liberated by the gracious rule of Christ. That is why I have the potential for amazing change and growth in my heart and life.

The Results for Daily Living: "The life I live in the body, I live by faith in the Son of God, who loved me and gave himself for me."

Here Paul drives home the present benefits of Christ living in our hearts. We live by a new principle – not the old principle of sin and death, but the new principle of the power and grace of Christ who now resides in us. This is what Paul means when he says, "I live by faith in the Son of God." We no longer live based on our assessment of what we possess in strength, character, and wisdom (from family, education, and experience). We base our lives on the fact that because Jesus lives in us, we can do what is right in desire, thought, word, and action, no matter what specific blessings or sufferings we face. Our potential is Christ! When we really believe this and live it out, we start to realize our true potential as children of God. We start to see new and surprising Fruit mature in our lives.

The Christian mom, who speaks with patience when she once would have spoken in anger, is experiencing the reality of Christ living in her. The husband, who comes home tired from work but still serves his wife, is living in the power of the indwelling Christ. The friend, who chooses to overlook minor offenses and stay in a friendship she would have once forsaken, is choosing to live on the basis of "Christ within me" faith. What Paul lays out here is intensely practical. It has the potential to radically alter the way we live and respond every day.

Cross 1: New Identity and New Potential

Three Redemptive Implications

What will your life look like if you measure your potential based on your union with Christ? What will it look like to face life really believing that he lives within you, empowering you to do what is right? Let's briefly consider three areas.

You will live with personal integrity.

You will be willing to examine yourself in the mirror of God's Word, seeking practical, accurate self-knowledge. Do you know yourself biblically?

You will embrace the fact that change is a community project. You will live with a sense of need and thankfulness for your brothers and sisters in Christ, living an open, humble, approachable life. Are there places where you are still hiding, bypassing the spiritual resources of the people of God?

You will be honest in your struggles. Your faith in Christ will allow you to express godly emotions, including anguish, pain, fear, anxiety, jealousy, anger, happiness, gratitude, and anticipation. Are there places where you are putting on a front, afraid to admit and appropriately express what you are feeling?

You will create a climate of grace in your relationships.

You will forgive as you have been forgiven. You will be merciful about the sins of others, based on the mercy you yourself have received from Christ (see Mark 11:25, Matt. 6:1-15). Are you carrying around the wrongs of another against you?

You will be ready to ask for forgiveness, freed by Christ from defensiveness, rationalizing, blame-shifting, and other types of self-justification. Are you resisting admitting your sin against someone else?

You will seek to give and serve in tangible ways (Rom. 12:14-21). Where, right now, is God inviting you to serve others?

You will persevere even when you are tempted to quit. Endurance, forbearance, long-suffering, patience, and perseverance are on every biblical list of the character traits of a new heart. They all involve doing what is right even when the Heat remains. Are there any places in your life where you are tempted to give up, run away, or quit?

You will act with courageous grace and constructive truth.

You will speak with honesty in the pursuit of unity, peace, and blessing (Lev. 19:17, Eph. 4:29). Where are you tempted to cower in silence or trim the truth to avoid discomfort?

You will gladly forgive anyone who seeks it (Luke 17:1–10, Eph. 4:30–5:2). Is there a place where bitterness and vengeance seem more attractive than grace and forgiveness?

Your responses will be more shaped by the Savior's will than by your own selfish desires, the expectations of others, or the pressures of the situation. Where do you need to say "no" to your sinful nature and say a joyful "yes" to the call of your Savior?

"Christ in me," Cross-centered living gives a purpose and direction to all our actions and words. No longer motivated by our own agenda, by God's grace, we now want our lives to reflect what God is doing in us. We want our lives to be part of what he is doing in others' lives, here and around the world. This results in surprising new Fruit in our actions, choices, and words. Where we once made war, we now make peace. Where once we were ruled by fear of others and said "yes" far too often, we are now motivated by God's practical will and understand when we must say "no." Where once we used our God-given gifts for our own benefit and glory, we now use them for God's glory and the benefit of others. Where we once trimmed and twisted the truth to get what we wanted, we now lovingly speak the truth, even when it may be costly. Where once we held onto bitterness and anger, we now give the offense to the Lord and extend forgiveness to others.

As we examine such new Fruit in our lives, what should we say? "Wow, what good Christians we are"? No, we humbly affirm that these things are present in our lives because "it is no longer [we] who live, but Christ lives in [us]." The harvest of good consequences is a hymn to the presence, grace, love, wisdom, and power of our Redeemer.

Cross 1: New Identity and New Potential

What If You Fail?

Never a day goes by when we do not fail to do what Christ has enabled us to do. Despite all of the gifts flowing from our union with Christ, sin still remains in us. That's the reason you need to know that Jesus has broken the power of sin – because its presence still remains! We should not be shocked that the war still rages inside us. We have been changed, we have been empowered, but we have not yet been perfected.

What do you do when you sin and fail? Do you excuse and rationalize? Do you wallow in self-defeating guilt and regret? The Cross calls you away from both responses. It gives you the freedom to admit your sin and repent. It is impossible for your sin to shock the One who died because of it. The Cross also gives you the freedom to seek and receive forgiveness each time you fall. We do not have to carry the sins Christ took on himself. He paid the price we could not pay so that we would never have to pay it again.

When you fail, keep Jesus and his work in view. Run to your Lord, not away from him. Receive his forgiveness, get back up, and follow him once more, knowing that each time you fail, you can experience your identity as one for whom Christ died. Each failure reminds us of why he had to die; each confession reminds us of the forgiveness that only the Cross could provide.

In the next chapter, we will consider our ongoing need to exercise faith and repentance as a lifestyle. We will also consider more of the amazing blessings that are ours through Christ. We not only have a new heart through the Holy Spirit, we have a new foundation that gives us confidence and hope as we live the Christian life on a daily basis.

CROSS 2:
THE CROSS AND
DAILY LIVING

Some babies enter the world quickly, screaming from the moment they arrive. Others come slowly and don't cry much at all. The manner in which they are born varies, but the fact that they are born is the same. The same is true of every person who becomes a Christian.

In the previous chapter, we celebrated the fact that when someone comes to Christ, he experiences something profound on the inside. God, in his powerful grace, gives the Holy Spirit to spiritually dead people, making them spiritually alive. For some, this experience is marked by intense, immediate change and strong emotions. For others, the moment seems quite ordinary, and change unfolds over time. Regardless of the outward manifestation, the Bible says that the inward reality of new spiritual life is the same for every believer. Peter says that we "participate in the divine nature" (2 Peter 1:4). John, quoting Jesus, says that we are "born again" (John 3:3). Paul says that we become a "new creation" (2 Cor. 5:17). The Old Testament describes this spiritual reality in terms of a new heart (Ezek. 36:26, Jer. 31:31-34). In Romans 2:29 and Colossians 2:11, Paul uses the Old Testament rite of circumcision to explain the New Testament reality of being made alive from within. It is a circumcision not done by hands but by the Spirit.

If a Christian is going to make progress in the Christian life, she must be convinced of this powerful new reality. We are personally united to Christ through the Holy Spirit. We have new resources and potential because God has moved in. The basic spiritual DNA of every believer has been radically altered, and we are part of a new story of redemption that includes the entire creation!

The Work of the Spirit: Magnify Christ

One of the new experiences that come with this indwelling work of the Spirit is the ability to see something we couldn't see before conversion. The believer can now understand spiritual truth. In 1 Corinthians 2:6-16, Paul says that we are given wisdom. Notice, specifically, the focus of this wisdom.

> [6]We do, however, speak a message of wisdom among the mature, but not the wisdom of this age or of the rulers of this age, who are coming to nothing. [7]No, we speak of God's secret wisdom, a wisdom that has been hidden and that God destined for our glory before time began. [8]None of the rulers of this age understood it, for if they had, they would not have crucified the Lord of glory. [9]However, as it is written:

> "No eye has seen, no ear has heard, no mind has conceived what God has prepared for those who love him" [10]but God has revealed it to us by his Spirit.

> [11]The Spirit searches all things, even the deep things of God. For who among men knows the thoughts of a man except the man's spirit within him? In the same way no one knows the thoughts of God except the Spirit of God. [12]We have not received the spirit of the world but the Spirit who is from God, that we may understand what God has freely given us. [13]This is what we speak, not in words taught us by human wisdom but in words taught by the Spirit, expressing spiritual truths in spiritual words. [14]The man without the Spirit does not accept the things that come from the Spirit of God, for they are foolishness to him, and he cannot understand them, because they are spiritually discerned. [15]The spiritual man makes judgments about all things, but he himself is not subject to any man's judgment: [16]"For who has known the mind of the Lord that he may instruct him?" But we have the mind of Christ.

The Spirit aids us so "that we may understand what God has freely given us" (v. 12). We have been given Christ, along with everything that goes with him. In other words, biblical wisdom is a person, Jesus himself! In John 16, Jesus elaborates on what the Spirit helps us to know and experience.

> [5]"Now I am going to him who sent me, yet none of you asks me, 'Where are you going?' [6]Because I have said these things, you are filled

with grief. [7]But I tell you the truth: It is for your good that I am going away. Unless I go away, the Counselor will not come to you; but if I go, I will send him to you. [8]When he comes, he will convict the world of guilt in regard to sin and righteousness and judgment: [9]in regard to sin, because men do not believe in me; [10]in regard to righteousness, because I am going to the Father, where you can see me no longer; [11]and in regard to judgment, because the prince of this world now stands condemned.

[12]"I have much more to say to you, more than you can now bear. [13]But when he, the Spirit of truth, comes, he will guide you into all truth. He will not speak on his own; he will speak only what he hears, and he will tell you what is yet to come. [14]He will bring glory to me by taking from what is mine and making it known to you. [15]All that belongs to the Father is mine. That is why I said the Spirit will take from what is mine and make it known to you."

The Holy Spirit enables us to see Jesus and all that we have and are in him.

Daily Christian Living

Why is it so important to understand this work of the Holy Spirit? Because we still struggle against sin. In Chapter 3, we considered the great hope of our inevitable glorification, when we will be completely changed into the likeness of Christ. In Chapter 11, we looked at God's work of regeneration – the way Christ's death for our sins makes us new creatures with new hearts. The process has already begun, and, in terms of our standing with God, it is already complete.

But if you are like me, you know that the reality of this great new life bumps up against the present reality where sin is all around us and the remnants of sin remain in us as well. You may be asking, "If all of these things about the Spirit are true, why do I and so many other Christians struggle so much with sin? If I am new on the inside, why does it feel like so little has changed?"

This is exactly why it is so important to understand the Spirit's ongoing work. He connects our hearts and minds to Jesus and all he has done for us. The Holy Spirit comes to help us to live Cross-centered lives. The reason we need to see Christ daily can be seen in many moments of everyday life. The following story is an example of my own.

The Real World, Take One

I like comfort. No, I love comfort! After a hard day's work, I head for home, looking forward to a nice, quiet time to rest and relax. The Heat of my life prompts me to want a time of respite from life's cares. Now, there is nothing wrong with comfort. God wove the blessing of rest and leisure into the fabric of his creation. God himself rested on the seventh day.

But as I am marinating in the prospect of comfort, something happens. My heart begins to morph along the lines of Romans 1:25. Something good becomes an object of worship, replacing the only true God in my heart. I don't just think about enjoying a good thing, I begin to feel entitled to it. After all, haven't I worked hard all day? I deserve a break! I treasure it and meditate on it. By the time I pull into my driveway, I have already been seduced by comfort, and I willingly place myself in its arms. Comfort is no longer a good thing to be properly enjoyed, but something I want more than God.

As I walk into our house, my idol of comfort is immediately threatened! Two of my children come running to me. They don't greet me with hugs, but with complaints that the other is not sharing the computer. In the middle of their complaining, my other two children request help with their homework. My wife completes the scene by saying that she is tired from working all day too. It's up to me to sort things out.

When comfort is reigning supreme in my heart, a scene like this turns me into a drill sergeant. I turn to the first two children and say, "You let your sister have it for thirty minutes, and then you can use it for thirty minutes!" I am harsh and forceful. If they protest, I get louder. I may even threaten to turn the computer off. As soon as these two "comfort robbers" are squashed, I turn to the other two children and bark out commands about their homework. If they protest, I can use the same strategies that seemed to work so well with the first two kids. Now that all four children are acting decently and in order, I have time for a few choice words for my wife. "How come you didn't handle this before I walked in the door? I don't deserve to come home and be barraged with this nonsense after working hard all day!" At this, my wife may have some provocative words of her own to share!

What has happened? My heart has been entangled in sin, and it is showing in my behavior. My object of worship has been comfort instead of God, and this vertical orientation quickly expresses itself in my horizontal relationships with my family. I use control to get what I want, sinning against my family and dishonoring God. I break commandments 4-10 because I have already broken commandments 1-3 on the way home. I have allowed something other than God to reign in my life. My worship needs to be radically reoriented so that I can love my family in ways that bless them and honor God. This can only happen if I live a Cross-centered life.

The Cross-centered Life

What do I mean by a Cross-centered life? Notice how Paul uses the language of the Cross throughout his letters. In 1 Corinthians 1:23 he says, "But we preach Christ crucified: a stumbling block to Jews and foolishness to Gentiles." In 1 Corinthians 2:1–2 he says, "When I came to you, brothers, I did not come with eloquence or superior wisdom as I proclaimed to you the testimony about God. For I resolved to know nothing while I was with you except Jesus Christ and him crucified." In Colossians 1:28-29 he says, "We proclaim him [Christ], admonishing and teaching everyone with all wisdom, so that we may present everyone perfect in Christ. To this end I labor, struggling with all his energy, which so powerfully works in me."

When Paul says that he focuses on the crucifixion, this is his shorthand summary for the entire work of Christ. He isn't saying that he only teaches people about Jesus' death. If you look at Paul's teaching along with the other biblical writers, it includes everything from Jesus' heavenly glory, the incarnation, his life of suffering and obedience, his death on the cross, his resurrection, his ascension, his present intercession on our behalf, and his future return! When Paul and the other biblical writers focus on the cross, they do it to emphasize that, without Jesus' sacrificial death for sin, none of the other benefits that are ours in Christ would be possible! We needed a substitute. So when we talk about living a Cross-centered life, we include everything about Jesus, his work on our behalf, and all the benefits we enjoy because of him: our election, calling, regeneration, justification, adoption, sanctification, and ultimate glorification.

Let's start by thinking about it this way. All of us live our lives based on some identity, some functional sense of who we are, what we are like, and what we are worth. Most of us are not particularly aware of our view of ourselves, but it nevertheless determines how we will respond to everything we face during the day – especially to the Heat in our lives.

Chapter 11 showed us that the Christian is meant to define himself or herself as a new creation in Christ. The heart of stone has been replaced with a heart of flesh. This chapter shows how a Cross-centered perspective enables you to grow in grace as you struggle against and repent of sin. The Cross must be central, because it defines who you are, who you are becoming, and who you will be!

Your Identity: "I am?"

Many Christians have very little idea of what it means to live a Cross-centered life. How about you? How much of the way you view yourself is shaped by what Jesus did for you on the Cross? When you awaken each morning, what functional identity shapes the way you face the day? Is your identity grounded in what you do or certain skills you possess? "I am a businesswoman." "I am a pastor." "I am a parent." Notice how these things begin to function as identities rather than callings. Or do you define yourself in light of a past event? "I am a survivor of sexual abuse." "I am an alcoholic." "I am a person who grew up in a dysfunctional family." Maybe you define yourself in light of a current struggle. "I am depressed." "I am bi-polar." "I am an angry person."

While a Christian should never minimize personal gifts, past problems, or current struggles, these do not displace his or her more fundamental identity of being in Christ. "I am a new creation in Christ who happens to be a businesswoman, pastor, or parent." Jesus defines me, not my particular calling or vocation. "I am a Christian who was hurt by someone in my past, who struggles with depression, who struggles with anger." My fundamental identity in the Cross of Christ supersedes whatever struggle I am going through now.

Do you know what it means to live a Cross-centered life on a daily basis? Some Christians think that the Cross is what you need to become a Christian and get to heaven. They think, I need my sins forgiven so that I escape God's judgment when I die. But once that is taken care of, what matters is that I follow Christ's example. I need to roll up my sleeves and get to work! The tricky thing about this perspective is that it is partially correct. Once you become a Christian, you do participate in your ongoing growth. You do actively pursue the obedience that comes from faith (Rom. 1:5, 16:26; Gal. 5:6). You do engage in spiritual warfare! However, you are never to minimize your continuing need for the mercy and power of Christ in the process of becoming like him.

The Normal Christian Life?

Consider Andy, who became a Christian five years ago. For the first three years, Andy woke up early every morning to pray and read his Bible for an hour. He faithfully sought out fellowship with other Christians and shared his new faith regularly. But for the past two years, Andy has struggled with guilt. He has grown distant from his Christian friends and lost his incentive to talk to others about Christ. In addition, Andy has begun to struggle with overeating. Occasionally he will visit internet shopping sites and buy needless items online. He says it picks him up when he is down. In other words, Andy has slipped back into habits that dominated him before he became a Christian.

Andy's friends say that his problems started about the same time he missed his first quiet time. Therefore, Andy has redoubled his efforts to read his Bible and pray, but it just doesn't seem the same. The Bible seems dull, and his mind wanders when he prays. What has gone wrong? Most would conclude, like Andy's friends, that he has grown lazy and that he is not using the things God has provided to help him grow: the Bible, prayer, fellowship, ministry, and service. And it's true: These are factors that have contributed to Andy's slow downward spiral.

But Andy's problem is much deeper that that. In fact, his problems started long before he missed his first quiet time. What happened is that Andy lost sight of his need for the Cross of Christ almost as soon as he became a Christian. If you had known Andy during the first three years of his Christian life, when he was faithfully engaging in the basic Christian disciplines, you would have met a confident and impatient man who rebuked others for struggling with their personal devotions or witnessing.

Although Andy had come to Christ for salvation, acknowledging that he was lost and without hope except for the mercy of Christ, he quickly began to live as if progress in the Christian life was all up to him. "Jesus got me in, and I have to do the rest" was Andy's functional identity. "It's all up to me." For the first three years, he was proud because he was working hard to grow. He saw very little need for the Cross of Christ because he had already been forgiven. His sense of acceptance before God had quickly shifted from what Christ had done for him to what he was doing for Christ. Because he was successful, he tended to be self-righteous, judgmental toward those less disciplined, and defensive when criticized.

In the last two years, the external behaviors have changed, but the problem is the same. Instead of being proud of his righteous efforts, Andy is ashamed, guilty, depressed at times, and easily attracted by old temptations. He feels like a failure because he can no longer keep up the routine. What is Andy's real problem? In both phases of his Christian life, the work of Christ on the Cross was radically minimized by Andy's own efforts. The first three years evidenced a Christ-less activism that produced pride and self-sufficiency. While this may not appear that bad on the outside, it is as dangerous as Andy's recent behavior of Christ-less passivity, which has produced guilt, depression, and a host of bad habits.

The sad fact is that Andy is typical of many believers who begin the Christian life with a clear understanding of their need for Christ but quickly lose sight of how central Christ must be throughout it. If Andy had kept the Cross central in those first three years, it would have reminded him that anything good was the result of the grace of Christ working in him. He could have also handled his failures over the past two years because the Cross would have reminded him that Christ has given him a new identity and a safe place to deal honestly with sin.

Faith and Repentance Are the Keys

How do you avoid leading a Cross-less life? The answer is found in moment-by-moment faith and repentance. Faith keeps us laying hold of the grace and mercy of Christ and thereby avoiding despair. Repentance keeps us facing our ongoing struggle with sin and thereby avoiding pride. This is just what Andy needs – throughout his Christian life. This is just what every Christian needs. And yet so many believers only think of faith and repentance as the way to enter the Christian life. They fail to realize that faith and repentance link us to Christ on a daily basis. Faith is another way of saying, "seeing Christ's glory and grace and turning to him." Repentance is another way of saying, "admitting and turning from sin." They are two sides of the same coin, and both are essential for the Christian life.

Faith: Seeing Who You Are in Christ

Repentance, or turning from sin, is never easy. It means admitting that you are wrong. Something in every human heart avoids this. When was the last time you had to admit that you were wrong and ask someone to forgive you? What was most difficult? No doubt your own pride was a major stumbling block. There may also have been fear that the other person would not forgive you, or possibly use your confession against you. But what if you knew that the person would be welcoming and full of joy? Would that make admitting you were wrong and asking for forgiveness an incredibly freeing experience? Of course it would!

In 1 John, a letter that unrelentingly calls us to examine our Christian life, we find rich pictures of who we are in Christ. Seeing Christ is essential if we are going to admit and turn from our sin. First John teaches us that we are new on the inside due to a new birth (2:29), a profound truth we considered in Chapter 9. First John also teaches that we are going to be completely changed one day (3:2), something we studied in Chapter 1. As if that were not enough, 1 John says that we have a new status. We have been justified and adopted by God the Father. All of these elements are critical to the Christian life. Let's consider our new legal status in detail. Understanding this will enable us to repent and pursue holiness.

You Are Justified

In 1 John 2:1-2, we have a clear description of our justification.

> My dear children, I write this to you so that you will not sin. But if anybody does sin, we have one who speaks to the Father in our defense – Jesus Christ, the Righteous One. He is the atoning sacrifice for our sins, and not only for ours but also for the sins of the whole world.

In verse 1, we see that Christians continue to struggle with sin. John refers to his readers as his children in the faith. They are Christians in whom he longs to see progress in holiness, but sin is still a reality in their lives. As we saw in Chapters 7 and 8, our need for the Cross is not over!

But verse 1 goes on to say that Jesus is our defense lawyer. When we sin, Jesus speaks to the Father on our behalf. He defends us, saying that we should not be punished for our sins because he has already atoned for us. He says something like this: "Father, I know that _____ has sinned and that change needs to happen in his life. But it would be unjust for you to condemn him. You would be exacting judgment twice for the same sin – from him and from me." First John 1:9 says that when we confess our sins, God is faithful and just to forgive us. He is just because Jesus has already made atonement for that sin.

One aspect of our justification that many Christians fail to see is that we are not just forgiven because Christ has paid for our sins. God also treats us as if we had perfectly obeyed the law, because Christ has obeyed it perfectly for us. He is our righteousness. This is truly mind-boggling!

You Are Adopted

As if our justification were not enough, God has done even more! In 1 John 3:1-3, we find a vivid description of our adoption.

> How great is the love the Father has lavished on us, that we should be called children of God! And that is what we are! The reason the world does not know us is that it did not know him. Dear friends, now we are children of God, and what we will be has not yet been made known. But we know that when he appears, we shall be like him, for we shall see him as he is. Everyone who has this hope in him purifies himself, just as he is pure.

Verse 1 delights in the fact that Christians have a radical new relationship with God. Because we have been justified, we are now welcomed into God's presence and family. God is no longer our judge; he is now our Father. John's joy spills over at the fact that God has done more than justify us. We see his exuberance in three ways:

1. Though not evident in most translations, John begins verse 1 with "Behold." He is saying, "Stop and think about this! Don't miss this incredible truth."

2. The phrase translated "How great" literally means "from what country." A modern interpretation of this phrase would be "from what planet!" The Father's love is so immense that it is hard to conceive of where it could originate – except in God himself.

Cross 2: The Cross and Daily Living

3. When John says, "And that is what we are," he can hardly contain himself. He is saying, "Can you believe it? We have not just been justified; we have been made God's children. What amazing love!"

Verses 2 and 3 go on to say that this amazing love of the Father compels us to live for him. When rightly understood, God's love will propel you toward holiness and growth in grace. The order is essential: I am a new creation, accepted, adopted, and free; therefore I want to please God. We do not say: I will try to please God so that I may become a new creation, make myself acceptable, and hope that God adopts me and sets me free.

The truth is, you are already dead to sin (Chapter 11) and in a new relationship with the Father because of what Christ has done for you (Chapter 12). This is how you are to think of yourself every day. Father, Son, and Holy Spirit have done something truly amazing: They have made it possible for sinners to draw near! What should this produce in the Christian? It should produce a deep gratitude along with a new confidence to look honestly at sin and engage in daily repentance. The fact of my adoption also reminds me that I am part of a new family, the body of Christ. The change process must take place in the context of my relationships with brothers and sisters in Christ.

Repentance: Turning From Sin

If the Christian is grounded in his or her new identity (Chapter 9), it will show itself in a life of repentance. In the story of the Prodigal Son in Luke 15:11-32, the Bible gives us a picture of what faith and repentance look like. We understand the ugliness of sin and the beauty of the Cross.

11Jesus continued: "There was a man who had two sons. 12The younger one said to his father, 'Father, give me my share of the estate.' So he divided his property between them.

13 "Not long after that, the younger son got together all he had, set off for a distant country and there squandered his wealth in wild living. 14After he had spent everything, there was a severe famine in that whole country, and he began to be in need. 15So he went and hired himself out to a citizen of that country, who sent him to his fields to feed pigs. 16He longed to fill his stomach with the pods that the pigs were eating, but no one gave him anything.

¹⁷"When he came to his senses, he said, 'How many of my father's hired men have food to spare, and here I am starving to death! ¹⁸I will set out and go back to my father and say to him: Father, I have sinned against heaven and against you. ¹⁹I am no longer worthy to be called your son; make me like one of your hired men.' ²⁰So he got up and went to his father.

'But while he was still a long way off, his father saw him and was filled with compassion for him; he ran to his son, threw his arms around him and kissed him.

²¹"The son said to him, 'Father, I have sinned against heaven and against you. I am no longer worthy to be called your son.'

²²"But the father said to his servants, 'Quick! Bring the best robe and put it on him. Put a ring on his finger and sandals on his feet. ²³Bring the fattened calf and kill it. Let's have a feast and celebrate. ²⁴For this son of mine was dead and is alive again; he was lost and is found.' So they began to celebrate.

²⁵"Meanwhile, the older son was in the field. When he came near the house, he heard music and dancing. ²⁶So he called one of the servants and asked him what was going on. ²⁷'Your brother has come,' he replied, 'and your father has killed the fattened calf because he has him back safe and sound.'

²⁸"The older brother became angry and refused to go in. So his father went out and pleaded with him. ²⁹But he answered his father, 'Look! All these years I've been slaving for you and never disobeyed your orders. Yet you never gave me even a young goat so I could celebrate with my friends. ³⁰But when this son of yours who has squandered your property with prostitutes comes home, you kill the fattened calf for him!'

³¹"'My son,' the father said, 'you are always with me, and everything I have is yours. ³²But we had to celebrate and be glad, because this brother of yours was dead and is alive again; he was lost and is found.'

Three Ingredients

There are three essential ingredients in faith-driven repentance.

Wake Up: "He came to his senses" (v. 17)

Real repentance means that you see that your biggest problem is you, not your circumstances. No matter how difficult things may be, your deepest need is to know and be known by God. In the case of the prodigal son, it took difficulty and poverty to awaken him to his true condition. Doesn't God often use Heat to bring us to self-awareness? What may begin as shallow repentance begins to grow and deepen. When you "wake up" in some of the following ways, change is beginning.

- You see life as a moral drama of immense proportions.
- You have a new sobriety about the reality of sin, suffering, and your need for grace.
- Momentary pleasures no longer hold your attention.
- Biblical truth begins to make sense as you think about your situation.
- The Bible gets personal. It's not just talking about them; it's talking about you.
- You begin to make connections between your heart and your behavior.
- You begin to see that God is a God of grace and mercy, and he becomes increasingly attractive.

Own Up: He admitted his sin (v. 18)

The prodigal's wake-up call is followed by repentance. If this is happening, we will not treat God's grace lightly. Three things are involved:

- **Godly sorrow, not worldly sorrow.** The prodigal son saw that his sin was against his father. This is godly sorrow as opposed to worldly sorrow (see 2 Cor. 7:10). Worldly sorrow is only sorry that you were caught, or that you failed to live up to your own standards and potential, or that you are experiencing the consequences of your sin. Worldly sorrow is self-centered, while godly sorrow focuses on how God was offended and others were hurt. Godly sorrow especially sees that God's love (not just his commands) has been treated lightly. Worldly sorrow produces tears of self-pity, but godly sorrow produces tears of true humility.

- **Seeing the sin beneath the sins.** You begin to see the heart sins beneath your behavioral sins, the idolatrous lies that drive you to do what you do. Remember, before you violate commandments 4 -10, you violate commandments 1-3 by forsaking God for something else. When you see this, you begin to see how spiritually blind you have been. There is no more excuse making or blame-shifting; instead, there is honest self-examination. You start to be self-critical without getting defensive or depressed.
- **Repenting of sin *and* righteousness.** You start repenting of your righteousness, not just your sins. What does this mean? Every time we try to build our lives on who we are apart from Christ, it is an attempt to justify ourselves. It is a way to create a righteousness apart from Christ so that we can feel we earned our acceptance before God, others, and ourselves. A Christian not only sees the Thorny behavior that results from these false identities; he also sees the many outwardly good things that may be motivated by the worship of something other than God. He repents of those things as well. For example, suppose you do not feel accepted by God, others, or yourself unless you are doing something kind or thoughtful for someone. You are placing your hopes for acceptance not on Christ, but on your image as a truly sacrificial person. Biblical repentance will lead you to repent even of these efforts, because they cannot make you right with God, either.

Shift Weight: Receiving his father's gracious embrace (v. 20)

When you admit the depth of your sin and repent, as the prodigal son did, the love of the Father, Son, and Holy Spirit gets increasingly attractive. The false identities and idols that were once so alluring lose their appeal. You start to experience the love of Christ, and change results. Notice how the father's lavish love is so prominent in the story. He runs in the direction of his repentant child. What does this tell us about what true repentance looks like?

- You begin to rest in Christ's work as you confess your sins, asking for forgiveness and grace.
- You get smaller and Christ gets bigger. You have a godly self-forgetfulness that is very different from self-loathing.
- You look at Christ, not just at your sin.

Cross 2: The Cross and Daily Living

- You receive new energy, joy, gratitude, hope, perseverance, and purpose.

In Chapter 11, we saw that God makes us new creatures in Christ and defeats sin's power in our lives. In this chapter we have seen what it looks like to depend on the Cross as we deal with ongoing sin. We grow when we remember our new identity as regenerated, justified, and adopted sons and daughters. This new identity and power enable us to admit and turn from sin and to pursue the things that please God. This brings amazing freedom into the life of the believer!

Daily Living and Your New Identity in Christ

Good theology has power when it is applied to daily life. Let's return to my battle with the idol of comfort that I talked about at the beginning of this chapter and bring a Cross-centered perspective to it.

The Real World: Take Two

After a long day at the office, I begin to dream about some rest and relaxation at home. But the Spirit helps me to remember that I am not entitled to comfort. I remember all too well how living for comfort can lead me to respond to my family in sinful ways. As I drive home, I take a look at my heart. First, I realize that my biggest problem is me, not my circumstances, and that I have everything I need in Christ to live in ways that please him. Second, I notice that comfort is something I tend to worship above the Lord. I need to repent, and I need something more glorious to recapture my straying heart. I compare and contrast comfort with Christ's glory and who I am in him. My heart responds with gratitude.

To get my heart where it needs to be, I often use a series of questions based on Philippians 2:1-11. They highlight what Christ did when he left heaven to suffer, die, and be raised for us. Here is what it would sound like in this case:

1. Comfort, you look beautiful to me right now, but when did you ever leave your place of prominence and glory to humble yourself for me?
2. Comfort, when did you ever enter my world to suffer on my behalf?
3. Comfort, when did you ever shed your blood so that I could be cleansed from my sin?

4. Comfort, when were you ever raised from the dead on my behalf? When did you ever promise to give me new life and power?
5. Comfort, when did you ever promise to send the Holy Spirit to fill me with true comfort that would help me to please God, even when my earthly comfort was threatened?
6. Comfort, when did you ever promise to intercede for me to my Father in heaven, so that I could be strong in trial?
7. Comfort, when did you ever promise to come again and redeem me from the things that capture me and make me their slave?

When I do this by faith, I can see Christ in his glory and my benefits in him. I am able to repent of making comfort my god, and it gets put back in its proper place. Comfort is something to be enjoyed, but not worshiped!

I have experienced the work of the Spirit on my drive home. I have engaged in intelligent repentance and faith, identifying the heart sins beneath the behavioral sins. I have applied the powerful realities of the gospel to my life. The roots of comfort idolatry begin to wither, and I sink my roots more deeply into Jesus, the true Vine.

This vertical reorientation back to God will change the way I interact with my family as I get home and face the same set of circumstances. I will seek to be kind, patient, and gentle as I begin to serve my family. I may need to be firm with my children, but they will encounter a shepherd who cares for them, not a drill sergeant. My wife will not face a spouse who thinks it is her job to deliver the comfort I deserve. She will encounter a partner who intends to shoulder the challenges of our life together. She will meet a man who is living out of his identity in Christ, and that will encourage her to do the same.

The life of repentance and faith puts to death the deeds of the sinful nature and lives more and more in righteousness. The Father who calls us to obedience has provided everything we need in Christ to live it out. When we fail, he promises never to leave or forsake us. He wins us back by the Spirit and gives more grace when we confess and repent of sin. For that, this Christian husband and father is grateful!

CHAPTER 13

FRUIT 1: REAL HEART CHANGE

Chapter 2 began with this statement: "Nothing is more obvious than the need for change. Nothing is less obvious than what needs to change and how that change happens." We hope that, by now, that statement is less true than it was when you began reading this book! Change can and does happen when we live in relationship with our Redeemer and embrace all the benefits he brings.

Diagnosis: Just the Beginning

But we are not through yet. It would be tempting to stop at analysis and pretend that we have finished our work. But that would be a travesty, according to the Bible. Real change does not take place until it is visible in our lives and our relationships. Our understanding of something does not mean we have solved the problem.

Suppose your car does not work. You take it to a mechanic and he hooks it up to all kinds of sophisticated machinery. He gives the diagnosis: a bad crank case. Now suppose he takes the car off the hydraulic rack, hands you a bill, and tells you the car is fixed! More than likely, you would tell him to put the car back on the lift and replace the crank case.

The same is true in the Christian life. It is not enough to diagnose the problem. You need genuine, concrete change in your behavior. James puts it bluntly when he says that "faith without deeds is dead" (James 2:26). Paul says the same thing when he says that faith will lead to obedience (Rom. 1:5; 16:26). In Galatians 5:6, he says that "the only thing that counts is faith expressing itself through love."

As you look back over this book, can you see how God's love for his people overcomes sin and its destruction? Good Fruit is absolutely possible, even in trying circumstances. Living God-centered, Christ-dependent lives that display God's power and beauty is not something reserved for uniquely godly persons. Any believer can experience godliness when he relies on Christ. In this chapter, we will look at the kind of heart that produces good Fruit. In Chapter 14, we will see what the Fruit itself looks like.

The Overflow of the Heart

The Bible uses the word heart to describe who we are at our core. The Hebrew and Greek words translated as heart are used in several passages to talk about "being at the center of something." Jonah is in the center of the waves (Jonah 2:3). Jesus is buried deep in the earth (Matt. 12:40). When the Bible talks about the Christian life, it talks about loving God with all of our hearts. God is not content to live on the periphery of our lives. He will settle for nothing short of the center!

This is in stark contrast to other popular views of the Christian life. For most non-Christians (as well as many Christians), the Christian life is a matter of keeping the rules. God does have concerns about a person's behavior, but the Bible gives us a much more redemptive picture of a believer's life. It describes the Christian life in terms of a new relationship with God that brims with hope and flows from the core of our being into our daily lives!

A Christian is someone whose life has been invaded by the holy love of God. God intends to create in us a pure love that flows from a new heart. We have seen that God even uses the metaphor of marriage to describe our intensely personal relationship with him. Marriage only begins to describe the relationship he wants to have with us, but it helps us understand why we obey God's commands and pursue a life of holiness.

Love and Rules Are Not Mutually Exclusive

Suppose a single woman starts working in a large company. She has not yet met her new boss. At one end of the office area, she sees a door with a bulletin board next to it. This is her boss's office. He posts directions and rules for his employees on the bulletin board. What does she think of her boss and his bulletin board? Most likely, she has a sense of awe and possibly some fear about her boss. The rules on the board could, therefore, be looked upon with similar fear and possibly distaste. The rules intended to govern her behavior and maximize her performance might not inspire or motivate her, but she would follow them to avoid being fired. The rules themselves seem impersonal and cold.

Fruit 1: Real Heart Change

Now imagine that months later, the boss, a single man, develops a personal relationship with her. Eventually they marry. During that time, she notices that her perspective about the bulletin board changes to the same degree that her heart changes toward her new husband. She now sees the guidelines as wise and loving directions from someone who cares for her well-being. She no longer views them as burdensome. They are specific ways she can honor and please the husband who happens to be her boss.

What has changed? Not the rules. The nature of her relationship and her attitude towards the rule-giver have changed. This is an imperfect illustration that ignores the issues involved in dating in the workplace, but it does point to some truths about the Christian life. A new lifestyle – the outward Fruit of a believer's life – does not grow out of a stoic obedience to God's commands, but from a heart that has been captured and captivated by the Giver of those commands. There will still be times when obedience is difficult. But even the struggle will grow out of a sense that the rules are there because a personal God cares for you.

Throughout the Bible, the heart is mentioned as the seat of motivation. There are over 900 references to the heart in Scripture. Let's consider a few passages to see how Scripture emphasizes the importance of a renewed heart in obeying God.

The Heart of Obedience

What would you say if you were asked to summarize what it meant to be a Christian? When pressed by the teachers of the Law, Jesus says that all true obedience grows out of a transformed heart. He echoes hundreds of years of God's revelation by emphasizing the centrality of heart obedience. Anything less is empty and hypocritical because the heart is central to change.

> One of the teachers of the law came and heard them debating. Noticing that Jesus had given them a good answer, he asked him, "Of all the commandments, which is the most important?"
>
> "The most important one," answered Jesus, "is this: 'Hear, O Israel, the Lord our God, the Lord is one. Love the Lord your God with all your heart and with all your soul and with all your mind and with all your

strength.' The second is this: 'Love your neighbor as yourself.' There is no commandment greater than these." (Mark 12:28-31)

In these verses, Jesus focuses on the heart and emphasizes the first three commands of the Ten Commandments. True godliness begins in the heart.

The Heart in the Old Testament

In 1 Samuel 16:1-13, God tells Samuel what to focus on when he assesses David and his brothers. God's gaze on the shepherd boy, David, goes straight to the heart.

> The LORD said to Samuel, "How long will you mourn for Saul, since I have rejected him as king over Israel? Fill your horn with oil and be on your way; I am sending you to Jesse of Bethlehem. I have chosen one of his sons to be king."

> . . . When they arrived, Samuel saw Eliab and thought, "Surely the LORD's anointed stands here before the LORD."

> But the LORD said to Samuel, "Do not consider his appearance or his height, for I have rejected him. The LORD does not look at the things man looks at. Man looks at the outward appearance, but the LORD looks at the heart."

> Then Jesse called Abinadab and had him pass in front of Samuel. But Samuel said, "The LORD has not chosen this one either." Jesse then had Shammah pass by, but Samuel said, "Nor has the LORD chosen this one." Jesse had seven of his sons pass before Samuel, but Samuel said to him, "The LORD has not chosen these." So he asked Jesse, "Are these all the sons you have?"

> "There is still the youngest," Jesse answered, "but he is tending the sheep."

> Samuel said, "Send for him; we will not sit down until he arrives."

> So he sent and had him brought in. He was ruddy, with a fine appearance and handsome features.

> Then the LORD said, "Rise and anoint him; he is the one."

So Samuel took the horn of oil and anointed him in the presence of his brothers, and from that day on the Spirit of the LORD came upon David in power. Samuel then went to Ramah.

God cautions Samuel not to place much stock in the outward appearance, but to look upon the inward disposition. In later life, David gives evidence of learning this truth in his psalm of self-examination. "Search me, O God, and know my heart; test me and know my anxious thoughts. See if there is any offensive way in me, and lead me in the way everlasting" (Ps. 139:23-24).

When you examine your life, how much emphasis do you place on your heart?

The Bible candidly depicts us as people who stray from God. Obedience requires radical change. Jeremiah 31 and Ezekiel 36 are filled with wonderful promises of an obedience that flows from hearts recaptured by the living God. These verses ring with the optimism of the new covenant and heart renewal.

"The time is coming," declares the LORD, "when I will make a new covenant with the house of Israel and with the house of Judah.

"It will not be like the covenant I made with their forefathers when I took them by the hand to lead them out of Egypt, because they broke my covenant, though I was a husband to them," declares the LORD.

"This is the covenant I will make with the house of Israel after that time," declares the LORD. "I will put my law in their minds and write it on their hearts. I will be their God, and they will be my people. No longer will a man teach his neighbor, or a man his brother, saying, 'Know the LORD,' because they will all know me, from the least of them to the greatest," declares the LORD. "For I will forgive their wickedness and will remember their sins no more." (Jer. 31:31-34)

In the same way, Ezekiel prophesies about the new covenant and the new heart.

For I will take you out of the nations; I will gather you from all the countries and bring you back into your own land. I will sprinkle clean water on you, and you will be clean; I will cleanse you from all your impurities and from all your idols. I will give you a new heart and put a new spirit in you; I will remove from you your heart of stone and give you a heart of flesh. And I will put my Spirit in you and move you to follow my decrees and be careful to keep my laws. You will live in the land I gave your forefathers; you will be my people, and I will be your God. (Ezek. 36:24-28)

Notice how both passages connect God's law and the heart. Ezekiel 36:27 is particularly powerful in its description of a new heart compelled by the Spirit to obedience. It is a voluntary obedience springing from a heart that has been transformed and captivated by the Redeemer.

The Heart in the New Testament

These Old Testament passages foreshadow things to come. In Ephesians we find the fulfillment of these promises. In his prayer for the Ephesians, Paul says:

For this reason, ever since I heard about your faith in the Lord Jesus and about your love for all the saints, I have not stopped giving thanks for you, remembering you in my prayers. I keep asking that the God of our Lord Jesus Christ, the glorious Father, may give you the Spirit of wisdom and revelation, so that you may know him better. I pray also that the eyes of your heart may be enlightened in order that you may know the hope to which he has called you, the riches of his glorious inheritance in the saints, and his incomparably great power for us who believe. (Eph. 1:15-19)

As Jesus echoes the words of Moses in Mark 12, Paul sees Christ as the fulfillment of all the promises in the Old Testament. Jesus is the one who has reconciled us to God by perfectly obeying the Father's commands from the heart, and suffering the penalty that we as law-breakers deserve. Jesus also sends the Holy Spirit, who comes to give the believer a new heart, to write the law on that heart, and to give a new power and desire to obey God's commands. In Ephesians 4, 5, and 6, Paul describes in detail what the Christian life will look like as a result.

Fruit 1: Real Heart Change

Nothing could be more hopeful and freeing than the picture we have in these passages. My life is not determined by my upbringing, physiology, culture, emotions, or anything else! Because God has made every provision to address my most fundamental need – redemption – I can have confidence and joy that change is absolutely possible for me. My biggest problem and hindrance – my wayward, sinful heart – has been addressed! God has redeemed me and given me a new one.

How are you responding to life's circumstances? Where do you see good Fruit in your life? Where have you been patient with someone who tempts you to anger? Where have you lovingly confronted someone who makes you fearful? What recent difficult situation has tested you and proven your faith genuine? What recent blessing has tested you and proven your faith genuine? Choose one of these questions and reflect on the kind of heart that produces such Fruit. In what way did you intelligently rest in and rely on your Redeemer? What specific things were you repenting of (putting off) and believing in (putting on) that energized and encouraged you to act? What new truths about your Savior began to fill your heart and transform your life?

A Case Study

It is one thing to think about change on a purely theoretical level. It is another to bring it down to where you live. With that in mind, let's look at someone who faced hardship and learn from his experience. The apostle Paul dealt with physical weakness, hardship, and sin. In his letter to the Philippians, we see how he responded.

Acts 16 tells us that Paul and Silas planted the church in Philippi. While there, they were thrown into prison for healing a slave girl. Later, in prison again (probably in Rome), he wrote this letter to the Philippians, encouraging them to have joy in difficult circumstances. How could he do this? What enabled him to maintain his peace and joy in the face of such hardship? If the gospel could work in Paul's life under these circumstances, it can do the same for you and me.

Read the book of Philippians and then consider the seven questions that follow. Each considers Paul's response and follows with a personal application. As you do this exercise, you will reflect on what you have been learning in this book. It will be a practical way of applying the Big Picture of

Heat (Chapters 7 and 8), Thorns (Chapters 9 and 10), Cross (Chapters 11 and 12) and Fruit (Chapters 13 and 14) to your life. Pick an area of personal difficulty. Look at Paul's life and apply what you see to your own.

Heat

1a. What is Paul's situation?

What are Paul's burdens, pressures, hardships, pains, and temptations, both actual and potential?

Paul is in prison. He cannot carry out his mission. He is distraught over the rivalries and competition in the churches he cares for. Paul's circumstances are disturbing. What is truly in his heart will come out.

1b. What is your situation?

What hardships do you face right now? Are you struggling with health, a family relationship, a work-related problem, criticism, the pain of being sinned against? What temptations are you dealing with? Do circumstances in the near or distant future have you concerned and even fearful?

Paul could not avoid living in a world of sin and suffering, and neither can you. Be honest about your circumstances. Face them. Before you can experience the grace of Christ, you must identify where you need his help. Glance back over Chapters 7 and 8 to locate yourself in your world.

Thorns

2a. What responses would you expect from people in difficult circumstances?

Because Philippians pictures someone who responds in godly ways, we do not see ungodly responses. But if you were in Paul's shoes, how would you be tempted to respond? A few possibilities might be: anger, frustration, despair, questioning God's goodness and wisdom, forsaking the faith, self-sufficiency, self-righteousness, preoccupation with protecting your comfort, and more. The possibilities for sin vary with every individual.

2b. What are your responses in difficult situations?

How do you typically react to the pressures you listed in the first question? What are your thoughts, words, attitudes, emotions, and actions? Next, think about how you typically react when things are going well. What temptations do blessings present? Do you get frustrated with God when he does something that seems to get in the way of your glorifying him? When difficulty enters our lives, we often question God's wisdom, goodness, power, and compassion. This is not a "little" sin. It assassinates God's character and impugns his motives. Do you wallow in self-pity when you face difficulties? Do you put God on trial when he doesn't run the universe the way you would? Review the typical responses outlined in Chapter 9. Do you see yourself there?

3a. What cravings and beliefs tend to rule the human heart and produce ungodly reactions?

What false masters can rule in situations like those Paul faced? Here are a few Paul encountered:

- Philippians 1:17; 2.3, 2.21; 3:19: selfish ambition.
- Philippians 3:1-7:self-righteousness.
- Philippians 2:28; 4:6, 12: anxiety.

3b. What cravings and beliefs rule your heart?

When pressures increase, do you try to get the upper hand on the situation or people involved? Is it hard for you to trust God because you think you will be used or manipulated? Do you lack courage in Christ because you are afraid of what people might think, say, or do? Are you judgmental and critical of others, gossiping or complaining about them? Are the typical ways you respond to trials comfort-driven, fear-driven, or people-pleasing reactions? Go back to Chapter 10's outline of what rules your heart. Identify the specific things that surface in the situation you have chosen.

4a. What consequences follow sinful reactions?

What vicious circles threaten the Philippians? How would their sinful reactions compound hardship, create new problems, or spoil blessings? What do you reap when you react sinfully?

- Philippians 1:15-18: envy and rivalry.
- Philippians 3:18-19: personal destruction and eternal punishment.

Our reactions to our circumstances have consequences. Our responses, whether godly or ungodly, help create a new set of circumstances to deal with. If I get irritated with my son when he doesn't do what I say, I create a new set of circumstances. When I sin, I make the problem worse, even if my son obeys me. When I respond in godly ways, it doesn't guarantee that my son will respond as I would like, but it does ensure that I am not a hindrance to the work of God in his life.

4b. What consequences do you face after sinful actions?

As you look at the way you have responded to your own situation, what consequences do you see? How have you compounded the problem because you were ruled by something other than Christ? In what ways have your efforts to fix the problem made it worse?

Cross

5a. What changes lives, inside and out? What rules the heart and produces godly responses?

How specifically does God reveal himself in Philippians? Who is he? What is he like? What has he done? What is he doing? What will he do? While you won't see everything there is to know about God in this book, what stands out? More specifically, what does Paul see about Christ? What rules Paul? How is his life determined by faith? What controls his interpretation of (and response to) his circumstances? What is the "secret" of contentment, peace, thankfulness, and joy? In what did Paul believe, trust, fear, hope, love, seek and obey? How does faith in the Redeemer make the whole world look different? How does faith change us in practical ways? How do thankfulness, peacemaking, and contentment flow directly from believing, trusting, and fearing God?

- 1:2: grace and peace are ours through Christ.
- 1:6; 2:13: a faithful, sovereign God.
- 1:19: the Holy Spirit of Christ.
- 1:20-21: confidence in the resurrected Christ.
- 2:1-11: Christ's humble service for his people.

Fruit 1: Real Heart Change

- 2:1-8; 3:10-11: identifying with Christ's sufferings. (If he suffered, why do I think I wouldn't? Suffering should not be avoided. It is redemptive and proof of my union with Christ.)
- 2:9-11, 16: trusting in the exalted Christ. (If he was exalted, so shall I be one day! This world is not my home.)
- 3:1-9: resting in the work of Christ for me.
- 3:12-14: Christ's secure hold on my life.
- 3:20-21: Christ's return and my transformation.
- 1:1, 5, 14, 25; 2:19; 3:17; 4:10, 18: the example of others.
- 1:9, 19: others' prayers.
- 2:12-13: God enables us to change.
- 4:4-7: true worship of God.
- 4:8-9: meditating on the truth.

5b. What changes your life? What rules your heart?

If you identified what tends to replace Christ in your heart in Question 3, you are on your way to Spirit-directed repentance and faith. Remember, you have to see how you have broken the first three of the Ten Commandments before you can repent of violating the other seven. In other words, you must repent of more than just the surface sins, as serious as they are. When you see what you specifically need to repent of, it helps you to see where Christ needs to come to the forefront of your heart and life. Use Chapters 11 and 12 to consider what you need to see about Christ again. What truths in Philippians stand out as you reflect on your own heart and life? These truths are not just cognitive tools to adjust your thinking; they are intended to increase your love for Christ!

Fruit

6a. What specific good Fruit do you observe?

How does Paul respond to negative and positive circumstances? In what concrete ways are you told to obey God?

- 1:3-11: love and prayer for others.
- 1:12-13, 15-18: concern for Christ's reputation, not his own.
- 1:3: thanksgiving.
- 1:6, 12, 19-26; 2:9-11; 3:13, 20-21: courage.

- 2:1: encouragement, comfort, and fellowship with Christ and the Spirit.
- 2:2-4: humility, tenderness, compassion.
- 2:12-18: pursuit of holiness amid difficulty.
- 4:11-12: contentment, not acting like a victim, though he has been flagrantly sinned against.
- 2:19-30: godly emotions in struggle.

6b. What specific good Fruit do you observe in your life?

Do you see good Fruit in your life? Are you growing in personal integrity? Can you face your sin and bring it to the Lord? Do you reach out for help? Do you express godly emotions? Do you move toward people you need to forgive or seek forgiveness from? Are you patient as you deal with their weaknesses and sins? How is the gospel shaping your speech? Can you rejoice as God uses this situation to make you holy?

7a. What good effects result from the way Paul handled his situation?

What gracious circles does he create? What positive consequences do you see? What challenges still remain? What new tensions will arise?

- 1:13: people are evangelized.
- 1:14: Christians are encouraged to be bold.
- 1:19: believers are encouraged to pray.

Present day readers have the same experience!

7b. What good effects result from the way you handle your situation?

Living in godly ways may not always make life easier. Paul was in jail! But there are many times when godly behavior brings peace and wholeness to life. In your situation, how have your actions created positive feedback? How have your actions made your world more challenging?

The Bible shows us how Paul responded in surprising and godly ways in trying circumstances. This Fruit grows out of a heart that drinks in the gospel. These responses are available to each of us when we seek them by faith. Paul's life shows us that the Christian life is so much more than obeying the rules. It is lived in relationship with the living Christ. When we trust and obey, we honor God, we are given more grace, and others are helped as well.

FRUIT 2: NEW AND SURPRISING FRUIT

Are you ever tempted to think that the commands and principles of Scripture don't work in the real world? Sometimes we doubt that the grace of Christ is really powerful enough to produce good Fruit in us in such a troubled and troubling world. Have you ever said anything like this?

- "I know a 'soft answer turns away wrath,' but whoever wrote that didn't have my children!"
- "If I turned the other cheek, people would take advantage of me."
- "I've tried my best to forgive her, but whenever I see her, I am flooded with the memories of what she did to me."
- "I know the Bible says that God's grace is most powerful in weakness, but in my moments of weakness, I just feel weak."
- "I tried being the servant, and now people always expect me to be the one who gives."
- "How can I love my enemies if I can hardly love my friends and family ?"
- "I know I'm supposed to love my wife like Christ loved the church, but sometimes she drives me crazy!"
- "It seems impossible to be kind to a teenager who is so rude."
- "It is very hard to treat my boss with respect when he cuts down everyone who works for him."
- "It's difficult to stay committed to a church that has never recognized my gifts for ministry."

The Bible intends to shock us out of our tendencies toward fear, complacency, and unbelief. It begins with a startling honesty about the poverty, injustice, bondage to sin, violence, corruption, shattered relationships, and decaying creation we encounter every day. The Bible is also very blunt as it talks about the temptations of blessing and abundance and the difficulty of handling them wisely. Plenty can be as big a source of struggle as need! But more than anything else, the Word of God shocks us with its hope, as it presents us with possibilities far beyond anything we would expect this side of eternity. Again and again, the Bible describes God's children as Fruit-laden trees fed by streams of living water (see Isaiah 55:1-2, 58:11; Jeremiah 31:12; Hosea 14:5-7). Given the trials and temptations of this life, we would expect God to describe us as parched earth and withered plants. Instead, the Bible reveals an oasis of grace in the midst of the desert.

In this chapter we will examine the fundamental changes that take place in our actions and responses when Christ changes our hearts. The hope of the New Covenant is a new heart that is daily being renewed. But even after all we have learned, some of us are still tempted to limit our expectations of what God can do in us. We say things like:

"Because of what I have experienced, good things are not possible for me."

"God's 'rules' may work for others but not for me. I have tried to keep them during this trial, but it has just produced more frustration."

"I have fought and prayed to conquer this sin, but I just can't beat it."

"I get excited when I read the stories in Scripture, but what those people experienced hasn't been my experience at all."

When we assume such things for ourselves, we tend to assume them for others, too. We quit believing that good Fruit can grow in the Heat of difficulty, so we give up on one another. That's why it is so important to be reminded of how God's renewal of our hearts helps us deal with life's Heat in new ways.

In the Cave and Okay

Consider this situation. A man is a highly respected leader with power and influence over thousands of people. Yet within his own family he is powerless. Something is very wrong with his son. It is not just that his son is rebellious; he is doing all he can to usurp his father's position. The father comes to the devastating realization that his son has turned many loyal subordinates against him. Then, just when he thinks that things are as bad as they can be, he learns that his son is planning to kill him! He knows that he cannot fight for his position and kill his own son, so he flees his home and goes into hiding.

Fruit 2: New and Surprising Fruit

Put yourself in this father's position. Imagine the depth of his grief and pain. Wouldn't you expect to find a bitter, angry man recounting all the good things he did for his ungrateful son? Wouldn't you expect him to question God, especially since he had sought to be faithful to him? Wouldn't you expect this exiled man to be hopeless, cynical, and unresponsive to the spiritual counsel of others?

Perhaps you have already realized that we don't have to imagine this situation. It is recorded for us in 2 Samuel 14–18. (Take time to read this tragic family story.) The father was King David and the son was Absalom. In David's actions and responses, we find little of what we would normally expect. There is something surprisingly hopeful about what he does and says, something meant to shake us out of our cynicism. Psalm 4 gives us a window into David's heart as he undergoes this profound family tragedy.[1]

> [1]Answer me when I call to you, O my righteous God. Give me relief from my distress; be merciful to me and hear my prayer.
> [2]How long, O men, will you turn my glory into shame? How long will you love delusions and seek false gods?
> [3]Know that the LORD has set apart the godly for himself; the LORD will hear when I call to him.
>
> [4]In your anger do not sin; when you are on your beds, search your hearts and be silent.
> [5]Offer right sacrifices and trust in the LORD.
>
> [6]Many are asking, "Who can show us any good?" Let the light of your face shine upon us, O LORD.
> [7]You have filled my heart with greater joy than when their grain and new wine abound.
> [8]I will lie down and sleep in peace, for you alone, O LORD, make me dwell in safety."

Psalms 3 and 4 were written as morning and evening psalms when David was hiding from Absalom. When you know the story behind Psalm 4, you cannot help but be impressed by what you learn about David's heart and behavior. David is in one of the most personally painful experiences of his life, and what do we see him doing?

1. He does not run away from God. He does not question God's faithfulness or bitterly rehearse how the promises and principles of

Scripture have failed. David places himself in God's hands once again. In trial, it is tempting to doubt God's goodness and turn from him in discouragement. But David turns toward God, pleading for him to hear and act (vv. 1-2).

2. He reminds himself of his identity as God's child. You cannot escape the fact that your sense of identity shapes your response to life. David tells himself, "I must remember that I am one of God's 'set apart ones.' I don't know why God put this difficulty in my life, but I know that he hears me as I cry out." The core truth of David's identity is "I am his, he is mine, and he will hear me" (v. 3).

3. He examines his own heart. David does something very different from what we instinctively do in times of trial. Normally, we take the trial as a valid excuse to question God's goodness, faithfulness, and love. We endlessly rehearse the problem and criticize other people's roles in it. But David does not rehash how bad his circumstances are or how evil his son is. David examines his own heart. In difficulty our hearts are exposed. Trials give us an opportunity to know and guard them more effectively. What we do in times of trial is not forced on us by the situation, but by what we desire in the middle of it (v. 5).

4. He worships. When we are in pain and difficulty, we are tempted to skip personal devotions and corporate worship. We allow ourselves to miss small group meetings and to ignore ministry opportunities. In subtle and not so subtle ways, joyful worship is replaced by doubt, anger, fear, discouragement, envy, bitterness, and cynicism. But when you peek into the cave of Psalm 4, you don't find David wallowing in a pool of complaints. You find him worshiping God (v. 5)!

5. He ministers. In Psalm 4 it is clear that David is not alone. He had been followed by a band of faithful supporters. But as David worshiped God, these men began to panic: "Who can show us any good?" (v. 6). Compare David's response to these fearful complaints with your typical response to hard times and problem people. David isn't judgmental, impatiently telling them that they should know better. He doesn't say, "You guys are driving me crazy," and then go off by himself. Even when David's heart could be sinking and his mind racing, he is drawn to the struggle of those around him. He

serves them in the best way he can: He prays for them, asking God to shine his presence on them so that they too can rest (v. 6).

6. He rests. In difficulty, we expect worry-filled days and sad and sleepless nights. Certainly David was grieving. His son was against him. He was about to lose everything God had given him, including, perhaps, his life. How could he not be deeply saddened? Yet, amazingly, David talks about joy and about sleeping in peace! Why isn't he overcome with fear, bitterness, anger, and dread? The answer is simple yet profound: because David's heart is controlled by God. He hasn't lost the one thing most precious to him. Because the Lord is with him, David knows he is just as secure in that cave as he was in the palace. He can lie down and sleep even while he experiences crushing disappointment.

As you read about David, how have you responded? Have you found yourself saying, "Come on, this guy just isn't real!"? Actually, David's worst choices did not come amid difficulty, but amid the temptation of blessing. When he was in the palace in an unchallenged position of power, he ended up stealing another man's wife and arranging his murder. David was not a plastic, perfect man. David was a vulnerable sinner, just like us.

Like us, there were times when he remembered who he was and lived out his identity as God's child. There were other times when he did not. That is precisely why this psalm holds out so much hope. It reflects God's grace to sinful people like you and me. Fruit trees do grow in the harsh Heat of trial in the lives of ordinary people.

Don't read Psalm 4 and say, "This is what I should be doing, but I'm not!" Say, "This is what God is doing in me, too. These things are possible for me, because David's Redeemer is my Redeemer. The God who ruled David's heart and gave him peace in a time of torment is in my heart as well. I can make good choices, do good things, and harvest good Fruit, even amid the hardest challenges of life!"

Psalm 4 does not picture a man's mechanical obedience to a set of biblical principles. If all we needed was information about how to do the right thing, Jesus never would have needed to come. What we actually see in this psalm is God's grace at work in a man's heart, empowering him to do things that would be impossible on his own. Christ's work on the Cross makes that same grace available to us, no matter what we may be facing.

The point is, God does more than deliver us from the Heat. He delivers us from ourselves so that we don't simply survive the Heat, but bear good Fruit. Under the pressure of family difficulty, love can grow. Under the Heat of unappreciated sacrifice, perseverance can grow. In physical suffering, peace and sturdy faith can blossom. In the midst of want, giving can grow where Thorns of greed and selfishness once flourished. Peace can live in the middle of financial disappointment. Humility can thrive in times of personal success. Joy can live under the burning sun of rejection. Hope can even blossom in times of grief.

Streams in the Desert

In John 7:37–38, Jesus says something very encouraging: He tells us that whoever believes in him will have streams of living water flow from within him. John says that Jesus was referring to the Holy Spirit. Through him, spiritual rivers of living water produce life where there was death. Galatians 5:13–6:10 pictures the kind of Fruit that grows through the Spirit's work.

> You, my brothers, were called to be free. But do not use your freedom to indulge the sinful nature; rather, serve one another in love. The entire law is summed up in a single command: "Love your neighbor as yourself." If you keep on biting and devouring each other, watch out or you will be destroyed by each other.
>
> So I say, live by the Spirit, and you will not gratify the desires of the sinful nature. For the sinful nature desires what is contrary to the Spirit, and the Spirit what is contrary to the sinful nature. They are in conflict with each other, so that you do not do what you want. But if you are led by the Spirit, you are not under law.
>
> The acts of the sinful nature are obvious: sexual immorality, impurity and debauchery; idolatry and witchcraft; hatred, discord, jealousy, fits of rage, selfish ambition, dissensions, factions and envy; drunkenness, orgies, and the like. I warn you, as I did before, that those who live like this will not inherit the kingdom of God.
>
> But the fruit of the Spirit is love, joy, peace, patience, kindness, goodness, faithfulness, gentleness and self-control. Against such things there is no law. Those who belong to Christ Jesus have crucified the sinful nature with its passions and desires. Since we live by the Spirit,

let us keep in step with the Spirit. Let us not become conceited, provoking and envying each other.

Brothers, if someone is caught in a sin, you who are spiritual should restore him gently. But watch yourself or you also may be tempted. Carry each other's burdens and in this way you will fulfill the law of Christ. If anyone thinks he is something when he is nothing, he deceives himself. Each man should test his own actions. Then he can take pride in himself without comparing himself to somebody else, for each one should carry his own load.

Anyone who receives instructions in the word must share all good things with his instructor.

Do not be deceived: God cannot be mocked. A man reaps what he sows. The one who sows to please his sinful nature, from that nature will reap destruction; the one who sows to please the Spirit, from the Spirit will reap eternal life. Let us not become weary in doing good, for at the proper time we will reap a harvest if we do not give up. Therefore, as we have opportunity, let us do good to all people, especially to those who belong to the family of believers.

You may be thinking, I understand that the Holy Spirit lives in me and that the Bible likens him to living water. But I am not sure how this helps me when I face trials and temptations. Galatians 5 and 6 explain what Christ meant in John 7.

Did you notice that this passage begins with a warning against self-indulgence (vv. 13–15)? We all know that sin causes us to be more committed to ourselves than to anyone else. That is why we compete with one another in traffic and the checkout line, for the first shower in the morning or the last cookie on the tray, for someone's affection, or for the promotion at work. Sin causes us to be more concerned about our own welfare than anyone else's. Such self-centeredness destroys relationships and does great harm.

But this passage does not end on a note of struggle. Rather, it pictures people who are committed to ministry, who look for ways to bear others' burdens and do good (6:1–10). The passage that begins with Thorn bush responses ends with Fruit tree living. What makes the difference? The living water of the Holy Spirit! The Spirit battles our sinful nature on our behalf. Because of him, we do not need to yield to it (vv. 19–21). We can say "no" to motivating emotions (passions) and powerful cravings (desires) and go in the opposite direction (see v. 24).

As we say "yes" to the Holy Spirit, his living water produces new Fruit in our hearts: love, joy, peace, patience, kindness, goodness, faithfulness, gentleness, and self-control. These character qualities aren't an ideal standard that God holds over us. They are gifts the Spirit produces in us. This change within us changes the way we respond to the things around us (Heat). And this is the Fruit that results: Kind people look for ways to do good. Patient and faithful people don't run away when people mess up. Loving people serve even when sinned against. Gentle people help a struggler bear his burden. Galatians 5 and 6 are filled with hope.

We must reject a view of the Christian life that emphasizes what we should do more than what God is doing in us by his Spirit. We should reject any view of the Christian life that says that the change God calls us to is impossible, or only takes place in eternity. We should reject any perspective on the Christian life that minimizes the war that rages in our hearts every day – or ignores the fact that God is fighting it for us and with us! The biblical picture is that God meets us in the trials of life, and he doesn't just give us rules – he gives us his Son! Because of him, what we are called to do is not unrealistic.

The Bible teaches us that a Fruit tree bears Fruit under the scorching Heat of difficulty. Now remind yourself, As a child of God, I am that tree. Its Fruit is God's gift, produced by his Spirit. I need not be satisfied with Thorn bush responses. It's not impossible to be who God says I am – a tree bearing Fruit in the middle of the desert.

New and Surprising Fruit

What will this Fruit of heart change look like in your life? As we consider this Fruit – these changes in our living – keep in mind that we are not simply listing things we should do as believers, but rather, what we have been given by Jesus. He gives us new life, new wisdom, new character, new hope, new strength, new freedom, and new desires. The Bible summarizes all of these things by saying that Christ's work on the Cross gives us a new heart. Our heart has been brought to new life through the Holy Spirit. When we think, desire, speak, or act in a right way, it isn't time to pat ourselves on the back or cross it off our To Do List. Each time we do what is right, we are experiencing what Christ has supplied for us. In Chapter 11, we introduced some of the Fruit Christ produces. We will expand the discussion here.

I will live with personal integrity. The complete forgiveness that Christ provides means I no longer need to be afraid to look at myself in the mirror of God's Word. I no longer need to defend or excuse myself, to rationalize away my sinful choices, or shift the blame to someone or something else. I no longer need to deny or avoid my sin. Why? Because if the God of forgiveness, wisdom, and power actually lives in me, why would I be afraid to face my weaknesses and sin? Instead, I can be committed to grow in self-understanding. I can be glad that God's Word is a mirror into my heart and that God puts people in my life to help me to see myself more accurately. I can be excited about my potential to learn, change, and grow.

I will also seek godly help. The Cross not only frees me from my slavery to sin, it opens me up to the resources of God's grace. One of those resources is the body of Christ. If I am encouraged that the ultimate Helper lives within me, I will take advantage of all the resources he gives me in the body of Christ. I will not live independently. I will take advantage of biblical teaching available to me. I will seek the fellowship of a small group. I will ask to be shepherded by my elders. I will pursue the wisdom of mature brothers and sisters. I will try to benefit from the accountability a close friend can provide. And I will take advantage of all of these resources by being honest about my struggles of heart and behavior.

As I do all of this, I will express godly emotions. There is no scene more filled with emotion than the scene at Calvary. Christ cried out to his Father as he suffered and died. The Cross invites you to cry out to the Father as well. Christ cried to a Father who was silent as he let him die, so that you could cry to a Father who will hear you and give you what you need to live.

The more you understand who God is and who he has made you to be, the more you realize that the Christian life is not an emotionless, stoic existence. On earth, Christ expressed a whole range of emotions and, as you grow in Christ, you will too. Maturity expresses the right emotion in the right way at the right time. As Christians, we should be the saddest people on earth (because we understand the ravages of sin), and the most joyful people on earth (because we experience the grace of the crucified Christ).

There is a proper time for sorrow, joy, anger, fear, jealousy, happiness, gratitude, anticipation, remorse, grief, and excitement. The life of faith is a stained glass window, rich with the color of many different emotions, through which the light of Christ shines.

I will let the Cross shape my relationships. As people who have had God's grace poured out on our lives, it only makes sense for us to share that grace with others. Jesus told a wonderful story illustrating this principle in Matthew 18:21-35.

> Then Peter came to Jesus and asked, "Lord, how many times shall I forgive my brother when he sins against me? Up to seven times?"
>
> Jesus answered, "I tell you, not seven times, but seventy-seven times.
>
> "Therefore, the kingdom of heaven is like a king who wanted to settle accounts with his servants. As he began the settlement, a man who owed him ten thousand talents was brought to him. Since he was not able to pay, the master ordered that he and his wife and his children and all that he had be sold to repay the debt.
>
> "The servant fell on his knees before him. 'Be patient with me,' he begged, 'and I will pay back everything.' The servant's master took pity on him, canceled the debt and let him go.
>
> "But when that servant went out, he found one of his fellow servants who owed him a hundred denarii. He grabbed him and began to choke him. 'Pay back what you owe me!' he demanded.
>
> "His fellow servant fell to his knees and begged him, 'Be patient with me, and I will pay you back.'
>
> "But he refused. Instead, he went off and had the man thrown into prison until he could pay the debt. When the other servants saw what had happened, they were greatly distressed and went and told their

master everything that had happened.

"Then the master called the servant in. 'You wicked servant,' he said, 'I canceled all that debt of yours because you begged me to. Shouldn't you have had mercy on your fellow servant just as I had on you?' In anger his master turned him over to the jailers to be tortured, until he should pay back all he owed.

"This is how my heavenly Father will treat each of you unless you forgive your brother from your heart."

Because the people around you are (like you) still sinners, they will fail, they will sin against you, and they will disappoint you. That is when you can extend to them the same grace you have received. Our anger, irritation, impatience, condemnation, bitterness, and vengeance will never produce good things in their lives (or ours). But God can produce good things in them when we are willing to incarnate his grace. We become part of what he is doing in their lives, instead of standing in the way. So, what does it mean practically to let the Cross shape your relationships?

It means being ready, willing and able to forgive (Mark 11:25; Matt. 6:12-15). The decision to forgive is first a heart transaction between you and God. It is a willingness to give up your desire to hold onto (and in some way punish the person for) his offense against you. Instead, you entrust the person and the offense to God, believing that he is righteous and just. You make a decision to respond to this person with an attitude of grace and forgiveness. This vertical transaction (between you and God) prepares you for the horizontal transaction of forgiveness between you and the offending person, when you are given that opportunity.

Let's face it – we are sinners living with sinners, so there is never a day when forgiveness isn't needed. The refusal to forgive, the temptation to replay an offense in our minds, and our thoughts of punishment and revenge all damage the relationships God wants to use to make us more like him. They are workrooms for his grace. In this important area of forgiveness, (1) the Cross causes me to want others to know the same forgiveness Christ purchased for me, and (2) it changes me, enabling me to genuinely forgive others.

The Cross enables me to humbly ask for forgiveness. When I ask for forgiveness, I admit my responsibility for a sin against you, without any justification, excuse, or blame. Here is what it sounds like: "I was wrong for _____. Please forgive me. I am sorry for the pain I caused you." The three parts of this request define what it is to seek forgiveness. First, seeking forgiveness means coming to someone I have wronged with an attitude of humble honesty. ("I was wrong for _____.") Second, seeking forgiveness acknowledges that I have sinned against another person, and I therefore need to ask that person to be part of the forgiveness process as well. ("Please forgive me.") It is not enough to say you are sorry. When we only do that, we deny people the blessing of actually granting us forgiveness. Third, a request for forgiveness always should include a compassionate acknowledgment of the pain my sin caused. ("I am sorry for the pain I caused you.") Here again, I am experiencing the results of the Cross of Christ. It reminds me that I am a sinner – if I weren't, there would be no need for Christ's death. But the Cross does more: it changes my heart, making me sensitive to the sin I was once blind to, and ready to admit what I would once have excused.

When the Cross shapes my relationships, I respond to the sin and weakness of others with grace. Do you hold people to higher standards than you hold yourself? Do you tend to forget you are a sinner, while remembering that others are? Do you fail to overlook minor offenses? Do you spend more time catching people doing wrong than doing right? Do people feel accepted and loved by you, or criticized and judged? How do you tend to respond to the weaknesses, sins, and failures of those around you?

The Cross enables me to serve others out of a heart of compassion, gentleness, forbearance, kindness, patience, and love. The closer I get to people, the more these attitudes are needed, because that is when I am affected by their weaknesses and sin (and vice versa). The closer we are to one another, the more our hearts are revealed. Thus we all need to ask, "What attitudes shape my closest relationships?" Christ lives in us to rescue us from ourselves, so that we can be loving and gracious with one another even though we are sinners. Every time I lay aside my own desires to minister to another, I am living out the results of Christ's death on the Cross.

The Cross gives purpose and direction to my words and actions. God calls his children to actions that reflect the grace we have received in Christ. The question is, "Does this grace shape my relationships?" Let's look at some of the Cross-based actions to which Christ calls us, actions that are part of the new Fruit of faith in our lives.

- The Cross enables each of God's children to make peace (James 3:13-18). Where do you need to be committed to peace?
- The Cross enables each of God's children to speak the truth (Eph. 4:25). Where right now can problems be solved, relationships restored, and people blessed by your clear speaking of truth?
- The Cross enables each of God's children to serve others (Gal. 5:13-15). Where right now is God calling you to be a servant?
- The Cross enables each of God's children to grant forgiveness to those who seek it (Luke 17:1-10). If I have given the offense to God and refuse to seek revenge, my heart is ready to grant forgiveness when the offender seeks me out.
- The Cross enables each of God's children to learn to say "no." In the Gospels, Jesus did not do everything others wanted him to do (John 2:3-4; 4:43-54; 6:15, 26-27, 30-40; 7:3-10; 8:48-59; 10:30-39; 11:1-6, 21-27; 13:8-10; 18:19-24, 33-37). Instead, he was motivated by his Father's will. Christian love does not make us slaves to the agenda of others; it makes us slaves and servants of Christ, and therefore willing to serve others. There will be times when my allegiance to Christ means that it is loving and right to say no to other people's requests.
- The Cross enables each of God's children to recognize, develop, and use the gifts he has given for his glory and the good of others (see Romans 12:1-8). What are your God-given gifts? How can they be used where God has placed you?

Putting It All Together

As she sat across from me, Bettina looked tired but not discouraged. In the previous six months she had watched her idyllic life completely fall apart. The suburban estate she once lived on was now a hazy memory. The circle of friends that had made life so enjoyable had evaporated with her marriage. Her husband had not only forsaken her for someone else, he had done everything he could to leave her destitute. She once had a healthy bank account and endless credit, but now seldom had enough money for the bare essentials. Her country club days had given way to ten hours a day at a menial job. She even had to change churches! But as she sat across from me, she did not look discouraged or angry.

I remember thinking that I was watching the grace of God in action. Nothing else could explain the character of this woman in the middle of this sad story. God had used the scorching Heat of marital trial not only to expose Bettina's heart but to transform it. The woman who once got her security from her situation now knew what it meant to rest in the Lord. The woman who once complained at the slightest difficulty now lived with courage and endurance. This woman, once given to bitter gossip, was now a picture of true forgiveness. She had once lived for herself, but now joyfully served others.

Bettina summarized it this way: "I hope I don't ever have to go through this again. It has been harder than I ever imagined it would be. There were times when I wondered if God was there, and I worried that I would not make it. Sometimes it seemed impossible to do what God says Is right." Then she hesitated for a moment and said, "But I would go through it all again to get what God has given me. He has so completely changed me, it almost seems like the old Bettina was someone else!" Bettina was incarnating the truth that God doesn't simply cool the Heat in our lives, he transforms us in the middle of it. Although some of the Heat of this marital trial would remain in Bettina's life until she died, she was not wasting away in anger, doubt, bitterness, and envy. By God's grace she was in the process of personal renewal, producing fundamental changes in the way she responded to life.

Bettina's story is your story. You, too, face difficult trials, tempting blessings, and struggling relationships. But you, too, have been given the gift of Christ, the Redeemer. He is at work, right now, changing your heart and the ways you respond to life. Remember these realities:

1. You are already a Fruit tree because of what Christ has done for you. There are already evidences of godly character and strength in your life. By faith, recognize the good Fruit that results from responding to the gospel and the Spirit's work.

2. The Christian life is about living by faith in Christ, with the possibilities and privileges he brings. It is not about grudgingly keeping the rules in a "grin and bear it" lifestyle.

3. Because Christ has made you a new creature, good things are possible even in difficulty. His work enables your heart to respond with good Fruit.

4. Because you are united with Christ and inhabited by his Spirit, trials and temptations are opportunities to experience the power of God at work.

5. God calls you to a new identity in Christ ("This is who I am") and therefore a new way of living ("This is what I can be"). Change is not rooted in a body of knowledge, a set of rules, theological outlines, or behavioral techniques. It is the result of your heart's transformation by the risen Lord. As his grace rules our hearts, we can keep his commands.

There is hope for us because Jesus is all we need. These words capture our lives with the Lord.

Each morning that greets me is full of hope
Not because I am successful at what I am doing,
Or because the people near me appreciate me,
Or because circumstances are easy,
But because God is, and he is my Father.
To look at the morning any other way
Is to believe a lie.
To live in hope is to live in truth;
To live in truth is to bring him glory;
To bring God glory in my daily living
Is the highest form of worship.

ONE COUPLE'S STORY

These last two chapters will take the model described in this book and apply it to one couple and one church. We hope that this will help you to apply what you have read to your own life and to the life of your church.

When you first hear a person's story, it can feel as if someone has dumped a thousand-piece jigsaw puzzle on the table. You have no idea how the pieces fit together; the thought of organizing them is daunting. In the same way, knowing how to understand the details of a person's struggle can seem overwhelming and confusing. But if what we have been saying in this book is true, that need not be the case. Let's apply what we have been learning to Ted and Ginny's marriage.

Ted and Ginny

This weary young couple asked if they could talk with the pastor for one hour, but it only took a few minutes for him to realize that they needed much more help than an hour would provide. Ted was embarrassed to admit that his life was a mess. He maintained a stiff upper lip, but anyone could tell that he was completely lost. Ginny wasn't so stoic. Tears and frowns had long since replaced her smile. The look on her face said, "I don't know how I got here or how to get out." One confusing detail tumbled over another to create a chaotic mass of difficulty that would overwhelm the best of us.

Ted and Ginny had simply gotten married too young. They had not considered the consequences of marrying each other. Ted had been a very new Christian; the ink of his conversion was still wet when they first met. He still had the bad-boy edge that had been such a big part of his former life. Sure, he had trusted Christ, but he didn't have a clue as to what a radical, life-altering decision he had made. Ginny, meanwhile, had been raised in a fine Christian home. Her social and spiritual life had revolved around the church her family had attended her whole life.

Ted and Ginny met while standing in line for a ride at an amusement park. From the first moment, Ginny felt a dangerous attraction to Ted. He was like the forbidden cookie in the cookie jar: she just had to have him! To Ted, Ginny seemed so different, so pure. They exchanged numbers and went their separate ways.

Ginny never thought she would actually hear from Ted, but she did. Soon they were talking every night. Ginny's mom was suspicious and inquired about the frequent and lengthy phone calls, but Ginny always managed to be safely evasive. Before long, Ted and Ginny agreed to meet. Ginny swore her closest friend to secrecy and told her it had been the most exciting night of her life. The secret meetings continued, but Ginny knew they could not go on forever. She began searching for a time to talk to her mother about Ted.

A few nights later, Ginny was at the supper table alone with her parents. She blurted out, "I've met a boy I really like. I would like to date him." The conversation did not go well. When her parents realized that she had already been seeing Ted behind their backs, they were hurt and upset. Ginny was forbidden to see Ted again until they met him. Three nights later, Ted came to the house. In many ways he was every Christian mother's nightmare. Ginny's parents soon realized that Ted was a troubled kid who knew almost nothing about Christianity. As a consequence, Ginny's parents forbade her to continue the relationship. Ginny was crushed and angrier than she had ever been. A chill descended on her relationship with her parents. Ginny grew more and more disrespectful and counted the days until she would graduate high school and leave home for college.

The minute Ginny arrived on campus (an hour from home), she contacted Ted. They were together on her first weekend away from home and went on to spend every weekend together. Ginny shared her faith with Ted, but he had little understanding or interest. Ginny kept telling him how important it was for them to share the same faith, so Ted agreed to go to church with her. The first time Ginny's parents heard about her renewed relationship with Ted was when she called to tell them that Ted had gotten "saved." (Despite his earlier profession, he had gone forward during an altar call to reassure Ginny about his salvation.) Although they wanted to respond positively to this news, Ginny's parents were hurt that Ginny had deceived them again. They were also concerned about the authenticity of Ted's conversion.

Without the support of parents or friends, Ginny continued her romance with Ted. The school year ended and the relationship continued over the summer while Ginny lived at home. The next January, Ginny called her parents to say that she and Ted were getting married. Of course, her parents were very concerned and expressed this. Ginny failed to tell them that she was pregnant.

Despite their reservations, Ginny's parents did what they could to give the couple a decent wedding and get them off to a good start. But there were problems from day one. Ted went from one bad job to another. Ginny often didn't know where he was. He began drinking again with friends he had promised to drop. Soon, with three children under the age of five, Ginny was a lonely, bitter, and angry woman. There was seldom a night without a fight. One night the battle became physical when Ted punched Ginny several times in the face.

Ginny took the kids and left that night, determined to get help for the mess she had made. From her parents' house, she called Ted and asked him to go for counseling. Ted reluctantly agreed. A week later, they saw the pastor for the first time. With faith and courage, Ginny's pastor waded into the swamp of difficulty that was their lives. He worked hard to hear their story and help them to see that God does understand our deepest disappointments and struggles (Heat). Over time, he helped each of them to admit the ways they had wrongly responded to their situation and their relationship (Thorns). He explained that those wrong responses were not forced on them by the situation, but came out of their hearts. He helped them begin to see that the same Christ who had forgiven them was ready to change them. In so doing, he would radically change their relationship (Cross). The pastor encouraged Ted and Ginny to become committed to a new way of living with each other and with God (Fruit). Though their marriage began as a Thorn bush withering in the Heat of struggle, it gradually became a tree, laden with the Fruit of changed hearts and renewed faith.

Confusion or Clarity

As you read Ted and Ginny's story, do you feel lost? Do the number of details and disconnected facts leave you frustrated and confused? Seeing life with biblical clarity is not usually natural or easy. Life blows by so fast that most of us don't take the time to reflect on our own lives in ways we should. We can thank God that the Bible does not leave us in the dark when it comes to living life well. It urges us to think about what it looks like to grow in grace. Paul is doing just that in Ephesians 5:15 when he says, "Be very careful, then, how you live – not as unwise but as wise. . . . " He is emphatic in his desire that we pay attention to what is going on around us and in us.

The model of change outlined in this book can bring clarity and insight to Ted and Ginny's confusion. It brings hope that change is possible. Let's consider how it points to Christ as the source of lasting change when we grapple honestly with our sin.

Present Trouble: Consequences of the Heart

One of Scripture's most humbling and helpful observations is found in Galatians 6:7-8: "Do not be deceived: God cannot be mocked. A man reaps what he sows. The one who sows to please his sinful nature, from that nature will reap destruction; the one who sows to please the Spirit, from the Spirit will reap eternal life." Ted and Ginny are living in the midst of their own harvest, reaping what they have sown. You, too, are living with a harvest of some sort. What were the seeds of that harvest? We need to acknowledge both before change can begin.

Unfortunately, we are often quite skilled at denying our own harvest. And if we are skilled at denying the obvious, how much easier it is to deny what's happening in our hearts, which is less obvious! Nevertheless, change will only begin when Ted and Ginny acknowledge that the harvest of their lives is the result of the seeds they planted. Let's examine that harvest.

One of the first things that stand out is how cut off this couple is from God's normal resources of wisdom and help. This has accelerated the downward spiral of their relationship. Their cold, formulaic, distant Christianity has no connection to a real relationship with God or the issues of their lives. There is no one to speak into their lives since they are outside the Christian community in which God designed this to happen. They have no spiritual center to connect them to God, to each other, or to other believers. This lack of connection deprives them of the restorative cycle of repentance, forgiveness, and reconciliation in which the Spirit of God works. Rather, their relationship is characterized by self-protection, anger, keeping a record of wrongs, and a lack of forgiveness. The devil has ample opportunity to work his schemes of trickery and enslavement.

Ted seeks comfort in negative friendships and bad habits. Ginny gives in to self-pity and bitterness. As each gives in to these temptations, their harvest worsens and they become more enslaved. Anger increasingly dominates their marriage. This happens because neither one forsakes anger; they just try to control it. Meanwhile, Ted and Ginny's children are exposed to the fallout of their sin and caught up in the confusion and anger. No wonder Ted and Ginny are looking for ways to escape.

But don't be too hard on this couple. They are a graphic picture of what all of us are like. We all tend to live with boundaries between our public and private lives. There is something in all of us that wants to live in the shadows rather than in the light. We want to minimize how bad we are and maximize how bad others are. It is always easier to blame the other person rather than look at ourselves. If we keep God on the periphery of our lives, our Christianity will become an empty shell of rules and beliefs rather than a relationship of grace, hope, and change. Let Ted and Ginny be a mirror into your own life. Let God show you where you need to grasp the depth and power of his grace.

Heat: Ted and Ginny's World

The consequences in Ted and Ginny's marriage are a result of their responses to the Heat of life. This Heat includes both difficulty and blessing. As we put the pieces of their puzzling life together, identifying the Heat is similar to finding all the border pieces of a complex puzzle. These are the boundary pieces that define Ted and Ginny's world. In some way, they are always responding to what is in that world, so we need to ask, what were the significant influences to which they have responded?

Heat Past

Take a look at Ginny's world. She was raised in a Christian home by concerned and active parents and exposed to the gospel at an early age. These are blessings. In addition, Ginny lived in a world with values different from those she learned at home. At the amusement park, Ginny was tempted by Ted's attention. He had a "bad boy" image and she wanted what she could not have. Ginny knew her parents would not approve of

Ted. Her parents' approval and expectations collided with the temptation of Ted's attention.

Meanwhile, Ted had no knowledge of the Bible, the church, or the gospel. His values were from the world. This was Ted's Heat, the environment in which he was raised. Ted was attracted to Ginny's purity and innocence. His "bad boy" image served him at the same time that it alienated him: it attracted Ginny but he knew he would never be accepted in her world.

The Heat intensified when the Heat of Ted's world collided with Ginny's. Each one was the other person's forbidden fruit. Almost immediately, they had to respond to Ginny's parents and their decision that they could not see each other. Yet Ginny was about to leave home for college, where she would be free of her parents' restrictions.

Can you relate to Ted and Ginny? Who hasn't faced the temptation of wanting something God forbids? The magazine we shouldn't read, the third piece of chocolate cake, the gossipy phone call, the emotional relationship with someone besides our spouse, sexual flirtations at work, the harboring of bitterness, or the promotion that pulls us away from marriage, family, and the body of Christ. The subtle hook in the temptation is not simply that I can have something I want, but that I can have it without any consequences. The temptation presents itself as the way to freedom and life; actually, it is a path to slavery and death. Both Ted and Ginny succumbed to the temptations and this is where we find them in the present.

Heat Present

Ginny now finds herself married to a man who is out of control. He is rarely home, drinks too much, gets violently angry, has no interest in the Lord, can't keep a job or have a calm conversation, and is making more and more contact with old friends. She is parenting the children alone and becoming increasingly hopeless. Ginny feels the pressure of financial debt every time the phone rings. This is Ginny's Heat.

Meanwhile, Ted wakes up every day to an angry wife. She is sullen, bitter, critical, and unpleasant to be around. Ted finds her very hard to talk to, since Ginny's bitterness and hopelessness color every conversation. Because they burned their relational bridges to family and church, they have no one to turn to. They are living with the consequences of their past and present deceit. And it's true: other than God, no one understands or cares because no one knows what is going on! Because they can't fix things, Ted and Ginny are in despair.

Ted and Ginny's experience is not foreign to the way the God of the Bible describes life in this world. Like them, the biblical characters were not moral heroes who always made the right choices. They were flawed people struggling with temptations and repeatedly rescued by God. Think of Cain, Jacob, David, Moses, Jonah, the disciples, Paul, Timothy, and James. When the gospel addresses these biblical characters, it also addresses Ted, Ginny, and us. But to see how the gospel addresses their sin and confusion, we need to see how, specifically, Ted and Ginny are responding to their Heat. This helps us understand what drives their behavior.

Thorns: Ted and Ginny Respond to the Heat

Four themes organize the way Ted and Ginny responded to their circumstances.

1. **They rebelled against God-given authorities.** God did not put Ginny's parents in her life to be a trial or an obstacle, but to be an ongoing source of guidance and protection. But when Ted and Ginny encountered her parents' concerns about their relationship, they did not see their authority as a good thing. Instead, they saw them as an obstacle to overcome.

2. **They ignored wise counsel.** One of the sweet promises of Scripture is that God makes his wisdom available to his children: he never plays favorites. The counsel Ginny's parents gave her was not their opinion; it was God fulfilling his promise to give wisdom to Ginny. Her strong attraction to Ted made it hard for her to think wisely about their relationship, so God gave her parents to help her.

3. **They broke the rules to get what they wanted.** This couple tried to build a healthy relationship on a shared commitment to break any rules necessary to get what they wanted. They were not deterred by the fact that this involved disobeying a parental command, planned deceit, and bold-faced lies. They ignored God's rules and wrote their own, pursuing their definition of personal happiness.

4. **They lived in secrecy.** The secrecy required for a forbidden relationship became the trap in which the relationship became ensnared. Their decision to disobey meant they had to conduct their relationship in secret, which cut them off from the help, guidance, and care of the Christian community. Instead, they were always looking over their shoulders, rehearsing their stories and retracing their steps. They could not benefit from the things God gives us to protect and guide us.

We have looked at how Ted and Ginny responded to the Heat in their lives and we want to examine why they responded as they did. But before we do, let's look at ourselves again. Do you see yourself in this story? Are you ever tempted to see authorities in your life as obstacles to get around rather than benefits to be enjoyed? Are you tempted to ignore wise counsel, because it questions what's in your heart? Where are you tempted to break the rules to get something you want? Where do you keep secrets because you really don't want people to know where you are struggling? Ted and Ginny's temptations are common to us all. How are you doing with them?

Thorns: The Heart Behind the Responses

Assessing Ted and Ginny's responses to the Heat in their lives is just a beginning. It is not enough to counsel them to change those responses, because it is not enough to stop at outward behavior. Rather, we need to delve into the heart and ask questions about motivation.

What could possibly cause Ginny to take this significant turn in her life? She was raised in a home where the gospel and biblical values were primary shaping influences. From all accounts, it seemed that Ginny had made the faith her own. Why would she turn and move in this direction? If you do not seek these answers, your understanding of her problem will be shallow, and so will the solution. The same is true of Ted. This is where a biblical model helps you; it gives you a comprehensive model from which to view life. Proverbs 20:5 says, "The purposes of a man's heart are deep waters, but a man of understanding draws them out."[1] This gives us biblical warrant to ask deeper questions about the motivations that direct behavior. A failure to pursue these issues assures a solution that omits Christ and his grace as central to change.

A verse like Romans 1:25 makes you wise as you see the many ways we replace the Creator with something in creation. We learn something utterly profound about the world God has made, who he is, and who we are. For Ginny, her attraction to Ted and a potential relationship with him became more attractive than a relationship with God. This is why she was willing to rebel against authority, ignore wise counsel, break the rules, and live in secret. She did these things because her desire for Ted ruled her heart, not God. What is amazing is how subtly this shift took place. In Ted's case, Ginny represented a world he never thought he could enter. She was pure, educated, and from a good family. Though Ted did not see it at the time, his motivation for a relationship with Ginny was selfish. Apart from the grace of God, it was virtually inevitable that Ted's selfishness and Ginny's dreams for marriage would collide. And they did.

The biblical category discussed in Romans 1:25 is idolatry. Human beings are worshipers; they will always worship something. Apart from God's grace, they will always choose something in creation over the Creator, as Ted and Ginny did. The typical patterns of false worship include:

- The physical is more important than the spiritual.
- The temporal is more valuable than the eternal.
- Relationship with a person is more satisfying than relationship with God.
- My desires overrule what God says I need.

This model shines a spotlight on the heart to help you understand why you do the things you do. This gives Ted and Ginny an opportunity to see the depth of their struggles and to hunger for the grace and mercy of Christ.[2]

Cross: The Hope for Change

The minute you realize that the root of a person's problem is in the heart, you also realize that telling them what behavior to forsake and what behavior to pursue is not enough. While our behavior matters and it is important to give people concrete directions, change will not last unless it is rooted in the Cross and its promise of a new, transformed heart.

What will it look like for Ted and Ginny to live with the Cross of Christ as their hope and motivation? The first thing they need is to understand that

Jesus came for people just like them! They are stubborn, confused,
enslaved, and committed to themselves and what they think they need.
Romans 5: 6-8 brims with hope when it says:

> You see, at just the right time, when we were still powerless, Christ
> died for the ungodly. Very rarely will anyone die for a righteous man,
> though for a good man someone might possibly dare to die. But God
> demonstrates his own love for us in this: While we were still sinners,
> Christ died for us.

Ted and Ginny are neither alone nor hopeless. Father, Son, and Spirit offer
them cleansing from sin and power for change. In this context, Ted and
Ginny can grow in daily repentance and faith, confessing their sin and
loving their Redeemer. As they start to understand how much God loves
them and how much hope Christ offers them, the things in their lives that
took God's place are demoted to their proper position. Christ is promoted
to the place where he belongs: as the only One worth living for. On a
practical level, this means that Ted and Ginny need to:

1. **Acknowledge that the bad Fruit in their lives is their own
   harvest and responsibility.** Ginny blamed her parents for driving
   her away. She blamed Ted for lying about his faith. Ted blamed
   Ginny for never being satisfied and making him chase a dream he
   could never attain. As a result, nothing changed: neither would
   admit the active role they played in their situation. Once they began
   owning their responsibility for their choices and behaviors, they
   could participate in the Spirit's work in their hearts and lives.

2. **Acknowledge the roots of that harvest in the thoughts and
   motives of their hearts.** Both Ted and Ginny wanted an external
   solution. Ginny wanted Ted to be her perfect companion. Ted
   wanted Ginny to give him his "needed" space. They wanted these
   "solutions" because they were still holding onto the idols of their
   hearts. Finally, Ginny began to realize that it had been a long time
   since God had been the primary desire of her heart. She began to
   confess not only sins of behavior but sins of desire. With that, she
   started becoming less critical and demanding. It was hard for Ted,
   but he began to admit how selfish he had been from the start. His
   attraction to Ginny had always been about wanting his own way;
   Ginny had just been part of that agenda. Ted's honesty before God

about his motives helped him to see how he had helped create the mess in their marriage. He began to desire a better way.

3. **Embrace Christ's forgiveness.** It was not easy for Ted and Ginny to see how destructive their idolatries and resulting behavior had been. It was humbling and frightening to admit it all. But rather than denying their own roles in the problem, they decided to trust Jesus and believe his promises of forgiveness and transformation. They began to see that God was inviting them to something better than they had ever dreamed for themselves. The magnitude of God's grace began to overwhelm the skimpy, shallow god-substitutes they had been chasing for years. Ginny's quest for human love and the ideal husband began to be overshadowed by Christ's love and her identity as God's child. Ted's insistence that the universe was meant to serve him began to crumble as he saw the self-giving, sacrificial love of Christ on his behalf.

4. **Follow his call.** As Ted and Ginny were transformed by the power of the gospel, God's commands became more practically attractive. This happened in at least four ways:

   - **Thoughts.** Ted and Ginny began to see that the wisdom found in God's Word was more reliable than their own. They decided to believe it and obey it.
   - **Motives.** They became more aware of the war within their hearts between their desires and God's purposes. They did not assume that their instinctive responses were right and good. They asked God to show them what was right.
   - **Actions.** They started treating each other in ways that reflected the way Christ had treated them.
   - **Words.** They began to talk to each other in ways that brought peace, love, unity, forgiveness, and hope.

5. **Trust his presence and provision.** Ted and Ginny's marriage had functioned in ungodly ways for years. The roots of their problems were deep and things did not change overnight. The process of change was hard: it beat at the borders of their faith every day. That is why they needed to know that Christ was with them in the midst of their struggles. Instead of putting their hope in techniques or systems, they began to grasp the fact that Christ in them was

their real hope. Psalm 46:1-2 became more meaningful as they continued to grow.

> God is our refuge and strength,
>> an ever-present help in trouble.
> Therefore we will not fear, though the earth give way
>> and the mountains fall into the heart of the sea . . .

Only Christ can work changes like this in a person's heart. Ted and Ginny were on a new trajectory together. Hope began to emerge as they thought about their marriage and family.

New Heart, New Fruit, New Harvest

In the weeks and months that followed, obvious changes began to take place. Ted's heart became more like a servant's. He stayed home more and became more responsible at his job. He had fewer temper tantrums and, when he did get angry, was more willing to come back to admit and confess his sins, ask for forgiveness, and be accountable to others. As Ginny began to forsake her idol dream of a perfect companion, she became less critical and more willing to encourage and serve Ted. As they became more aware of the depth of their sin and the sufficiency of Christ's provision, they came out of hiding and connected themselves to the communities of family and church.

This new lifestyle led to a harvest of new consequences. Ginny reconciled with her parents and enjoyed a relationship with her family that she hadn't had since her high school years. Ted began to make friends with other men in the church. His story was used to encourage others in hurting marriages. In addition, Ted and Ginny's children began to benefit from the new ways grace was shaping their family.

Ted and Ginny also continued to face daily struggles. That is the way change is. This side of eternity, it is a mixture of gold and dross, just like we are. Yet God allows us to experience the blessings of his grace in the here and now.

These truths are not new – they are as old as the Scriptures in which they are found. They offer us true knowledge of ourselves, true insight into the path of change, and true hope that it can actually take place. All of it rests on Christ our Redeemer and King. If you are in him and he is in you, there is hope for you, too!

Oh, the depth of the riches of the wisdom and knowledge of God!
How unsearchable his judgments,
and his paths beyond tracing out!
"Who has known the mind of the Lord?
Or who has been his counselor?"
"Who has ever given to God,
that God should repay him?"
For from him and through him and to him are all things.
To him be the glory forever! Amen. (Rom. 11:33-36)

ONE CHURCH'S STORY

It's Sunday morning and a congregation of five hundred is making its way to services at Lake Glen Presbyterian Church. There are families, singles, the elderly, and loads of young children heading towards the sanctuary. In many ways it looks like a typical Sunday at a typical evangelical church, but LGPC was in the midst of a significant revolution.

There would be no new theology, and the worship service would look pretty much the same. Children would still attend Sunday school and the youth groups would continue their weekly meetings. Evangelism and missions would remain strong emphases and mid-week home fellowships would keep multiplying around the city. There would still be a commitment to a clear exposition of the Word and the discipling of new believers. Yet in a real way, LGPC was changing at its very core.

Since it was founded, LGPC had only had two pastors. The founding pastor had stayed for twenty years, and the second pastor had served for a little over a decade. The founding pastor and the original members were committed to a church with a strong teaching ministry, and this brought many to LGPC over the years. The church continued to grow, purchased land, built a building, expanded the staff to three full-time pastors, and multiplied its ministries. In many ways it was a history of healthy beginnings and solid growth.

Yet the current staff had become concerned. As they took an honest look at the church, they saw signs of ill health. There had been a series of all-too-public separations and divorces within the congregation that made the staff question the relative health of the marriages at LGPC. They seemed to be losing their teenagers, and a smaller percentage of members were joining home fellowship groups. The men's and women's ministries remained vibrant but lacked direction. In terms of evangelism, well, there simply wasn't much of it going on. But what got the staff's attention more than anything else was the overwhelming counseling load that all three pastors were carrying.

All of these things caused the leaders to take a long, hard look at the ministry culture of LGPC. Such an intensive corporate study had never been done, but there were clear signs that it was needed. Despite all the positive things God had done in and through LGPC, the leaders knew that they could not be complacent. If the church was going to be a place where people could grow, a revolution needed to take place. But what would that revolution be and how would it happen?

A Quiet Revolution

In Chapter 1, we met Phil and Ellie and their "hole in the middle of the house." They illustrated the gospel gap that many believers live with unawares. We live with some sense of the past forgiveness of our sins and the future promise of heaven, but without understanding or experiencing the power of the gospel in the present. The monotony of life lulls us to sleep, and we miss the miraculous presence of Christ.

The same thing can happen to a local church. On a corporate level, the present power of the gospel can be forgotten.

But Scripture says that the opposite should be true for the individual Christian and for the church. We should not – and need not – live long seasons of life with "gospel amnesia." God has placed each of his children within the body of Christ, where we are meant to be constantly reminded of the value of the gospel for our daily lives. When the church is functioning as it is supposed to, the message of grace permeates every facet of the community. Wherever they turn, believers are challenged and encouraged to be transformed by the gospel's power. When the leaders at LGPC realized that this was not happening as it should, they took action.

Six Inescapable Facts

The leaders at LGPC were motivated by six basic facts of life in the local church.

- Fact 1: Each week, there are people in local churches with a multitude of problems.
- Fact 2: The Bible says we have everything we need to help these people (2 Peter 1:3).

- Fact 3: People usually seek help first from a friend, family member, or pastor before going to a professional counselor.
- Fact 4: These people will get no help, bad help, or gospel-centered help from that friend, family member, or pastor.
- Fact 5: If they don't get meaningful help, they will look elsewhere.
- Fact 6: They will seek to help others with whatever they found helpful.

The leaders at LGPC saw the significance of this progression. Do you? If a local church is not providing meaningful, gospel-based help, people will go elsewhere. Their experience will either encourage them (and others) to see the power of the gospel or convince them that the gospel is not enough to deal with life's problems. If the latter happens, the local church becomes a place of confusion. The impact and influence of the gospel is weakened significantly, or totally replaced by another message and method of change. In other words, people will find other means of change that are not built on the solid foundation of God's redemptive work in Christ. The apostle Paul was concerned about this when he wrote to the Colossian believers in Colossians 2:6-8:

> So then, just as you received Christ Jesus as Lord, continue to live in him, rooted and built up in him, strengthened in the faith as you were taught, and overflowing with thankfulness. See to it that no one takes you captive through hollow and deceptive philosophy, which depends on human tradition and the basic principles of this world rather than on Christ.

For Paul, this was no small matter. It was a compromise that robbed God of his glory and the people of God of their only hope for change. There is no room for compromise when it comes to what is available to us in Christ.

The Goal of Our Ministry

In Colossians 1:28-29, we find a clear, uncompromising goal for building a culture of grace within the local church:

> We proclaim him, admonishing and teaching everyone with all wisdom, so that we may present everyone perfect in Christ. To this end I labor, struggling with all his energy, which so powerfully works in me.

Paul's goal was to see church communities singly devoted to the message of the living Christ. Notice that he says he teaches everyone so that everyone may grow to maturity in Christ. Paul affirms this commitment in other passages, including 1 Corinthians 2:1-2:

> When I came to you, brothers, I did not come with eloquence or superior wisdom as I proclaimed to you the testimony about God. For I resolved to know nothing while I was with you except Jesus Christ and him crucified.

For Paul, it is inconceivable to have a community of Christians who are not immersed in the grace of God in Christ. To the degree that Christ is not central, that body of believers will function at a deficient level, because some other message is at the center.

Our Vision for Community

The leaders at LGPC realized that the lives of individual Christians are reflected in the corporate life of the church. Individual Christians must constantly struggle against gospel amnesia. Our hearts, though made new in Christ, still have a layer of sinful resistance that deflects the truth of the gospel while subtle lies remain and new lies are absorbed. We are duped into thinking that we can change without God's grace, or that we need something in addition to Christ to fight the good fight. There are many counterfeit gospels that can rise to a place of supremacy in a believer's life.

The same thing happens in a community of believers. The larger group must also unite to fight gospel amnesia. A church's gospel identity can be replaced by external emphases that direct the church, even while the church theoretically affirms the centrality of grace. Formalism, legalism, mysticism, activism, Biblicism, and psychological and social emphases can slowly gain prominence and influence the entire community. These replacements represent an aspect of truth, but ultimately they only emphasize part of what the Christian life is all about. They rob the church of its primary focus on Christ and weaken and impoverish its life.

In light of these realities, the LGPC leadership realized that they needed to guard the church from subtle gospel replacements and strive to saturate the church with the message of Christ-centered change. We too must be after nothing less than entire bodies of believers who keep the Cross central in every area of church life. For some churches, this will involve a complete paradigm shift. For others, it will involve refining and clarifying what it means to keep the grace of Christ primary. Figure 16.1 depicts what we are striving for.

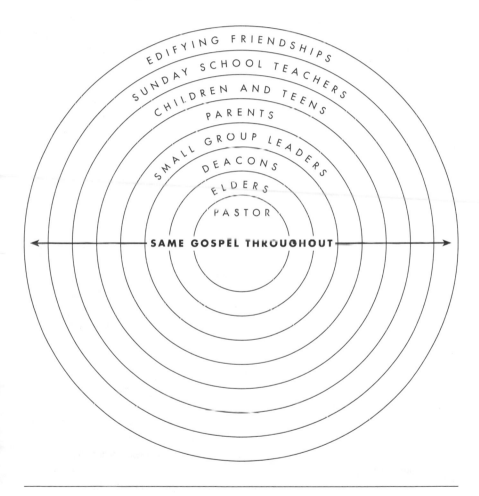

FIGURE 16.1 A Gospel-centered Ministry Culture

In every layer of congregational life, a consistent message of gospel change is present. From pastoral care and preaching to redemptive friendships, the gospel is the primary message and ministry.

In light of the trends they were seeing, the leaders decided to assess the life of LGPC. They knew that Luke 6:45 was true when it said, "Out of the overflow of his heart his mouth speaks." A person's functional identity will drive his behavior. What you worship will influence how you act. This is true for church communities as well. Figure 16.2 shows how a local church's identity will shape the way it functions.

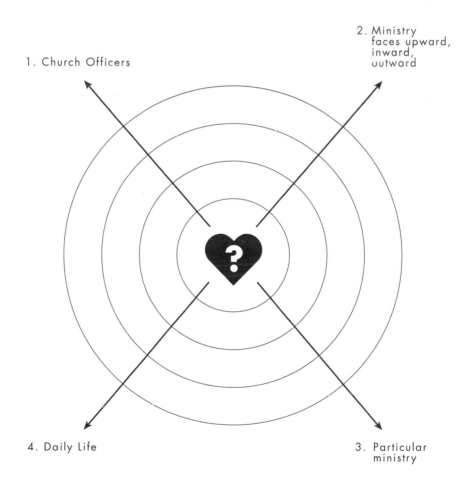

1. Church Officers

2. Ministry faces upward, inward, outward

4. Daily Life

3. Particular ministry

FIGURE 16.2 What Drives Your Church?

The church's functional – not theoretical – identity shapes the way it thinks and acts, what it teaches people and how it equips them to live. In some churches, sociological identities, such as race, class, education level, and age, are what drive the ministry. The question every church must ask is not, "Do we have an identity?" but, "What is our identity?" How does it shape the way we behave as a church? Is Christ at the center? If not, what has replaced him? Remember, even good things can displace Christ as the source of life and the head of the church.

In the case of LGPC, for example, the church started in a community where few if any churches proclaimed biblical truth. The people who started the church made every effort to plant a church that was doctrinally sound. This is a good thing, but it can also be dangerous. At LGPC, theological correctness (a good thing) so drove the preaching that the sermons became theological lectures to keep the faithful safe from error. The Christian life was reduced to affirming right doctrines that were not adequately applied to daily life. Soon people thought they were growing because they were acquiring more knowledge; they could agree with the specific doctrines of the church. But soon the cracks began to emerge. Scandals were revealed in the lives of leaders and congregants even though they espoused all the "right" things. The various ministries of the church were also designed more to guard against theological error than to show people how these truths should empower their lives. And Christ, the person with whom the believer and church are to be in relationship, was slowly turned into an abstract system of thought, although nobody realized it was happening. This is a sad but common example of how a good thing like sound doctrine can supplant Jesus Christ from the center of individual and church life. (Chapter 1 discusses other gospel replacements that rob individuals and churches of life and power.)

What About Your Church?

In light of these dangers, it is crucial to assess what is happening in your local church. Leaders cannot afford not to do this. Some other identity is always competing to become the dominant identity of the church. Individuals and churches are never neutral! When Christ is supplanted, whatever replaces him will usually allow us to remain in control, independent of him. When this occurs, churches become unwelcoming toward struggling people. They become places where like-minded, well-adjusted people pat themselves on the back for how well they are doing.

The church loses its ability to help people grow in the joys of daily repentance and faith while rejoicing in Christ.

Examining a Church's Ministries

When you examine the culture of your church, be sure to assess its various ministries and levels of leadership. The following categories, though not exhaustive, will stimulate your thinking.

Church Officers

What shapes the way we define the roles of the pastoral staff, elders, and deacons? It is easy for churches to move in one of three directions that diminish the centrality of the gospel. First, leaders are expected to function as CEOs of the church, casting vision and issuing directives. A second alternative treats leaders as managers in charge of structure, systems, and order. A third alternative sees leaders as those who set goals and objectives. Success is evaluated in terms of the bottom line and productivity.[1]

While all of these can legitimately be a part of a church officer's role, they can also blind leaders to what is most important: the growth in grace of people, people who are not your employees or customers! When the gospel is at the forefront, church officers are driven by a biblical emphasis on people and their spiritual formation. A sanctification agenda colors church life at all levels. When the Cross is central, both the individual and the community grow in grace and God is glorified.

The Upward, Inward, and Outward Faces

Every church has these three aspects to its life. The upward face involves the worship and preaching of the church. The inward face involves the fellowship and equipping of the church. The outward face involves the evangelism, mercy, and mission of the church to the world. If anything besides the Cross is at the center, the ministry of the church will be unbalanced.

When the upward face of the church is emphasized to the exclusion of the inward and outward faces, the church tends to become a preaching center, a large group gathering where the "experts" do all the work. This usually means that ministry and growth are limited to the stated formal meetings. When the inward face takes precedence, the church can become insular and self-congratulating. When the outward face is most important, the church places an emphasis on how non-Christians need the gospel to enter the Christian life. This can minimize the fact that the Christian also needs the gospel to continue in the Christian life. The gospel becomes something for "them," not "us." In each scenario, a good aspect of church life is dangerously overemphasized. Too much of a good thing can ultimately become a bad thing!

Let's consider the Cross-centered alternative. When the gospel functions at the core of each facet of ministry, the balance and health of the church is safeguarded. If the gospel is central in worship and preaching, people will be humbled as they are reminded that they are not superior to others, but needy recipients of the same grace they are called to share with others. The inward face is protected because the gospel reshapes the ways we think about our relationships with brothers and sisters in Christ. We exist not primarily for one another's happiness, but for one another's holiness! Relationships are seen through the lens of mutual service and ministry. The gospel also propels us outward to the world with mercy and compassion. The outward face is strengthened by the gospel because our calling to love the world is not driven by self-righteousness or attempts to merit God's approval. We move outward because God first moved toward us. Once again, people's spiritual growth is central when the grace of Christ is central. There is ministry balance because the humility-producing grace of God keeps us honest about our own sin, as well as hopeful and confident in God's commitment to use us in others' lives. Gospel worship continually reorients us to the living God in the vertical dimension, which moves us outward to others with a redemptive agenda in the horizontal dimension.

Particular Ministries of the Church

LGPC used a Cross-centered focus to look at all of its ministries. You can do the same with the particular ministries of your church: nursery, children, youth, adult, singles, families, small groups, new members class, leadership development, evangelism, mercy, missions, worship, shepherding, counseling, to name a few. Does the gospel propel these ministries? If you were to survey the entire life of the church, would you see a consistent emphasis on the gospel in each area?

One area that is often sorely lacking in gospel awareness is children's ministry and literature. I cannot count how many times my children have come home from church with a lesson that simply tells them to be kind to others and to obey their parents! While these are both biblical precepts, the emphasis on external obedience is often divorced from a basic understanding of the grace of Christ. This is the only thing that can change our hearts and sustain us when we fail. Unfortunately, many more grace-less examples could be given. Does the message of the Cross consistently equip the leaders of these ministries, as well as the content they teach each week?

Daily Life

When the gospel is not central to our understanding of everyday life, self-examination, repentance and faith are minimized. Marriage, parenting, work, leisure, citizenship, temptations, and struggles are not seen primarily as places where God wants us to work out our salvation with fear and trembling (Phil. 2:12-13). We will miss the daily implications of living in communion with Christ. If Christians are not being taught how the gospel works at this level, they will more easily succumb to temptation in the bigger moments of life. The purpose of this book is to get individuals and churches to think deeply, consistently, and biblically about the gospel's significance for the everyday matters of life.

Examining Your Church's Message

Although LGPC was known for its solid preaching, the leaders found it helpful to examine the message being communicated from the pulpit. This goes on to influence the message communicated by all the other ministries of the church. Let's examine the message being communicated by the various ministries of your church in terms of Heat, Thorns, Cross, and Fruit.

Heat (Chapters 7 and 8). Does your church take the Heat of your people's lives seriously, or are their struggles minimized, with change made to seem too easy? At the other end of the spectrum, do you place undue emphasis on people's struggles and communicate hopelessness? The gospel helps us maintain a realistic optimism. Life is challenging but the gospel gives us everything we need for life and godliness (2 Peter 1:3). Change is rarely easy but always possible. Change is rarely quick, but it happens over time as we depend on Christ's power at work in us.

Thorns (Chapters 9 and 10). Does your church help people engage in Christ-centered self-examination as they reflect on their sinful responses to life? Do you help people move beyond worldly sorrow to godly sorrow by helping them see what is going on at the heart level? Or are you satisfied with external behavioral change? If the gospel is central, people will grow less and less satisfied with external change, and more willing to ask why they do what they do, rather than simply resolving to change their behavior. The gospel liberates us to look more closely at our lives, and to face the things we treasure besides Jesus. The Christian life is more than just saying no to bad behavior. It is about being renewed from within with a growing spiritual passion!

Cross (Chapters 11 and 12). Are you helping your people engage in honest, confident, humble, and intelligent repentance and faith grounded in the gospel? Do you err on the side of repentance and just tell people to change? Do you err on the side of faith and just tell people that they are loved in Christ? Or do you combine heart-searching repentance with a faith that brings people face to face with God's holy love for them in Christ? When the gospel is central, people can look honestly at their sin – not just behavioral sin, but the heart sin beneath. Real repentance looks deeply at the ways we have forsaken Christ. This produces sorrow and humility for allowing something to displace Christ from the highest place. Faith then lays hold of the grace and love offered to the repentant person. When repentance and faith are joined in this way, the person's heart is recaptured by Christ. This is what produces lasting change from within.

Fruit (Chapters 13 and 14). Do you offer people hope by showing them what they can be and do through Christ? Do you show them what specific good Fruit will look like as they grow in practical godliness? When the gospel is central, you are not afraid to call people to specific acts of godliness. The more you ground them in their identity in Christ, the more you can confidently call them to change in the details of their lives. Because we sin specifically, the gospel intends us to grow in grace specifically. Every thought, action, attitude, and response to the pressures of daily life is of concern to our holy God, who desires to free us from every evil desire.

■How People Change

Summary

As you look at the ministries of your church, you must also examine the message being taught in those ministries. The questions that were helpful for the leaders of LGPC may be helpful to you too.

- What is being proclaimed each week in the preaching, teaching, and worship of the church?
- Is Christ central?
- How are we equipping current officers and ministry leaders? How are we training future leaders to minister in a way consistent with the gospel?
- Do we tend to stress doctrinal orthodoxy and skill to the exclusion of life-liberating, Christ-laden change?
- Are our ministries functioning with a Christ-centered view of change?
- What are we doing to insure that this is happening?
- Is there regular evaluation? Are we willing to make changes?
- Are all the members of our church being helped to live their daily lives out of the power of the gospel?
- Are our efforts to reach the unchurched guided by humble gospel outreach? Or do we tend to be content with techniques, programs, guilt, or false promises of a happy life?
- Do our members read their Bibles, pray, and participate in the sacraments in a Christ-centered way? Can they make specific connections between their hearts and lives and the promises and blessings that are theirs in Christ?
- What obstacles hinder this kind of culture? Where can we do a better job? How and where should we begin?

A Strategy for Change

Begin with Yourself!

Their season of evaluation convinced the leadership of LGPC that change was needed. While they affirmed the many strengths of the church and God's blessing over the years, they also wanted to face weaknesses that existed and do the hard work of addressing them. However, the pastor and staff were so committed to providing leadership and direction that they sometimes forgot that they, too, needed to change! Whenever this happened, they ceased to be useful to the church, their staff, and their families. This is a common temptation, so we encourage you to start at the beginning. Start by applying what you have learned in this book to yourself! Hebrews 10:19-25 helps us in this.

> [19]Therefore, brothers, since we have confidence to enter the Most Holy Place by the blood of Jesus, [20]by a new and living way opened for us through the curtain, that is, his body, [21]and since we have a great priest over the house of God, [22]let us draw near to God with a sincere heart in full assurance of faith, having our hearts sprinkled to cleanse us from a guilty conscience and having our bodies washed with pure water. [23]Let us hold unswervingly to the hope we profess, for he who promised is faithful. [24]And let us consider how we may spur one another on toward love and good deeds. [25]Let us not give up meeting together, as some are in the habit of doing, but let us encourage one another – and all the more as you see the Day approaching.

This passage ends with a familiar call to ministry, but this must not be divorced from the earlier verses. Before the passage calls us to minister to others, it reminds us to ground ourselves in the gospel. Verses 19-21 provide the gospel foundation for the commands that follow. We have been cleansed by the blood of Christ and have free access to God because of our great high priest, Jesus. He has opened a new and living way for us to know and be known by God. Once we have applied these truths to ourselves, we are invited and commanded to worship God (v. 23), witness to those who do not know him (v. 24), and engage in redemptive friendships in the body of Christ (vv. 24-25). When we do not begin with ourselves, we are of little help to others. Our efforts are skewed by self-centeredness.

Humbly Pursue Change in the Church

After you have examined yourself, ask some honest questions about your church. Systematically and prayerfully evaluate the various areas of church life. Begin by examining an area where you serve, and ask how you can be an agent of change there.

Level One: Pastoral Staff

The leaders of LGPC saw that there were ways they needed to grow in their gospel-centeredness as a staff. If you serve on the pastoral staff, how can you grow in your relationships with other staff members? How can you spend time thinking, sharing, and applying the gospel to your own lives? What gospel-based resources are you using to shape the way you live and serve together? You may want to read this book together or use the discipleship course that corresponds to it.[2] Staff leaders need to live out the gospel as part of their ministry to the church. Don't skip this level! It is key to shaping the church's identity.

Level Two: Elders and Deacons

LGPC took time to determine the primary focus of their gatherings as leaders. You too need to ask, "What drives the agenda when elders and deacons meet?" There are always plenty of decisions that need to be made when leaders gather, but is there any sense of excitement about what Christ is doing in his people's lives? On one occasion in a church I pastored, someone suggested that we go around the room and share where we had seen the gospel change a situation or a person's life. Every leader could think of at least one example from the previous week. What an encouragement this was! The leadership of a church needs clarity about its mission and purpose. We must take our lead from the apostle Paul, whose sole passion was for Christ to be central, and for everything else to be driven by Christ's grace and power for his glory. Does this dominate your meetings and ministry as leaders?

Level Three: Key Ministry Leaders

Wisely, LGPC did not stop with its elders, deacons, and pastoral staff. They also thought about their key ministry leaders, who in many ways are just as important. They may very well become tomorrow's elders and deacons, and they have tremendous influence in hundreds of people's lives now. These are the people leading small groups and serving in the various committees and ministries of the church, from nursery to missions and everything in between. How are these mid-level leaders being equipped in your church to think about their ministries as means of God's grace?

For example, when your worship team prepares for Sunday services, do they bring a sanctification agenda to the structure of the worship, as well as the content of the songs, confessions, prayers, and words that will be sung and spoken? How can the simple categories of Heat, Thorns, Cross, and Fruit inform the way they lead in worship? While it may sound spiritual, the common practice of telling people to forget their lives over the past six days so that they can truly worship God for the next hour smacks more of Greek dualism than a biblical view of a spiritual person. Our lives over the past six days are what God is most interested in! A recognition of the Heat we all face will lead us to bring our messy lives before him. This is a simple way for our worship to become more real and meaningful. Think about worship and the other areas of church life through these categories (Heat, Thorns, Cross, Fruit) to see whether the message of grace is prominent.

Level Four: Attendees and Members

Finally, LGPC thought about what every person in the church was hearing and learning. They wanted a gospel-centered culture that was more than a top-down movement; they wanted it to be a bottom-up, grass roots movement as well. This is important for your church too. Below the mid-level leadership is the vast majority of your congregation. They are participants in the church's ministries and potential future leaders. Where besides the pulpit are they reminded of the centrality of the gospel? What contexts do you have to shape the way they think about the Christian life? Your answers will include the obvious places like small groups, Sunday school classes, new member classes, church sports teams, and informal conversations. The rest of the list will vary with every church. The primary question to ask is how these areas of church life help or hinder attendees to understand what it means to be changed by the gospel. Do they understand the basic dynamics of the Christian life? What resources are available to your people at this most basic level, so that they hear and see what it means to grow in grace?

An Action Plan to Celebrate Grace

Their evaluation completed, the leaders of LGPC devised an action plan. This chapter can assist you to do the same. Begin as LGPC did, by thinking more broadly about the culture of your church. Step back to assess where change needs to occur, and then plot out a two- to three-year strategy to equip your people. You may want to consider the four levels discussed above and think of ways to involve each one in Christ-centered change. If you are a pastor, preaching a series of sermons on this subject is a good way to cast a vision. But don't stop there! Look for existing programs and structures where the material in this book can be taught, absorbed, and applied. Here are a few suggestions:

1. Have your church officers read this book and discuss it during your meetings.
2. Train small group leaders with this material.
3. Gather your key ministry leaders and show them how their ministry area can be guided by this material.
4. Identify the people in your church who are regularly sought out for help. Come alongside them to train them with this model of change.
5. Incorporate some of the material in a new members' class.
6. Teach a Sunday school class several times over the next three years so that this material is introduced to new people in the church.

A Quiet Revolution Begins

Today, those five hundred people gather each Sunday at LGPC. The same pastoral staff provides leadership. The same ministries, with many of the same leaders, organize the church's everyday life. The church's doctrinal statement remains the same. In fact, appreciation for it has increased! But underneath all of the apparent sameness, a significant revolution has taken place. In ways that were intentional and meant to be obvious, Christ has become more central and prominent in the ministries of the church. They are seen as means to an end, not ends in themselves. They are now truly means of grace. A Christ-centered view of the Christian life has begun to shape conversations between husbands and wives, parents and children, and brothers and sisters in Christ. A once passive congregation has become more active, since they have been equipped to explain and experience change as they live together in the body of Christ.

Be prayerful and patient as these ideas permeate the life of your church. As they do, it will become clearer to your people that change is possible and that God's grace is sufficient for all circumstances. The Bible emphasizes change within the community of faith as people apply the gospel to their lives and the lives of their friends, spouses, and children. Our desire is to see individual Christians and entire churches participate in a groundswell of gospel celebration – a celebration of the amazing grace available to us in Christ. Father, Son, and Spirit are at work to make the church a radiant bride, purified and glorious, ready for his appearing. This vision pulls us upward, beyond our personal happiness, so that we might enjoy his blessings and offer them to others.

Our hope and prayer is that this book will help you grow in grace as an individual within a community of faith. May you grow in the grace and knowledge of our Lord and Savior Jesus Christ. To him be glory both now and forever! Amen (2 Peter 3:18).

Endnotes

Chapter 2

[1] C. S. Lewis, The Problem of Pain (New York: Macmillan Publishing Co., 1962), pp. 46-47.

[2] R. C. Lucas, The Message of Colossians and Philemon, The Bible Speaks Today (Downers Grove, Ill.: InterVarsity Press, 1980), p. 110.

[3] J. C. Ryle, Holiness: Its Nature, Hindrances, Difficulties, and Roots (Cambridge: Redwood Burn Limited, Trowbridge and Esher, 1959), p. 49.

[4] J. C. Ryle, Holiness, p. 50.

[5] J. C. Ryle, Holiness, p. 21.

Chapter 5

[1] This testimony was given at New Life Presbyterian Church in Glenside, Pa., September 30, 2004 by Jan Powers.

[2] Tod E. Bolsinger, It Takes a Church to Raise a Christian: How the Community of God Changes Lives (Grand Rapids: Brazos Press/Baker Book House, 2004), pp. 22-23.

[3] Jonathan Edwards, Charity and Its Fruits (Carlisle, Pa.: The Banner of Truth Trust, 1998) pp. 327-328.

Chapter 10

[1] C. S. Lewis, Mere Christianity (New York: Macmillan Publishing Co., 1952), p. 106.

[2] These questions were formulated by CCEF faculty member David Powlison as part of CCEF's course, Dynamics of Biblical Change, and are used by permission.

Chapter 13

[1] The Bible uses words like mind, soul, spirit, thoughts, and motives to describe the inner person. The word heart is the more general word that encompasses all of the others.

[2] The Philippians Bible Study was developed by David Powlison in his course, Dynamics of Biblical Change, and has been used with permission.

Chapter 14

[1] In his commentary on this psalm Derek Kidner notes, "Absalom's revolt, which gave rise to Psalm 3, could still be the background here; for David is, as he was then, humiliated (2a) and surrounded by lies (2b), exasperation (4) and gloom (6). In Tyndale Old Testament Commentaries, Psalms 1-72 (Downers Grove, Ill.:IVP, 1973), p. 55.

Chapter 15

[1] This metaphor refers to the deep waters in a well, not in an ocean. It pictures a wise person drawing out what is inside a person. When someone is thinking rightly about God's world and the human heart, the depths of the heart can be known.

[2] Remember the "X-Ray Questions" in Chapter 10. Notice how creative we can be as we worship so many things in creation rather than the Creator!

Chapter 16

[1] E. Glenn Wagner, Escape From Church, Inc.: The Return of the Pastor-Shepherd (Grand Rapids, Mich.: Zondervan Publishing House, 1999), p. 94.

[2] CCEF has written a user-friendly discipleship tool designed for the local church. Both How People Change (which addresses the gospel gap) and Helping Others Change (formerly Instruments of Change, which addresses the ministry gap) have been written for this purpose. Get more information by going to CCEF's website at www.ccef.org.

Scripture Index